POETRY AND POETICS IN A NEW MILLENNIUM

Poetry and Poetics in a New Millennium:

Interviews with Clark Coolidge, Theodore Enslin,
Michael Heller, Eileen Myles, Alice Notley,
Maureen Owen, Ron Padgett,
Armand Schwerner, Anne Waldman,
and Lewis Warsh

edited by Edward Foster

Talisman House, Publishers
Jersey City, New Jersey

Published in the United States of America by
Talisman House, Publishers
P.O. Box 3157
Jersey City, New Jersey 07303-3157

 Manufactured in the United Sates of America
Printed on acid-free paper

Library of Congress Cataloging-in-Publication Data

Poetry and poetics in a new millennium : interviews with major contemporary poets /
edited by Edward Foster
    p. cm.
    ISBN 1-58498-015-X (alk. paper) — ISBN 1-58498-014-1 (pbk. : alk. paper)
    1. American poetry--20th century--History and criticism--Theory, etc. 2, Poets,
American--20th century--Interviews. 3. Poetry--Authorship. 4. Poetics.

PS325.P575 2000
811'.509--dc21
                                             00-056407

To the Memory of
Ted Berrigan
and
Douglas Oliver

CONTENTS

Preface

"The Bostonian of 1900 differed from [that] of 1850, in owning nothing the value of which, in the market, could be affected by the poet. Indeed, to him, the poet's pose of hostility to actual conditions of society was itself mercantile,—a form of drama,—a thing to sell, rather than a serious revolt. Society could safely adopt it as a form of industry, as it adopted other forms of book-making."
—Henry Adams, *The Life of George Cabot Lodge* (1911)

Writing early in the twentieth century, Adams may have thought his "Bostonian of 1900" was a passing thing, but a century later the type is universal, and the great majority of poets seem to consider themselves effective only when their books sell. The fact that poetry can have its own economy is for the most part no longer important, at least for those who consider publication a major reason to write. Poetry, as Adams phrased it, has become "a form of industry," and in its essentials, the business of promoting the poet and his or her work is then not much different from the business of promoting anything else.

The "serious revolt" Adams pointed to does not refer merely to the substitution of one economic or social priority for another but to something that originates within one's self and is brought about by language and in turn affects it. Interviews with writers generally follow a formula; certain kinds of questions are asked that involve personality and interpretation of the poems, but in this case, it is personality and interpretation as such, not the poetry, that matters. Such interviews suggests that a poem is interesting because of the life of the person who wrote it or that it is interesting as an excuse for those "form[s] of industry" we call criticism and scholarship. The interviews collected here were intended to avoid that kind of focus.

These interviews appeared originally in *Talisman: A Journal of Contemporary Poetry and Poetics.* They include all of that have appeared since those collected in *Postmodern Poetry* (1995). Three of the earlier interviews (the first interview with Alice Notley and those with Clark Coolidge and Ron Padgett) are reprinted here to give a further context to certain questions that are central to the later ones. Basically these questions have to do with problems of lyricism and personality in poetry that is not "a form of industry" and is not written essentially to promote the poet and his or her politics. The underlying problem has to do with how personality is transformed into words and poems.

Ideally, it would be best to reproduce all of the interviews, since all deal with these matters at some point (the interviews with William Bronk and Gustaf Sobin particularly), and perhaps it will eventually be possible to do that. Those collected here, however, more obviously belong together: with the exception of Theodore

Enslin, all of these poets have been associated primarily with the New York poetry community, and the majority have been associated with the Poetry Project at St. Mark's Church, especially in its early years. Their work correspondingly reflects shared interests and premises about poetry, though often pursued in very different ways, and it is on these points that the interviews repeatedly converge. Enslin provides the contrast: the poet who has worked mainly without a community but whose work, following its own route, essentially answers the same questions.

Edward Foster
1 August 2000

∾∾∾

The interviews were initially published in this order: Alice Notley (1), issue #1 (1988); Clark Coolidge, issue #3 (1989); Ron Padgett, issue #7 (1991); Michael Heller, issue #11 (1993); Theodore Enslin, issue #12 (1994); Anne Waldman, issue #13 (1995); Eileen Myles, issue #17 (1997); Lewis Warsh, issue #18 (1998); Armand Schwerner, issue #19 (1998); Maureen Owen, issue #20 (2000). The second interview with Alice Notley will appear in issue #21-24 (2001).

POETRY AND POETICS
IN A NEW MILLENNIUM

CLARK COOLIDGE

EF: In *The Crystal Text*, one of the lines is, "How much of poetry is unprovoked thought?" Do you have any . . .

CC: How much of poetry is unprovoked thought? Well, god, that's such a weave. I mean, that whole work must somehow be taken together. To pull out something like that, that's really dumping me cold into my procedures. It's hard to reconnect. Well, I suppose I meant "unprovoked" as trying to make thought not be a kind of rational thought or discourse. It's more the kind of poetic thought, which may not be thought, depending on how you define thought. I mean, all the statements that come up in a work like *The Crystal Text* are a product of the poetic process, not sitting down and thinking, Now what do I think about this? But what did you think of that so-called statement? And I'm not sure it is a statement.

EF: I would say that all poetry is unprovoked thought.

CC: How do you see "unprovoked"? I mean, that seems to be the key, which I can't dredge up.

EF: I'm not the one who's supposed to be interviewed.

CC: I know, but it would be interesting to me to know why "unprovoked," since that's the modifying word.

EF: Yes, "unprovoked" since it doesn't participate knowingly or intentionally in any rational system, cause and effect.

CC: You could ask, Provoked by what? I guess, but . . . "provoked." I almost don't know what it means at the moment. Possibly that poetry is the free play of thought without assignment or containment.

EF: What, if anything, provoked the structure of *The Maintains* and *Polaroid*?

CC: Well, *The Maintains* came first, and that was, as I recall, one of the periodic attempts I used to make to widen my vocabulary. I mean, it really used to annoy me that it seemed like most poets were stuck with a vocabulary, and it was almost some kind of poetic ethic not to go outside of that, as though that was your domain or your personality or character or whatever. A sort of authenticity was thought to come from having certain words be yours. And so it struck me, Why should a poet be stuck with that? I was complaining about this once in an interview and went on to say that, after all, a painter has all the colors. But then Norma Cole, who is a painter as well as a poet, wrote me and said, Are you kidding? I can't use *all* the colors. I knew what she meant right away, but on the other hand, I think that we were both right. You know, why not go out and get some vocabulary, stir up some vocabulary? Like the thing de Kooning said about hunting for environment, though I'm not sure those are his exact words. But, anyway, why be limited? Why not use the whole keyboard? This is what I was trying to do in *The Maintains*. So *The Maintains* was a dictionary work, looking in the dictionary and using those pages as a source directly. And so I got a lot of words in there that I didn't know at all, that I'd never used, a lot of nouns and adjectives primarily.

EF: What made the relationship between the words?

CC: Well, for one thing I found out that there was a syntax in the dictionary which I hadn't noticed before. You might think dumbly of the dictionary as a list of words with nothing in between, but of course in its definitions it has phrases like 'that which is blank,' that sort of syntax. So that kind of thing got in there and helped hook the work together. Of course I was still close to that time earlier when I was trying to use words that didn't go together, to see what could come from that kind of resistance. Say there are no rules, let's see what can be written. *Polaroid* was almost the reverse of that impulse. I mean, a backlash against so many nouns, so many descriptive words. I picked a set of words—prepositions, connectives of various kinds, which's and that's and conjunctions—and thought I would limit myself to those, but what happened was that after a while I began to find nouns and adjectives and brighter words creeping in, and I decided to let that happen. So, particularly at the end, the third section, those long lines have a lot of other sorts of words. But each of those long-line pages is based on a seed phrase from the original set of words which it makes variations on. Boy, this goes back so far I have to dredge up memories. I mean, this is early seventies, which seems a long time ago in my work.

EF: So in a sense *that* poetry is provoked. It starts from a proposition or a riff and follows it through and discovers what course it takes.

CC: You mean the seed phrase I was talking about? Yes, not provoked though by what you might normally think poetry was provoked by: feeling or something happens or something you see. Of course, that could all eventually become part of it. You're using your mind but it's almost a project to not start with that, at least not begin there. But talking about it this way makes it sound a lot more constructivist than it really is. I mean, I never adhere to my own rules that consistently. I find it boring to say, Every time you do this you do that. Why do that unless you're using pure chance? Very early under the influence of Cage I did some purely chance-generated work, but it didn't have enough variety. It didn't have enough energy somehow. I guess that's when I discovered that I really am a writer, you know, and have a writer's expectations, not a musician's. I don't know if you know John Cage's word things he's been doing, like the Thoreau piece in which he sometimes generates individual letters, gets something that he sort of sings or chants. I mean, I think it's fine from his aesthetic, but it doesn't satisfy me to do that. I think when you do that to language you have no longer language. You have something else made from the particulate ruins of a language, which can be performed as a purely sound composition that sometimes nudges against literature, but it's not. And that can be fascinating to experience, but if I did that I think I would discover that I wanted something more like literature, that had the energy of word art rather than purely sound art. Obviously, I'm somebody who has always been in between arts in a sense. Played drums very early. Interested in painting. Visual, a lot of audio, everything, and actually didn't start to write until I was about twenty, to really say OK, this is now it, I'm going to do this. And then actually went ahead and wrote words *and* played music simultaneously for a while. In fact I still play but just by myself in the basement.

EF: With Cage, the thing was to eliminate the self as much as possible, and that didn't have appeal for you.

CC: Yes, I mean that's an interesting question because do you really eliminate the self? Thinking of eliminating choice, I immediately think of Burroughs who was sort of half doing that, he was choosing from those cut-up generations ultimately, but he actually fled from the extremes of cut-up fairly early. You can see it if you look at the French edition of *The Soft Machine*, for instance, and compare it to the Grove edition. He took out most of the cut-up. But that's a giant question, Are you satisfied with randomness? I think I like to push as close to that edge as I can and not quite give it all up.

EF: Is randomness possible?

CC: Well, I think John would say nonintention is possible. I'm not so sure about that, or let me say for myself I don't think I would want that one hundred percent. I mean it's fun to be suddenly faced with a cut-up combination of words that wouldn't have come out of your mind and then use it, and that's kosher. But I mean everything's kosher, I'm just speaking from my point in all this. Inevitably you come up against your own laws, limitations, resistances. Or your own desires certainly. I could have gone, I suppose, further in that direction. And in fact I did get to some pretty skinny works at one point, but they didn't generate anything. David Melnick once told me he thought I had chickened out and not gone on to the inevitable next stage. And I thought, Well, what next stage? Why are we so logical? It sounded like some sort of Clement Green-bergism or something. You know, you go from sentence to phrase to word to letter, and once having stepped into the next garden, you can never go back, which isn't the way art works.

EF: It isn't that Melnick was working in the same field at all. He completely misconceived the nature of what you were trying to do.

CC: I thought so, but he may have wanted some kind of back-up. You know, you look at somebody who's been working before you and think, Can I see this impulse in him? It might lend some kind of determination to what I'm doing. I think we all look over our shoulders or look back because nobody can really tell you if it's viable. You do it, and then if it stands up to some people then it is viable. I mean, I can't think of anything that anybody did enough so that everybody talked about it, where everybody said no and just totally rejected it and that was the end of it. I mean, can you? That's strange. Maybe there are cases of that. I mean, there could be weak art, you know, but not impermissible art. At least I hope that there wouldn't be. I always want somebody to show me something, and I would go, That's ridiculous, wait a minute, wait a minute, let me look at it again.

EF: I think mathematicians have finally discovered the possibility of real random order with the computer, but I don't think it's possible in language. Any combination of words is an order.

CC: Yes, that's what I wonder about, because it seems like in music you can have it, although that's questionable, too.

EF: Could you?

CC: Well, you know that funny thing that happened in the fifties when Pierre Boulez decided to totally serialize every parameter of a musical composition, not just the pitches as in the Schoenberg idea but the dynamics, the tempo, everything. And he made a piece like that and it sounded totally random, like a Cage piece.

EF: It sounded random, but in fact . . .

CC: It was totally determined. So then everybody got all mathematically excited. In fact, probably some mathematicians had interesting things to say, if they were paying attention to that, and probably a few of them were. I can't remember exactly, but that would seem to be close to what you were saying. Mathematicians conceived of a total randomness or *produced* it . . . ?

EF: I think with a computer they've found a way to induce . . . For the first time ever, you can actually get true randomness. Absolutely no order at all.

CC: Now you get guaranteed randomness. I mean one hundred percent. Sue them if it isn't.

EF: Is the point that the field of organization is larger than people conceive—in language as well as anything else?

CC: What do you mean, "field of organization?"

EF: Field of forms. There's greater variety than people have conceived possible. That what has been considered random in fact has its unrecognized order.

CC: Probably. If there were a feeling in their minds that they did conceive of it, I'm sure that their conception of it was limited. At least I can't imagine conceiving of all forms, all possible forms, a limit of forms. Unless you're breaking it down and abstracting it and saying, you know, metrical form, random form. Sort of broad categorizations, and then filtering out things like iambic pentameter.

EF: *At Egypt* seems to have a fairly regular structure, certain kinds of stanzaic forms and patterns. Was that intentional, provoked?

CC: Well, it is in the sense that I remember waking up one morning with the look of that page in my mind. That it would have these little inroads of short segments between the long-line sections, and that these short segments would hopefully feel almost like another voice coming in. I think for a while I even entertained the idea that it was the voice of some Egyptian spirit, something very ancient that was speaking—because I did use some texts that I rewrote from *The Book of the Dead*, *The Book of the Caverns*, *The Book of the Tombs*, all that sequence. But those are heavily rewritten, I don't think there's anything recognizably quoted. Anyway, I was obviously looking for a way to interest myself in writing that, instead of just writing it as usual line by line. Who knows how those things click in your mind? But I often wake up in the morning with the results of something that's been brewing maybe in my unconscious during dreams, and then it's either useful or not to the project at hand, but in this case I did get this visualization of the page structure. I think it was Schoenberg who said he used to get images of a kind of structure that was not filled in by notes yet. It was almost like a phantom, a kind of overall envelope of the form of a piece, which he would then find the pitches to make. And I think this was a case very close to that. I had no idea what the words were going to be, but I could see the way that page would look. And I think I also realized that I wanted a polar back-and-forth thing happening for some reason.

EF: Had you done any of the phrasing or any earlier work before you came up with the form?

CC: Well, I had written some things which didn't turn out to be part of the final work, which were attempts to make some kind of work along the lines of the Egyptian memory and imagination working from my notebooks of the trip. But they all became false starts and I didn't really write the work until I had that overall form click in. Also I had pages of lines from the rewritten Egyptian texts I spoke of before, which I wanted to use somehow but had no specific idea how to use until I was well into the writing.

EF: Were there any notations made in Egypt itself?

CC: Well, the basic framework is quite an extensive journal that I kept on the trip, which got heavily transformed in the writing. If you took them side by side you could see things I used. And it's written in sequence, eleven sections for the eleven days of the trip. That's one of those things nobody really needs to know to read the book.

EF: But your earlier work . . . You said one time in an interview that you did not generally revise, but in this instance, there's a considerable amount of revision, reshaping.

CC: Well, not so much really once I got going. Once I got that shape in mind I pretty much wrote it right out. I did change a few words here and there, as I usually do when I make the final typescript. In fact I may have rejected some sections and some stanzas which just weren't working out. But if I do that I tend to just go on, keep writing and just not use those parts. But I have to keep going, I can't keep stopping to consider. I'm not good at looking at the same page for days and weeks, which some people do to great profit. This is just the way I work. There seem to be at least two main processes, mine being a sort of improvisational momentum, and then there's the heavier revision procedure. I was thinking at one point a while ago that the difference between myself and Michael Palmer, who is an old and dear friend, whose work I've paid a lot of attention to, might be that the freedom for me is to keep moving, while the freedom for him is to change what he has. At least I suddenly had this vision of "the freedom of revision," which I think must be true for him to some extent because otherwise he'd go crazy like I do if I try to revise too heavily. I get into a state where it seems like I could change each word endlessly. I mean, there would never be an end to this page or even to this word. Which is a kind of madness. Who was the great painter who ended up just doing abstract lines on one canvas over and over, and he said he was painting the universe, his masterpiece, but nobody could see it. And he just kept working on the same picture till he died. Was it Delacroix? At the beginning of Godard's *Pierrot le fou*, Belmondo is in the bathtub reading from this art book to his little daughter and it's a section about this guy. I think it was about Delacroix. No, it was Velázquez.

EF: Is there any descriptive way to distinguish between these as words on the page, an approach through considerable revision and some kind of . . .

CC: You mean could you tell just by looking at the finished work whether it was done that way? That's interesting. You mean you could look at somebody's work cold and tell that that's how they did it?

EF: Distinguish between . . .

CC: I doubt it. I mean, if it was really strong I don't think you could. I suppose I just think this about Michael because we've talked endlessly about these processes. I mean it's interesting to me increasingly, and as we all get older, that the processes are that different, and yet we might end up with quite similar results sometimes. Although I don't think anybody would mistake my work for his, probably.

EF: It's interesting. It's the distinction between Saroyan and Hemingway.

CC: You mean that Hemingway heavily revised.

EF: Over and over and over again.

CC: And Saroyan didn't.

EF: In fact isn't Kerouac the model for you in that?

CC: I suppose, yes, because of the improvisatory connection. I've said this before a million times. When I realized I could write, it was when I put jazz playing together with Kerouac's work, reading Kerouac and realizing he was improvising. He was not doing like Hemingway or like some teacher I must have had in highschool English instructed. In other words, the whole pedantic notion that you know what you're going to say and then you find the right word for it. That there's only one, and you find it and put it down. If you don't get it, you go and search and you can't go on until you do find it. All that just gave me a blinding headache. I never could conceive of being a writer that way. But when I read Kerouac, I thought this guy doesn't know where he's going, he's improvising, he's winging it. And that was the big discovery that enabled me to be any sort of writer at all. I hadn't even probably read much poetry, or certainly been taught any poetry in the sense of what I imagine Lowell must have taught his students in the fifties about how one builds a metaphor or uses the iambic line. In that scene, I probably would have decided that I couldn't do it.

EF: So you say he's just winging it, he's just going. Perhaps what Kerouac does is motion, time, and what Hemingway does is find a place where it doesn't go anywhere, where it stops.

CC: Why would he want to stop?

EF: He's trying to fix his life maybe, psychologically.

CC: Because, you mean, he also has that feeling of going on forever.

EF: He's afraid.

CC: He can't stand it. I mean, there's a terror about it. I've had this happen many times where I can't get loose from the work. I try to go to bed. I'm totally tired and it's three in the morning and I keep coming back to the desk. The words just keep coming and I can't stop it. And that is not a great state of mind. It's almost like an illness. But that's the risk of that kind of work. You take that on. You find ways of stopping it, of waiting until the next day so that you stay alive. But some people don't have that feeling. It must be very different for different writers. Maybe Hemingway had the idea of fixing something, like fixing a painting, fixing the pigment so that it stays that way for a hundred years or whatever. Fixing a painting like fixing a string of dialogue or something like that. I don't know, that just popped into my mind. Instead of, Let's see where this goes. And when you say that, when you propose that, you know that actually it never ends. It goes and goes and goes. It's just that you tire, and you're not going to reach the end of it. And you might come to write some work that would be impossible to read. You know, I'm sure I've been accused of that.

EF: Who else besides Kerouac do you know who's done this?

CC: It's hard to think of writers, cold.

EF: How about somebody like Breton?

CC: I know there are others. I don't know. Breton. Of course I don't read French well enough to feel comfortable with Breton. He does seem to sort of pour out, but there's a stiffness, an impactedness almost, to his prose anyway. Or are you in fact talking about automatic writing?

EF: But what you're talking about is not automatic writing.

CC: If I understand automatic writing, which I'm not convinced I do, or if I believe it's really automatic. I mean, how conscious is it in fact? Is it trance, like being in a literal trance? I don't think Breton did that, did he? Those things that he did look a little conscious to me. And it all has this French formality.

EF: But it's still not . . .

CC: Yes, I don't know. I remember some of the earliest writing I did was an attempt to do automatic writing under the influence of the surrealist concept of automatism. I had read that Motherwell collection of Dada painters and poets [Robert Motherwell, *The Dada Poets and Painters: An Anthology*, 1951]. But I couldn't figure out how to proceed. I just kind of started writing and it got awful right away, really gooey and either sort of (what would you call it?) substitute-sexual or sentimental or too easy in associative pattern. Nowhere near even something like *Soluble Fish*, which at least has its points of interest here and there.

EF: You said "substitute-sexual." What about *The Book of During*? What's going on there?

CC: Oh, you mean what state is it in? Or what's going on in it?

EF: What's happening in those words?

CC: Well, that's just pushing myself up against that subject matter, you know, to see . . . I mean, it's one of those great subjects, and people have told me for years that my work is sexual in the sense of rhythms or whatever. I'm not sure I'm totally in agreement or aware of that. But somewhat. And I thought, what if I just use that as a subject. Which is sort of the taboo subject not so much in the sense of a prudish taboo but that you can't write it, no? The supposed danger being that you immediately get into some sort of orgasmic state of writing where the mind goes blank or something, or it's just these awful substitutes for it that we're seeing all around. I guess I just felt like: try it. Maybe it's impossible. So let's take on the impossible, the unspeakable and see. Plus just getting interested in subject matter. I was just in Vancouver doing a talk with Lyn Hejinian, and we got talking about subject matter. She suggested we talk about sexual writing. We were trying to think of what subject to use for the talk, and she's doing this collaboration with Carla Harryman which has a lot of sexual stuff in it, and she knew I'd been doing *The Book of During*. But then I said, Wait a minute, because I'd done this talk duet a couple of times before with Michael, the last time with writing sex as subject, and it's very difficult to do. I mean, you get the audience reactions all the way from nervous tittering to sexist provocation, people just not taking it seriously or unable to deal with it somehow. So I thought, OK, why don't we just talk about subject matter, and maybe that's even more provocative because if they're thinking "language school" maybe they're thinking that subject matter doesn't matter. Also, I was thinking of that club the painters in New York City had in the fifties which for a while was called "The Subjects of the Artist," and it was all guys like de Kooning and Newman, when the public perception was that they were abstractionists so subject matter wouldn't mean a lot to them. But it turns out that that is a faulty polarity, as I think all those things turn out to be in making art. You look at those painters now, were any of them really abstractionists? I mean, what is pure abstraction? Mondrian thought he was going to save the world, and De Kooning said, What a stupid idea, but it was enough to make some terrific paintings. So how are you going to divide that? Anyway, subject matter. What if you propose, say, sexuality? So you hit it any way you can, from reading the de Sade texts to just improvising on image, feeling, whatever. Stick to no proposal but write against this wall and see what emerges. And I started in prose, I don't know why. And then in Italy I was writing a lot of shorter poems, so some poems came into it, and those have been published as *Mesh*. But the whole thing was started off by George and Chris Tysh, who a few years ago were teaching a course at the Detroit Museum in what they call pornography, which was writers like de Sade and Bataille, really pretty elegant and elaborate pornography. But that itself became an issue, all the assumptions getting shaken up in a great way. At the talk Michael and I gave at

St. Mark's somebody said, So you're *not* trying to write pornography? and we said, No, and then we said, Wait a minute, what if we did? In other words, no holds barred and nothing presumed. Could one write erotically stimulating material that would also be literature in the best sense? I began to feel like the whole thing is open again for grabs. But in the middle of it I got interrupted by some other work, and I have nowhere near finished it. I mean, it's the impossible work, and I probably never will finish it. But maybe it will just run out. I've thought that before, that books were going to go on forever and they've stopped. *Mine* was like that. That stopped.

EF: That's not complete?

CC: It is complete, in the sense that it came to an end. But originally I thought I would write at least several hundred pages of that. And then when I hit that last section—that Egyptian, strangely enough, image—it seemed the instruction to cease, the image itself a blockage of any continuance. And I did try to write beyond it, thirty or forty more pages, but none of that would attach to the work and I realized that I'd been given this instruction, whatever that might be, to stop. And so the work ended, which was shocking.

EF: What happened to the prosoid work?

CC: Well, that turned into other possibilities. I think *Mine* came directly out of that. I wrote about six hundred pages of the proposed thousand. But I think what happened was that I became tired of my own procedure. The structure that I started with as a kind of armature began to bore me. I just didn't want to keep feeding the words through that again and again. And therefore *Mine* and probably a couple other prose things I'm forgetting were produced out of that. It seemed right that the long prose caused those things to happen. That's what you hope, that something will grow from something. One problem with it was that I could never find a title for it. Sections of it have been published, some with titles. *Weathers* is a section of it and when that began appearing in United Artists magazine I found people mistaking its title as the overall title. I could understand the mistake; pieces of writing seem to demand titles. Has anyone ever gotten away with publishing a big prose book with no title? There is something seductive about the idea.

EF: Well, do you intend to publish this as it is?

CC: Maybe, except that I've done a lot of things since then that I'd rather publish before that one, given the opportunity. And now it's beginning to look like we're not going to have so many publishers for such things.

EF: Is it your H.D. book?

CC: Oh, I don't think of it that way. That's a very different project, isn't it? This is *very* unprovoked thought. And it seems to me now to be part of another era of my work. I think I may have passed beyond it as a working procedure. I think I have, although you never know. I might wake up some morning and, Hey, I think I'll finish it. But I really doubt it. Too many things have come in between, unless I'm being led around some elaborate barn and back to it.

EF: You were talking before about pornography. The thing about pornography is it's always about objects. It's never about itself.

CC: You mean bodies are objects too, fetishism.

EF: It is always about something that is outside the pictures or the words, something that is outside the work. But that doesn't seem to me the way that most of your writing is done.

CC: You mean that it's more inner.

EF: Yes, it is an entirely different way of using language. It's not what *Polaroid* is.

CC: No. Except that I at least like to entertain the notion, let's put it that way, that I'm dealing with things outside myself, that I see the words themselves out there, that I hear them out there. But it's probably a kind of conceit, a way of dealing with what after all is an inner process. Does writing have a bridge effect, between inside and outside? If you're not writing just bald description, which even in itself is going to be inner to some extent, then you're probably perceived as turning on a flow, putting it out. But, I mean, sex *is* that problem. How much outer is it? How much is it inner? A lot of it is fixations on objects, visualizations, fantasies based on parts of the body. You know those Picassos that see the body from all points of view at once, which I always think of as a sexual need on his part. I don't know. That's maybe not for me to say how much it's inner or outer.

EF: But that change in language . . . Is that why the book is called *At Egypt* instead of *In Egypt*?

CC: Oh, that's for several reasons. One of them is silly in a way. I mean, it's not, but it's not directly a source. There is a jazz tune by Zoot Sims on a record I had in the fifties. I don't have it anymore, and now I wish I had it again. It was a song that he wrote that he actually sang, though he's not a singer, but he did on this one track, which had the lyric "Where you at?" Things like that, which was bop slang. Where's it at? I mean they still use it. Where you at, man? Or where is it at? So that's kind of native to me. And then I was thinking of, like, *at* the desk, or *at* work, engaged in. That kind of prepositional direction because I was at work on a kind of remembrance, or personal remnant, of Egypt. Bringing it back up through my memory and imagination a year after the trip. The work goes through that much of a set of changes. It's a kind of transformation into a *voyage imaginaire*. Or something one was at, like a movie or a show. Also at is an Egyptian syllable like Nut or Set. It rings like a fragment of those god names.

EF: From various things you say in that book I gather that what Egypt stands for is more important to you than Greek and Roman traditions. Because those traditions have sealed off something?

CC: Well, I was living in Rome and flew to Egypt. We'd been in Italy for four months and I was very attracted to Renaissance art—Piero, Uccello, and those people—and was not attracted to Imperial Rome, the Caesars. They seemed very fascistic, heavy-handed, not a very reflective civilization. Plus I went to Classical

High School in Providence and had four years of Latin, read Caesar's *Gallic Wars* and some of the less interesting things written in Latin. We certainly didn't read Catullus. Maybe a little bit of Virgil. Not Ovid. No Lucretius. So I never got interested through that. But I instantly made a connection somehow between the Renaissance and ancient Egypt, and in fact there is a bridge where you get the hermetic tradition coming in through people like Giordano Bruno. There's a very prominent statue in the old Roman Campo dei Fiori, the place where he was burned for heresy. He was an adept of the Hermes Trismegistus wisdom, which is thought of as probably a Greek derivation from the Egyptian magic tradition. So it comes around that way, there actually is a Renaissance-Egypt connection. I mean, you can jump over all that other stuff, which it seems I did. I didn't want to pick that stuff up. I could see Egypt. I mean there's a magic tradition in Egypt, and there is in the Renaissance in Italy, all over the Renaissance and ultimately in Shakespeare. So it's just a rift, a preference between one thing and another. Some people really get off on ancient Rome and do things with it. I couldn't. But there is that bridge.

EF: Magic. I wouldn't have expected you to use that word. For the kind of interests you have, magic doesn't fit with geology, Schoenberg . . .

CC: Well, I don't know, maybe. I probably avoided using the word because I didn't like the way I heard it being used, or felt like I was becoming a member of a club, or . . . You know, sometimes you avoid the terms.

EF: Well, talking about magic leads me to Duncan. What about him?

CC: Duncan. Very hard for me to get to initially. It seemed like he was from an entirely different tradition. And in fact he is—the whole hierarchy of fanciful powers that he lives in. It took a long time just to realize the way in which it's poetry and not so much that mind-set. I mean, now I read him. Maybe I finally found the way to get what I need from him. Which is another way of reading, the way poets read poets, and that could be a whole other book, right? What you need to eat, you know.

EF: The thing about Olson saying that San Francisco was an "école des Sages ou Mages."

CC: Where did he say that? Or when did he say that?

EF: "Against Wisdom as Such."

CC: He was thinking of Duncan particularly.

EF: Well, Everson, Spicer. What is your feeling about Spicer?

CC: More and more I realize what a big influence he's been.

EF: On you?

CC: Yes. I would say a major influence. I used to carry around *The Heads of the Town* and it became this irreducible work. I was continually drawn to it and puzzled by it, and I think there are things like that that are very useful if they retain their irreducibility as poetry. So you never use them up. I mean particularly *that* book of his, I think it's somehow stuck to my mind. In fact right now I'm trying to find a copy of the original Auerhahn edition because I don't like the way it looks in *The*

Collected Books. Somehow that grayness at the bottom isn't right. It was just so perfect, that size and that page shape. At least it's something I want to go back and look at.

EF: You know he didn't like it, thought it was too cramped.

CC: Yes, I know. I think I remember hearing that. Well, so what? I mean I'm talking about the way I first perceived it.

EF: But the poet?

CC: Well, yes, I mean it's his book and he's going to feel that way, or whatever way. But . . . I'd like to think that there's somebody more or less contemporary who will never be reduced to explication, who will never be drained in the sense that people will be so familiar with what that's "about". I don't think poetry "means" in the sense that you can derive a meaning and say, OK, lock it up, teach it. And Spicer seems to be one who resists that as well as just about anybody. I mean, you get somebody like Olson that includes all kinds of references and so they can pick him apart and make him seem something that I don't think he most strongly was. But anyway, Spicer doesn't have that sort of surface, can't be reduced to parts as easily. I mean, you can realize he was looking at Cocteau's *Orphée*, but that movie is not *the* entrance to that poem. You'd still have to wonder who is *his* Cegeste, for example. And then there's that great image of the poet picking up the code numbers on the radio and receiving the poems, which is like a great overall image for poets. A magic. I mean, he's a magic poet in that sense. And I guess I'm saying that that's what I would like to do, to leave something that was irreducible in the world, that couldn't be explained away. That's maybe a dumb phrase but, you know, "OK, move on to the next genius of the twentieth century." There's a few too many of them that can be dealt with like that.

EF: Spicer thought a lot about *logos*. Is that what you . . .

CC: Yes, well, of course he has a linguistic background, which I don't have. Which makes me think of that poem of his where he says, "People worry more about bitter than they worry about -ness/ Worry more about -ness,/ Damn you." ["Hokku," *One Night Stand & Other Poems*] I suppose that has a very easy meaning at first, but the linguistic pointing that he's doing is a wonderful kind of poet's expostulation. Like, what about "-tion" or "-ing" or whatever. I had a phase back there where I was thinking how we don't look at the "-ing," this little motor that's pushing the verb along.

EF: What about that linguistic training with him, and with people like Barrett Watten? What's your own . . .

CC: Well, I don't have much of that at all. I'm a relative ignoramus on those texts. In fact, I have a hard time reading any sort of abstract language, which I'm not proud of. I wish I could. A lot of philosophy too I find impenetrable for that reason. I seem to need a brighter, denser, in the painter's sense, language than that. My mind doesn't seem to retain a writer's particular redefinition, say, of a common abstraction or generic term, long enough to carry through a whole work. I feel like I'm back struggling through freshman sociology. Or maybe I depend too much on the slippage in language to respect anyone's rules of the game at this point.

EF: You don't take language as its own subject.

CC: You mean in the way you think of Watten? Not entirely, no. But I doubt that he does either.

EF: Even in *Polaroid* you're avoiding that.

CC: I hope so. That book became more of a performance piece, in fact it works very well vocalized. A few years ago the composer Alvin Curran and I did it in San Francisco. We modified it through all sorts of black boxes, added tape and piano to it. It does lend itself well to that sort of thing. So it has that outer dimension, which gets it away from the limitations of "language about language" hopefully. I guess I fight against that more or less. Not that poetry isn't reflexive at every point. But I don't have big theoretical ideas. Or if I do have them, I turn them over pretty quick.

EF: In *The Crystal Text* you come down pretty hard on critics. Is it the way they're talking about poetry, or is it the way they're talking itself that's the problem?

CC: Well, it's both, of course. I just don't . . . I mean it's not my gig. I suppose they have to do that, but I wish they would be more helpful sometimes. And I'm quoting there in a way. I don't know if you ever saw the transcript of that public talk Jean-Luc Godard did with Pauline Kael some years ago at the Marin Civic Center. It started out with her being very negative; she'd just panned his latest movie. They were going at it a little bit, and finally he said, I wish you could help me get some ideas for my next movie. And everybody laughed, and then Godard said, But all I get from the review is that Pauline doesn't like me. I suppose at its best criticism does provide some options, maybe. But a lot of it seems to be just saying: This shouldn't be that way. And if you wrote the thing, you know that they're probably not aware of what it was supposed to be anyway, so what are they comparing it with? They're comparing it inevitably with what their expectation is, which is often very askew. And the other thing to say about that is that you never write your expectations. To the point where now I wouldn't even be satisfied if I did. Or it would be weird if you had a notion to write a work and it filled itself out in exactly that way and then you were finished. I can't even imagine that happening. I wonder if it has ever happened to anyone, if they were honest talking about it. I mean you can say, Well, this turned out the way I wanted, but that conceals a lot of modification, transformation in the process. You know, the funny thing about *The Crystal Text*, I'd forgotten until I read somebody's review of it, is that some of those journal entries that Michael published in *Code of Signals* were actually the beginning of that work.

EF: I was going to ask about that.

CC: I had forgotten that completely, so I was sort of shocked when I went back and checked. I read this guy's review and I said, No, that's not true, he's wrong. And then I looked at the book and, Oh my god, he's right. I realized that the origin of that came out of some other impulse. I mean, I just kept writing in a notebook, and when I went back and threw out a lot of sections I kept those, so I must have felt that this was the beginning of the impulse. It's interesting. And so one thing I was thinking about that I find in the notebook around those early entries was an attempt to write a review of *Notes for Echo Lake*, which I was finally unable to do, and some of that got changed in the beginning of *The Crystal Text*. And so I was probably raving against what I thought the distortions and incomprehensions of the critics might be, and already getting ahead of myself. That shouldn't happen, but inevitably it does in some way. Anyway, this shows you how you can forget the impulses for your own work.

EF: So the same process as *At Egypt*. First a series of sketches and then a form, a book.

CC: Because the crystal probably occurred pretty quick but not right at the beginning. I'd have to go back and look at it to see in which paragraphs it actually gets mentioned first. But anyway, those other impulses were there. It's interesting to me that you bring that out and nobody else has because I thought that I'd covered my tracks a little bit better. But you really noticed that?

EF: I noticed it.

CC: Did you see that all the way through it?

EF: Which?

CC: This railing against critics.

EF: Oh, yes. There's always an enemy waiting somewhere in the woods, and he's a critic. I was wondering about this, though—that what a critic does is that he has a certain vocabulary, and he has a certain form, and it's simply another kind of writing.

CC: Well, that's what I started to hint at when I started talking about this. They have their materials. But it's hard to get used to looking at yourself in these other terms. I was thinking of what Philip Guston said when Dore Ashton wrote that book about him. He was someone who did not react very well to criticism in print, and it was a nervous situation. Finally the book came out and I asked him how he liked it and he said, Oh, that guy had a pretty interesting life. I thought, right, if you deal with it in the third person it can become a character to you, remove and defuse the inevitable encroachment somewhat. Jerome McGann recently sent me an essay on my work which I think will be in *Parnassus*. It had words like "truth" and "falsehood" in the title and so right away I thought, oh oh, since I don't use such words, but as I went on reading it I got quite interested. Once I got beyond the fact that it wasn't me at all, that it was somebody else's impulses, then it was actually fascinating to see the work from this totally other point-of-view, other references and other reading. I mean, I don't think of myself as someone who has spent much time with Blake, and McGann obviously has, but when he mentioned "The Marriage of Heaven and Hell" in this piece, I went back and looked at it and realized that I knew it almost word for word. I must have read it with some attention a long time ago. That's interesting to find out that someone you didn't think you paid much attention to is really solidly in there. Sometimes I think that bad memory is good. Guston used to value what he called the Angel of Forgettal. He thought it was good that he couldn't remember doing something because he might not have had the impulse to do it again if he'd remembered painting this shoe before, or the way he painted it. On the other hand, in certain moods he would claim that he remembered every detail of every single image he ever painted out, so . . . It's just a matter of recall, what pops into your front mind. I always say I have very bad recall because I remember school humiliations not remembering the thing on the page at the right moment. And now, of course, I'm old enough to have lost a few brain cells and so sometimes the name won't pop into the slot. And it's, like, your mother's name. I mean, things as absurd as that have happened to me in the last year or so. Well, I'm way off the whatever.

EF: None of the questions I planned got asked so far. But it seems as if you just got around to them anyway. Well, one thing I was going to ask about was music, you know, bebop and time, form . . .

CC: I was thinking of that in a certain way just the other day. A bunch of us were in Boston for The Figures reading and Geoffrey Young mentioned this very particular record, a Blue Note album under Cannonball Adderley's name called *Somethin' Else* with Art Blakey on drums. Now if you're familiar with Blakey's work, you won't hear him playing a lot of his usual figures on this session. He's mainly doing what they used to call "keeping time." Geoffrey was going on about how wonderful this was, and Stephen Rodefer said, Yes, but he's not *doing* anything. And I don't tell this as a story on Stephen but just that it's a good point. I mean that what Blakey was doing was miraculous because he was making time. He was shaping time in a very particular way and keeping it there. I mean you could say it swung. You could use such euphemisms for the shapeliness or the sensuality of a kind of synthetic time. As a drummer myself I am totally awed at this. And he wouldn't have to do any kind of figures or phrases or anything. If you could get that kind of time shape going in a room for however many minutes, that's what it's all about, the basis. That's what you're doing, you're creating a time phase within which things can get articulated, without which those things can not be articulated. In other words, if the bass player and drummer aren't playing the same groove you aren't going to be able to play certain things if you're the piano player or the horn player. I mean, the inner action is *that* dependent. So anyway that's one example of making time, which makes something like clock time seem totally silly. I never wear a watch, which I always think I gave up because I didn't like the feel of it on my wrist when I was playing drums. But I've noticed since that a lot of drummers wear very prominent wrist watches. So it probably went deeper than that. I've never been very comfortable with clock time. And now it's worse with the digital clocks because who cares if it's "two twenty-three," plus we've lost a certain spatial representation of time by reducing the clock face down to mere numerals. I've said *synthetic* time, but I meant synthetic in a positive way. You synthesize it, you make it out of its elements.

EF: The quality of the time.

CC: And there seems to be an infinite number of qualities to time. Just doing time.

EF: And that's what poetry does, too, necessarily.

CC: Yes.

EF: What happens when there isn't time?

CC: When there isn't time . . . You mean if you don't make the time?

EF: Or someone isn't making the time for you.

CC: So it's just stale poetry.

EF: Or in *At Egypt* you come back to the idea of silence.

CC: And stillness. It's funny, once you talk about motion and time passing, suddenly there's the notion of stillness, the desire for stillness. That's something it's almost impossible to talk about. As if there would be a kind of stillness in an incredibly rapid and sheerly articulated time or momentum, and which is what you're really trying to get to. I get that feeling largely from Beckett, of course. He has a great momentum and yet what seems to be wanted is some ultimate stillness. Not just the stopping of the voice, but that everything will be as I think he really conceives it to be, a complex static condition.

EF: No time.

CC: No time. No word after word. This kind of "nohow on" feeling he gets to. Where it's like you can't do it, and you do it. And if it doesn't go on, it goes on. It's always been his "at the same time" feeling. Language is inadequate to that. In the stillness, it goes. You know, poetry can sometimes hit obliquely into that, given an image. Although image is another difficult thing to talk about. Michael and I were on a panel on "The Image" that Geoffrey organized down at Tyler School of Art a few years ago, and in talking about it, we realized that we weren't really that concerned with writing images. I mean you'd have, say, house and orange, words like that in a work, but you didn't think of it as building an image, making an image wasn't primarily important.

EF: You mean just visual image, or do you mean more?

CC: Yeah, then you get rightaway into something like Zukofsky's definition of an image, or is it Pound's, or is it Zukofsky's modification of Pound's. You know, that intellectual-and-emotional-complex-in-a-moment-of-time sense of an image. But I guess we were taking it more simply as in "His work is full of images." And undoubtedly there are images all through our work, but they're more of a by-product of what we're doing. Whereas somebody like Burroughs seems to be more primarily an image maker.

EF: That, of course, comes all around full circle back to *Mesh* and *The Book of During* and the idea of objects. Objects imply images. They may not be specified, and they may be generalized, but they are there. You're not interested in them, and therefore, it's a strange . . .

CC: Well, of course, I was interested in the crystal in the sense of what the crystal might do to things, to me, to the writing, to the day, to the mood, to whatever might come along. And actually one of the things that I want to do in *The Book of During* is a description of a series of rooms which are imaginary, with objects of course, in which sex acts could take place, or have taken place, or are about to take place. Without bodies at all. Just a sequence of rooms.

EF: You don't like the word "metaphor."

CC: Unless it's, like, infinitely extended metaphor. Metaphor chains.

EF: So "Egypt" is not a metaphor? The "crystal" is not a metaphor?

CC: You mean like a big overall title metaphor? No, I think I'm too interested in particularities. I don't have much fun thinking of it as a big umbrella image. I usually get my titles last. In a shorter poem, say, the title would come directly after the last line. If you looked at the manuscript, you would see it written at the bottom of the page, circled. It would almost be like the last word of the poem, but it would go up, you know. And I sometimes thought how weird that is, because in the sense that it's written last it is the last. It's the first and the last, or the last and the first. You go back to the beginning with it. Maybe that's what titles are for, to lead you back through the process? I was reading through that manuscript of "The Waste Land" volume the other day and realizing what a different feeling Eliot must have had about that poem when he was calling it "He Do the Police in Different Voices," from Dickens. In fact I'm not even clear how that title shift happened. How did it become "The Waste Land"? Did Pound do that?

EF: I don't know. One thing that has always struck me about it is that it is two words. It's "Waste Land," not "Wasteland." And that determines the meaning in a very major way.

CC: Yes. It's not the one-word term. Actually in the footnote doesn't he say that the title comes from . . .

EF: Yes, Jessie Weston's . . .

CC: Which I've never seen, so I don't know what he means. Have you read that book?

EF: *From Ritual to Romance*? No.

CC: It's like grail legend, stuff like that?

EF: I guess so. I'm not sure all the scholars agree with her, though. But even if they don't, it wouldn't make any difference. To the poem, I mean.

CC: The great misunderstandings. Yes. That's a whole history of art, isn't it?

EF: So, is there anything else we should add?

CC: Well, we've got some more tape here.

EF: OK. Well, you describe your work as "arrangement" rather than "composition." Is that "arrangement" in the sense of musical arrangement?

CC: Part of that is the impulse you get when you're asked to give a lecture and you don't want to use a term like "structure" or "composition" again. I suppose "composition" could just as well be musical. [Clark Coolidge, "Arrangement," *Talking Poetics from Naropa Institute*, ed. Anne Waldman and Marilyn Webb]

EF: Sure.

CC: I think probably "arrangement" has a less positive musical sense to me than "composition," because an arrangement is usually an adaptation of some initial material, so it's secondary, and actually a lot of arrangements are hack work. But of course the main source for my title was that Lewis Padgett story, "Mimsy Were the Borogroves." The kids in there placing those random objects in a certain arrangement and so unlocking a dimensional gate. And I'm sure that was a very early direction, because I read that story long before I ever wrote anything and it stuck in my mind. In fact I spent years trying first to recall which story that situation was in, and then trying to locate the book. It was part of those thousands of sci-fi stories I read in junior high school. And it turned out that the author had two names. Henry Kuttner is the other one for Lewis Padgett. In fact I'm not sure which one is his real name. Plus there's a funny connection with Ron Padgett. Or I should say non-connection. I don't think there's any relation.

EF: You grew up near the Brown University campus.

CC: Yes, the East Side. My father being chairman of the music department, so of course I was a faculty brat.

EF: Is your father a composer?

CC: No, but he plays the violin. He told me a few years ago that when he was young he had some idea of being a composer, but he decided he didn't have what it took. Then he got married and became a teacher. But they always had a string quartet on campus, and he played in that and in the local orchestra. So I grew up surrounded by that kind of musical dimension, which I rejected as a child. Went to Spike Jones and then jazz. Drums instead of piano. But yes, I grew up eight, ten blocks from campus.

EF: There were some poets teaching at Brown then, but what you do is completely different from anything they would have felt. People like Samuel Foster Damon.

CC: Oh, well, Foster Damon was probably the most interesting one there, and I knew him through my father because they both had an interest in American music. They worked together on the sheet music collection in the John Hay Library right up until Foster's death. So I did see something of him, and he was a fascinating guy. I mean, Blake scholar isn't the half of it. I think he thought of himself as a kind of Blakean personage. He had a wild sense of his own character, made his own wine and the strongest martinis I've ever tasted, and he had this hearing aid that he would turn off when he didn't want to talk to you. He was a great character. I'm only sorry that I didn't take one of his courses. I think it was Bill Berkson who was telling me about taking his Blake, or possibly Melville, course, and how great it was. But I did hear him talk informally about some of these things. There was no one else really interesting there. Anyway, I was part of the beatnik gang at the time, reading

Ginsberg and Corso and Kerouac, yelling for Williams and against Eliot. I'm eating crow now because I realize that I used to put down Eliot without really having read him. Which I think was necessary though at the time. I don't regret that. I just hope nobody was listening to me for the truth about that poetry because I didn't know. Now I discover that Eliot is a terrific poet, but then I would have said he was bad without knowing. But that's just because I needed to avoid that area. I needed Williams. I probably wouldn't have been able to read Eliot then anyway, just as I wasn't able to read Stevens. And then, but sooner than Eliot, he became a favorite of mine. I carried that collected Stevens around for a long time without being able to read it but never got rid of it. I must have sensed that someday I would need that.

EF: Did you ever know Kerouac?

CC: Met him twice but never knew him. Kind of late. Well, I saw him read in 1959 and I just shook his hand backstage and then saw him later at Harvard when he was drunk out of his mind, very distressing circumstances. It's probably just as well because the Kerouac that I would have known then would not have been the one that I would have liked to have known. And anyway there's the division between the man and the work in the case of someone like him becoming increasingly wide.

EF: Who was there before Kerouac?

CC: You mean who did that sort of thing? Well, I don't know. I mean I suppose if you get into other languages . . . I always assume that Proust was like that, although I can't read French well enough. But people tell me that he has those great swooping endlessnesses like Kerouac. And I know that Kerouac read him in French, so there's a line there, though evidently he'd always rather talk about Balzac.

EF: Stein?

CC: Stein. I don't know if Stein works like that. She has a way of turning things, continually turning, like turning the objects on a table, which is different from going along at speed seeing things out of the car window. I don't think of her with that sort of momentum. It's a different kind of momentum, I guess.

EF: Do you know Sherwood Anderson's poetry?

CC: No. Do you think he . . .

EF: Oh, yes. I think so. His stories, too. Some of his stories move in big sweeps.

CC: Yes, I know those a bit. Possibly Whitman, although I'm not a big Whitman reader.

EF: No?

CC: In and out, you know. He's probably there, a bit in the way I was speaking of Blake being there before. He's just not somebody I refer to. Though I recently got the impulse to go and buy that big black Whitman collection, The Library of America or whatever it's called, because I only have some sort of old pocketbook edition of *Leaves of Grass*. Actually I have an old hard cover edition of *Specimen Days*, too. But there does seem to be that distinction between the ones you continually refer to and the ones that are just there, and then the ones that aren't. There are certainly different ways of them being in your head.

EF: Yes, and critics like to play the game of tradition. What do you come up with? What kind of tradition is there here? Is there anything that goes back for you before Kerouac?

CC: Yes, Melville's been a big thing with me.

EF: *Pierre*, I'd guess.

CC: *Pierre* and *Moby-Dick*.

EF: Not *The Confidence Man*.

CC: Or I should say *Moby-Dick* and *Pierre*, because that's the sequence. The book and the book about the book in a way, about the writing of the book. No, not so much *The Confidence Man*. Certainly not *Billy Budd*. I'm not much interested in the early voyage books. Clarel and some of the later poems are interesting. And his journals are wonderful, especially *The Journal up the Straits*, which has that wonderful description of the pyramids as not being created by man or nature. And I do think that *Moby-Dick* is the great American novel. I don't see why anybody ever had any doubt.

EF: So the book for you is *Moby-Dick*, not *Pierre*.

CC: Well, but *Pierre* is a wonderful appendage, I think, to *Moby-Dick*. He raced right into it after he finished with the whale. Still in the middle of that probably fairly terrible state of mind. He had written this great book and saw it, and even Hawthorne was telling him to keep his distance.

EF: *Pierre* has great passages on silence, everything coming out of silence. Would you connect that with *At Egypt*?

CC: Well, I should go back and read it. I haven't read it in a long time.

EF: When I was reading *At Egypt*, that seemed . . .

CC: I thought of that image of him sticking his head under the balanced rock.

EF: Which he calls the Memnon Stone. Egyptian.

CC: Now it's all covered with graffiti. At least the last time I was out there and it must be ten years ago actually. It was all day-gloed over. There were guys riding motorcycles around it.

(end of tape)

THEODORE ENSLIN

EF: I've never been to this part of Maine. It seems the absolute end of the earth, but it's incredibly seductive—a miracle there are still places like this. I suspect Thoreau helped you find it. In fact I suspect Thoreau of being responsible for a lot of places you've found.

TE: I certainly don't think of myself as someone who attempted to emulate anything Thoreau did. On the other hand, when I was a kid, when I was at music school, I studied Thoreau, and I actually read *Walden* on the shores of Walden Pond. I used to go there spring nights.

EF: Any particular reason you were drawn to him?

TE: I had heard about Thoreau because he had a connection with my family. My great-grandmother was Lydian Emerson's cousin, and great-grandmother disapproved of Mr. Thoreau very much. Apparently no one has ever really decided exactly what did or did not happen when Ralph went to think high thoughts with Carlyle. But there is that letter from Lydian to Henry saying she thinks he should not come to Sunday dinner.

EF: An attitude your great-grandmother shared, it seems.

TE: My great-grandmother: "There are things about that man that are not really known." And so I was raised to think of him as some sort of conceited, strange, reclusive man who happened to live in Concord. Then I started reading him, and I found that not the case at all. I read everything I could find, and it made very good sense to me because I had decided that . . . (at that point I was thinking of composing as well as writing.) I would live the life of an artist. OK, there are practical things that go along with such a decision.

EF: Which is when parents get involved.

TE: My father was a New Testament scholar, an eminent one, and he got into a great deal of trouble in academe in those years.

EF: Because of his ideas?

TE: Well, yes, both because he was considered a radical and because he was an honest man, and he was not one to play games. So eventually he was fired from the seminary where he was teaching.

EF: In Philadelphia?

TE: Yes, just outside Philadelphia. Crozer Theological Seminary, where he was for thirty years. He kept saying things like follow the truth wherever it leads you whatever is truth to you. Which he certainly did for himself. And also in his practical life, he was the same sort of man, so he got into trouble. I was impressed by what he said, and yet I also decided that I didn't want to get involved with the academic world. He and my mother had hoped that I would teach languages or be a philologist, certainly not something that I wanted to do. I was interested in languages, but as I grew towards manhood, I realized that the questions that were continually fired at me missed the mark . . . No one ever tried to dissuade me from doing what I wanted to do, but parents and teachers would say, OK, poetry and music are very fine, but how are you going to make a living? Are they enough? And I said, yes, they are. And so it's interesting that you should pick on Thoreau, because he gave me heart. I think that way of living modified to the age in which I live and the way that I want to live may be the answer.

EF: You also spent a lot of time on Cape Cod, which was Thoreau country.

TE: That's right. I had read *Cape Cod* earlier when I was twelve or something, and I had walked those same beaches with my father. That was one thing we did together. We used to take marathon hikes, twenty-five or thirty miles. Something that has been a joy to me ever since. I still like to take long walks.

EF: Did you read the journals?

TE: That's an interesting thing. Houghton Mifflin republished the whole fourteen-volume set basically for libraries. I think that would be in the late forties. I had certainly read excerpts before that. And there was a very blind ad in the *New York Times Book Review* saying there are a few sets left over, and if anyone is interested, inquire from the publisher. I did, and the response was very interesting. I was dead broke. Those journals are the only thing that I ever bought on time, *Thoreau's* journals! It wasn't that much; it was less than a hundred dollars, but a hundred dollars in, say, 1948, 1949 was a lot of money. And the whole attitude of those hundreds of pages was towards a living, how one made a living, what was important in one's relationship to other people. Here was something that in some ways was completely opposite to the atmosphere in which I was living.

EF: Which was?

TE: I was living in Boston, a student of Nadia Boulanger. Boston at that time was the Stravinsky capital of the world. And there was this, in some ways highly affected, Franco-Russian atmosphere, which certainly had nothing to do with Thoreau. As a matter of fact I was criticized: "Oh, you read *Thoreau*—that *nature* writer!" Yes, that was the attitude then. Very few people did take him seriously except for those involved in groups, I guess, in what became an ecological movement. So I was a maverick, of course.

EF: This must have been when you were at the New England Conservatory. That would have been . . .

TE: I was around there earlier from '42 until '46.

EF: At the conservatory?

TE: Yes. I went there first in 1942. I was slated to study composition. I would have studied with Quincy Porter. But there was a French Canadian composer—Jean Papineau Couture—people in Montreal speak a lot about him—and he lived in the dormitory, and I became friendly with him, and he said, "Look, Nadia Boulanger is in Cambridge. I'm studying with her. Would you like to study with her, too?"

"Yes," I said, "there are a lot of things I'd like to do."

"I'll talk to her."

So the next day he came around to chit-chat and said Boulanger would see me, and so I went. Took along some songs, Very bad. She was patient.

And so my poor family, who had suffered under my various vagaries for about ten years by that time had one more surprise. I called my father and said, "She wants $5,000."

EF: For private study?

TE: For private study. It included private study, a so-called master class. I would also continue a class in analysis under a man by the name of Francis Judd Cooke. You know him?

EF: The name is familiar, but no, I can't place it.

TE: He was a marvelous man, a student of Sir Donald Tovey.

My father would have made a good musician. He never studied music, but he was deeply involved in it. He knew many organists. He went and talked to one of them, and he said, "That crazy son of mine! What he wants to do now is to study with this French floozy. She wants $5,000."

And he said, "Nadia Boulanger? Will she take him? Send the $5,000."

Which he did.

EF: Putting you suddenly in the hands of the most famous composition teacher anywhere.

TE: And that was marvelous. This was something I'd been looking for—that kind of study, which I had never had with anyone in any of the things I was interested in doing. There were things about it that annoyed me because Nadia did invade the private lives of her students, told them how to live. I know that one time when I was waiting for a lesson . . . (I always brought a book along because I knew that I'd have to wait long.) I had Freud's *Outline of Psychanalysis*. I left the book behind. When I came back the next time, I did not get a lesson—I got a lecture about the enormities of reading Freud. She had known Dr. Freud, and he was a bad man.

But she certainly did give me the basis for many things, and those master classes were absolutely fascinating. The people who were drifting in and out of those classes! One day a young man with bright curly hair and sparkling blue eyes dressed in jodhpurs appeared. "Who's that?" It was Paul Bowles.

Bowles never studied with her; he studied with Copland . . .

EF: Who had.

TE: And at that time he was still involved with Copland. He was in Boston because of a musical, *Jacobowsky and the Colonel*, for which he wrote the music. Things like that happened all the time.

Stravinsky came to Boston regularly about twice a year, and he would always take us young ones out to dinner at the Athens Olympia. We never had menus. He could speak modern Greek, and he'd go into the kitchen and talk to the chefs, and eventually we were fed. He sat at the head of the table and pontificated on every conceivable subject. Mainly these had nothing to do with serious music but were very valuable. For one thing, he taught me how to eat flounder. It was served according to his specifications at the Athens Olympia. "Never the filet. Always the whole fish." He was right.

One time towards the end of that period something happened that was very important to me. This was a musical comment. Stravinsky didn't say much of anything, rather, all of a sudden, he slammed his hand down on the table and said, "Beethoven is a rotten composer!"

EF: What in the world did that mean?

TE: I was eighteen years old and starry-eyed: "What did he say?" And it took me a long time to figure out what he did say, which had nothing to do with the value of Beethoven's music. What he was saying was that at this point, I, Igor Stravinsky, am composing *The Rake's Progress*; I am completely involved with *belle canto*, and I cannot hear Beethoven.

I think that was a correct understanding. At least I've always taken it as such and felt that that was something that all of us should remember, our personal crotchets and our personal biases, which can change completely overnight if something else opens up.

But then after all, there is a story, one of the last stories, of Stravinsky at the age of eighty-nine spending an entire night when he should have gone to bed—far too weak to have done this—talking about the last quartets of Beethoven with Robert Craft.

Our bias is very important, and it is almost always misunderstood by those we talk to. We should be aware of this, and they should, too. If someone has the stature of Stravinsky, people take this as gospel. OK—Stravinsky says Beethoven's no good, so Beethoven's no good according to his followers, but *not* according to Stravinski.

EF: What about a student's biases? Like yours. Thoreau—or, for that matter, Mahler.

TE: I got into a lot of trouble. Even then I was much interested and involved with Mahler, and that was not done in the Stravinsky circle. But then, of course, ten years later . . . I would have loved to be around when this happened—when Stravinsky was honestly looking for a new way, and Craft said, "What do you think about these guys? How about Schönberg's stuff? How about that whole culmination of the German Romantic development?" So Stravinsky wrote *Agon*, and to the end of his life, he continued to write serial music. And it was no problem at all. But many of those in the group—Harold Shapiro, for instance—stopped composing completely. It floored him. He couldn't go any further. Arthur Berger and some of the rest of them took it in stride and eventually incorporated serial technique. Copland did.

But I think that was a very valuable lesson. I can't be sure that this is an exact interpretation, but it's pretty close.

EF: If we could go back to Thoreau for a minute, I'd like to ask why these people, some of the most brilliantly creative people around, had so little use for him.

TE: They simply weren't interested.

EF: How about Emerson and the rest of the New England tradition? They were living in the midst of it after all.

TE: In that group, with the possible exception of Shapiro and maybe Irving Fine, they weren't much interested in it.

EF: Were they in some sense living in Europe rather than Boston?

TE: Yes, they were, absolutely. Nadia was there simply because of the war. The Longy School was more or less formed to give her a teaching vehicle by Melville Smith, a former student. So it was very heavily biased toward a European tradition. Copland, who used to show up sometimes, would inject something else, and you could see that he was not thoroughly satisfied with this. Copland and David Diamond: "We've got something here, too, and we had better pay attention to it, our art is here. We'd better use what we have." Unfortunately I never had the opportunity to really talk much with them about this.

EF: How did your association with Boulanger end?

TE: It was a very bittersweet ending. Once I had enough of the technique to know a little of what I was doing I realized I had very little to say in music. Of course, she realized it. And I was more and more unhappy.

She had a breakdown and left. She stayed with the Stravinsky's. I think this was sometime in 1945. And so she was gone for about six months. We students were more or less thrown upon each other, so we studied together. And when she came back, I had decided I should really not try to compose. What she said I have never forgotten:

"Promise me you will not compose. You are literate. You should write." And eventually I did, but with a few accents from another discipline.

EF: So you were writing as well as composing at this time.

TE: Oh, I was always writing. I had the idea fully formed when I was fourteen . . . I don't know what sort of grandiose notions I had, maybe my own Bayreuth or something.

EF: Boulanger's criticism must have been horrible to accept.

TE: It was shattering. For almost six months it was impossible for me to do anything. I didn't write. I certainly didn't compose. I wouldn't listen to music. Scarcely read. And it was about three years before I could really listen again. Then one time I was with a friend, and it was absolutely impossible to avoid it. The piece was very dear to me anyway, but now it is doubly so, the B-flat quartet, opus 131 of Beethoven. Now I realized that I wasn't meant to compose. I could become involved in other ways.

EF: Where did you turn then?

TE: I went on and went to the Cape and lived there for fifteen years and wrote with very indifferent success, and I think very little of what I wrote was of much value.

There were some things that I picked up and later published. Very, very little.

EF: This would have been in the late forties.

TE: Early fifties, late forties.

EF: You had broken with Boulanger in . . .

TE: '45. I cut myself off from the musical life pretty much. The only person I was at all involved with in those days was Claudio Spies.

EF: I don't know that name at all.

TE: He is still at Princeton.

But as I say, I was running into another roadblock. The force of the New Criticism was felt in practically everything. I read religiously things like *Partisan Review, Virginia Review, Kenyon*. I kept getting this feeling: these people are telling me that they are the happy few. Their band has the real dope on what *it* is and the rest of us just don't. And I didn't believe it.

EF: Did you have any connection with any of those guys? Know them or correspond with them?

TE: No, I stayed away from the whole bunch. I did regularly send things to Poetry, and I got a very curious rejection from Karl Shapiro at one point. He said everybody else likes this poem except me, so I'm sending it back. I've got that letter somewhere.

I got more and more disgusted. I told a friend, if this really is what one is supposed to do, I'd better take up something practical like taxidermy. But there were little things. The magazine that . . . Three of them: Richard Emerson's . . .

EF: *Golden Goose.*

TE: Robert Beum and Fred Eckman. Well, that was a combination of two earlier magazines, *Chronos* and *Sybilline*. And they took a couple of things from me, and I kind of liked the sense of the way things were looking: "Maybe there is something outside." And then I found the first issue of *Origin* at Gordon Churnie's Grolier Bookshop in Cambridge. I read that and: "Lord! I'm not alone! There are plenty of people." And suddenly a great weight was taken off me.

Actually I read those first parts of *Maximus* going through Gloucester. I was on the train. I went to Cape Ann, and I came back, and a couple of days later I went to the Grolier, and I talked to Gordon about this. Gordon was an extremely politic man. He got along with everybody, and he never entered literary squabbles. But he kept asking me, "Well, what do you like about it? What do you think about this Olson?" It was late afternoon and a couple of people came in and out, and there was this tall, blocky young man, and finally Gordon says, "You want to meet the editor? That's Cid Corman." So we went out to a Hayes Bickford and had coffee, and that, of course, changed everything. That was the beginning of the opening up.

And I still . . . I wrote a letter to Cid yesterday. That correspondence has been unbroken now since 1951. It's one of the most pleasant parts of an ongoing conversation. We talk about everything, always have.

EF: Did you begin to identify yourself with any particular group of writers?

TE: I've never really been connected with groups, and I've always wanted not to be. One of the things that I noticed very early in *Origin* . . . This is perhaps not exactly what Olson wanted to happen, but it was *not* a group. These were really people who were writing as well as they could from wherever they were, and that was the big strength, particularly in the early years. I enjoyed that position.

EF: Yes, that's one thing I've always liked about Corman, his real integrity—he just wasn't interested in running somebody's else's magazine. There were all those people who thought they knew what he should be doing, and he just wasn't going to sit down and shine somebody's else's shoes. And poor Olson, he wanted so desperately to make that magazine his own, but look at all the terrific work that might never have been published if he had.

Did you ever know him? Olson, I mean.

TE: I never met him, and in a way, I'm glad. I think one of two things would have happened. Perhaps I wasn't then as cantankerous as I am now, but we might have fought. If not, I'm afraid he might have become a father confessor as he did to a great many other people, and I never functioned very well in that position.

EF: Did you correspond with him?

TE: I had a very interesting interchange by postcard with Olson, and I was never able to figure out just what was going on until years later. Olson was at Black Mountain, and I started getting a series of postcards. I tried to answer them, and the final one said, "Never mind, lad; it was a good poem." Fine. then several years after that I met Mark Hedden, who would have been in Olson's class then, and he said, "Oh, I knew all about you years ago because Olson came into class one day furious, banged his fist on the table, and said, 'There is some bastard up in Massachusetts writing about tansy. Tansy is mine!'" And in the seventh issue of *Origin*, there is a short lyric of mine called, 'Tansy for August.' And it was at the time when Olson was writing the *Maximus Poems* and the third letter with "Tansy buttons, tansy / for my city." And I said then that tansy is a pretty tough plant; there's enough of it around for all of us.

But that was the closest to contact. He did refer to me several times in letters to Cid, sometimes kindly, sometimes not.

EF: You mentioned elsewhere that you were once interested in Conrad Aiken's work, thinking you had something in common, particularly your interest in music, but that eventually you recognized that he was going in a very different direction.

TE: Well, because he used musical terms in those essays which are collected in *Skepticisms* . . . He said things about counterpoint, ear, and cadence. I was interested because I was dimly aware even then that I was using some of the things that I had learned in studying music. And I'm one of those people who felt early on that I needed some guidance. Well, he lived near where I did so I walked over.

EF: This was on the Cape.

TE: I was in Harwich, and he was in Brewster.

But I found very quickly that he was using these terms in a way that poets often do, something that still rather annoys me. They don't really talk in a musical sense. They think they do, but they really don't know what the fuck they're talking about. They don't really know what counterpoint is, and except in a very few cases, they don't really understand the different kinds of cadence. In a musical sense, there may be different kinds of cadence in poetry that are closely connected to the various musical forms. How many poets know what a plagal cadence is, or can use it properly?

EF: While you were looking for ways in which you could take musical cadence and adapt it to poetry.

TE: Exactly.

EF: Whereas he . . .

TE: He was using it in the same way as talking about "ear." It's a different thing. So I dropped that. We were friends for a while, and then I made the cardinal mistake of living in his house for a year. That was a good way of falling out with Conrad.

EF: This was when he was away?

TE: Yes, that was when he was at the Library of Congress.

So then I was stuck with Cid. I took Cid as more or less a mentor, and we got into some wonderful discussions, some by letter. I went to Boston about once a month, and I'd go out to Dorchester where he was living with his parents in those days. And finally we got into a real log jam, and neither of us would give an inch. I knew that I didn't want to do exactly what he wanted, and he knew that he couldn't move me. But that was when he was first in touch with Zukofsky, and he said, "Look, you seem still to want some kind of guidance. Why don't you send some stuff to Louis? I've talked to him about it. He has read your stuff, and he is willing."

I did, and that was again a blast of fresh air. OK, a guy is talking about these things in exactly the same way that I am. And he was extremely valuable to me. I would not want to echo anything that any man said, but when Oppen said that Louis was the only person who ever taught him anything about poetics, I would say exactly the same thing.

EF: Specifically in terms of his interest in music as it relates to poetry, or . . .

TE: In terms of everything. He would correct things. He was very patient. He would allow, if I argued for something that perhaps he didn't like, he would say all right. He was merciless so far as what he considered sloppy.

EF: What sort of things did he look for?

TE: Well, if he felt that a line break was something that had been reached as a sort of compromise, he could spot it immediately. He did the same thing with Williams. Williams sent him poems almost to the end of his life, and Louis would do things of that sort. And he was marvelous at it. He was an excellent teacher.

This was all by correspondence. I never met Louis until it was all over when I left the Cape and went to New York for a year.

EF: So he dealt with the specifics—word choice, line breaks rather than poetics generally.

TE: Absolutely, he was always specific. There was never anything cloudy. And he was also exemplary in detachment. I know that some of the things I was doing were not things that interested him very much. He never tried to say, "Well now, why don't you write a Zukofsky?" He tried to find out what it was that *I* wanted to write and to make it easier for me to do it. Well, I think that is one of the hallmarks of good teaching. He was invaluable.

EF: He had an understanding of your musical considerations.

TE: He simply sensed. He made the right decision whether he had formal training or not. He had that kind of mind.

EF: But also the ability to distinguish between conventional musical directions in language and the directions of music as such.

TE: Yes, Louis certainly knew what a fugue was, and there are many musicians who have studied for many years and who don't know it that well and would have been absolutely floored by something like *A*.

EF: Did you ever look into Thoreau's ideas about music?

TE: So far as organized music, he made some rather snide comments in the journals, and one of the real reasons that he went to Walden in the first place was to get out of his father's house because his sister Sophia was banging at Schumann on the piano all day. He didn't like it, but of course, that's something that gets lost until somebody brings it up again. The real reason that Thoreau went to Walden was to find out for himself if he should write poetry. That was one of the prime reasons. Ralph had that woodlot and told him, OK, you want to build a cabin—go ahead.

EF: I was thinking of the chapter "Sounds," or maybe it's "Solitude," where he says that storms can sound like music to anyone who knows how to listen. Nature as music.

TE: Yes, *that* musical sense he certainly had to a very high degree. So far as the more sophisticated development he didn't want anything to do with it. It was his choice. Apparently he liked to sit in his boat and play on the flute. But what did he play?

EF: I guess we have to defer to Ives on that, but personally I'd guess Thoreau hovered pretty close to C major.

What is it in your own work that determines the order of the words—a simulation of musical structures, musical cadences, qualities in syntax, the course of the idea . . .

TE: Certainly it is not primarily to state an idea. The development of the language, the cadence of the language, the musical cadence—those things. But I hope that very often when in something like "Late   As Budding Node" [*Talisman* 10], I am more or less at sea when I begin. I know pretty well where I want to go, even though I'm not sure whether I can get there. My hope is always, that the sense of the thing becomes clear both to me and, if it's going to be saved, to anybody else—will be clear not in the sense of making an idea: That can be, yes—I'm not ruling it out, but it is not my primary concern. After this happens with many (good people, too) as a poem builds towards some kind of climax, you get this memorable line, and that freezes my blood. I hate it, that memorable line, that whole . . . Well, maybe it's important to some people. It's not to me.

EF: Did you ever correspond with Robert Duncan or talk with him about musical structure?

TE: No. I talked with him a number of times about many cognate concerns at what he used to style the Summer Camp at the poetry festival in Michigan in 1973. Rakosi was there, all the old Objectivists except Louis. We talked quite a bit about music, and his sense was in some ways mine and in some ways not.

EF: For instance . . .

TE: I think he was in some ways impatient in trying to put this in terms of something that makes a musical exercise. I don't think that I was, but I think that . . . Anyway, his sense of music was something *other* because he didn't really study music either. I'm sure that in some ways this is a limitation as far as I'm concerned. I'm very glad that I did study, but I'm sure that I do look at things like this from a more literal stance.

EF: Your work seems to undergo a change, a break, in the seventies.

TE: I don't think there was really a break. I think it was simply that I had come to a place where I thought that if I continued to write what everybody expected me to write that maybe I could make very nice copies of things I had done, some of them much better. I've always resisted that. I dislike it. I don't want to do the same thing again and suddenly it came to me. Listen: there are all kinds of possibilities, and I had a very strong interest at that time in the development of serial music. I thought that there were certain things that I could take, certain things that I could use. I even went so far in a couple of things as to set up something comparable to a tone row. Now I have used modified forms of that in a lot of things. Actually "Node" has a pretty strong row.

Generally the way that works now is that a series will occur (this is nothing I can be held to, but it has happened in a number of cases); the initial statement is pretty much as that series is first set up, and then it is elaborated or broken down. Much more important is the little corpus of material. It's dangerous to use these musical terms. But if it is like a melody, then the thing that I plan to do very often is to vary it, and the whole principal of variation has become more and more important to me over the years. I think that it really is one of the foundation blocks of all art. That is *it*: variation. But variation is not the repetition in various registers of something that is appealing with embellishments and broderies and things of that sort. The material is used to the point where it cannot be used any longer. It has been used up. Now, if it had been set up in a slightly different way, you could do another set of variations, yes, but doing it this way—OK, there's no more to do. That is something that to students, to anyone who will listen, I will defend. I do not understand visual arts anywhere nearly as well, but I think that the same principles apply there.

EF: This exhaustion is an exhaustion in sound, I gather, not in ramification or application of what is being said—in ideas.

TE: The sounds. And in doing this, they, the sounds themselves, have said. It's not a superimposed idea. You're not being led by anything like that.

EF: Does the reader have to be aware of the way the structure turns the poem?

TE: No, no, absolutely not. As a matter of fact it might even be a deterrent. I mean at some point we should be allowed to cover our tracks.

But there should be a satisfying sense, and that satisfying sense should entail both the feeling that the material has not been exhausted in a sense, but it is being used as far as it can be. And at the same time that it has become very clear. It is a distillate at this point.

EF: Who do you see working in territory similar to your own?

TE: In a way, John Taggart, but it seems to me that he is dealing with the same sorts of problems in his own way. I think we inhabit a common aesthetic country. And young Mark Nowak. Yes, very much. He was at Bowling Green when I was there, and we became friends very quickly. Even now sometimes when I see him, he'll say, "How's that, teacher?" And I'll say, "All I ever did was say you're on the right track; it's all right—do it."

EF: What about *Axes*—where is that now?

TE: That has never been wholly published. Only parts of it have been. If anybody's interested in publishing it, it's there.

EF: It's done?

TE: It's done. The last part is *Bases*. I started the whole process in 1950, and I thought it would be nice to finish it in the year 2000. So maybe . . . I don't know. I haven't done anything with it for a couple of years. There have been other things that have occupied me. Now maybe I will.

EF: It's about as Wagnerian as anything any poet ever attempted. And there might be more? That's astonishing.

TE: I always go back to musicians for examples because it seems to me that composers—not instrumentalists—but composers of all artists have thought the most clearly about their art. And interestingly. Brahms said that after sixty, "There isn't much more." Then he modified it, as he well might have. There was quite a lot actually: "Yes, I can still do it, but it's a lot harder." And it is a lot harder. Every time you do something worth doing, it's as if there were a little valedictory note at the end: "Gentlemen, I have just slammed sixteen doors. I don't want to do this again."

This last winter was not a terribly good time for me except that Mark Nowak had needled me. He's always been very appreciative of the part songs, and we performed parts of them the way they should be once in Bowling Green. And he said, "I don't know how much further you'd like to take this, but I will give you a commission if you'd like." Well, unfortunately we don't have a piano, but our neighbors do. So it was a great joy.

I find this many times: I am not aware until I actually sit down how long things have been going on inside me. And another thing. I talked about this with Duncan. Apparently he had that same sense. The actual *revision* that everybody is so hot to find—the worksheets—OK, some people work that way. Other's do not. I mean plenty of things I've written all over, but I've never been as happy as with the things that simply seem to come from nowhere once I've started. And then at the end there is actual physical tiredness. A long journey.

Anyway, I did a set of inventions of various kinds. And I had more pleasure in doing that than I have ever had with any extended piece since *Ranger*. *Ranger* I loved, and I hated leaving it, but I knew damn well I had to; it was getting too easy to do.
EF: There's one final thing I'd like to touch on, Ted, and that's your statement various times that poetry is life and life is poetry. That's Thoreau again. Or Wagner. I mean your conviction that there's not a series of works but one continuous work.
TE: Yes, some people have appreciated that, and some have been very much disturbed by it. But I have said that many, many times. I do believe it. For myself at least I don't like the idea of isolating masterpieces; they're like tombstones, mega-liths. Maybe that is what leads me on and why I become interested in somebody else's work in toto.

But then I want everything—everything of that person—of myself.

MICHAEL HELLER

EF: You have written a great deal about the objectivist poets and spoken of Oppen's importance for your work. Your poems, meanwhile, appear, for instance, in a recent anthology of poets influenced by Buddhist thought, your memoir writing deals with language and Judaism, and in both your poetry and prose there are citings and references to Benjamin, Celan, Montaigne, Montale and to certain philosophical traditions. The field of reference is unusually broad, but also constructed largely of references to the past. How do you place yourself in connection with contemporary poetry, to some of its directions or movements?

MH: How? Uneasily. That is, I tend to think first in my poetry about meaning or personal and public discovery, and in terms of a vocabulary of self, history, the emotions, terms which in the present critical climate are often viewed as irrelevant or debased. I find it hard to picture myself as an art or cultural worker. Rather, I'm someone on a quest, my energies directed at what can be said about one's life or about how the act of writing might impinge or enlarge on one's life. Questions of poetic form are related to this goal. My relations to other poets is primarily based on friendship and/or a deep feeling for their work which cuts across the poetic spectrums or lines drawn between poetic 'schools.'

EF: In your essay, ``Avant-garde Propellants in the Machine Made of Words,'' in an a issue of *Sagetrieb*, you criticize language poets as formalists.

MH: I was trying to say something about poetry, its traditions, about reading and language, but yes, I spoke of some language poet practice as formalist, to a certain extent. Formalists in my sense of the word as being concerned with certain procedures and creating certain forms before actually writing. In other words, about these poets having some preexisting notion about the shape, the kind of content or exclusions thereof concerning the poem.

EF: At the same time, you admire Williams's notion of the poem as machine.

MH: Yes, but I make a qualitative distinction between the language poets' use of ``machineness'' and Williams's metaphor. . . . What I was really after in that piece, among other things, was a critique of the declared assumptions that language poetry was being written under, not so much whether it was good or bad poetry. I tried to avoid that type of judgment. As with any other genre, we have the good and the bad. And I guess I had a polemical notion in mind in some parts of that essay because many of the language poets and their theorizers seemed so polemical and dismissive about all sorts of other kinds of writing. They were re-enacting that classic avant-garde trope of defining poetry solely in their own terms, and that not only rankled but had its wonderful ironies, not the least of which is that their rhetoric has been comfortably normalized to the rhetoric of the academy.

So yes, one hinge of ``Avant-Garde Propellants'' is the question of machineness, something that people like Bakhtin have discussed with more thoroughness and rigor. I contrasted the way Williams saw that term, at least the way I thought he saw that term, and the way that the language poets, if we can use that broad brush, saw that word.

Williams, in my view, saw the machine notion as an ethical or spiritual demand placed upon the poem; the writer had to be kind of ruthless almost in trying to make a poem get to its point, do its job, so to speak. He uses that term metaphorically. And when I talk about someone like Barrett Watten applying the term to the work of Bruce Andrews or a couple of other people who actually invent a poem-making machine the way you would use Ractor, the poem generating software, you know, it struck me as a rather different sense of ``machineness.'' Between those two senses, something I thought essential to poetry was being lost, whether that is voice or risk or, you know, commitment or whatever. In its place, I found a language that was personally difficult to read in that it wasn't leading anywhere in particular or going beyond anything other than its kind of surface zippy zaps, *frissonville*, so to speak.

EF: And yet, in spite of the differences between Williams's sense of the poem as a machine and what one finds in language poetry, there is a common perception of the poem as a mechanism-a very twentieth-century perception, I think. Certainly not very useful in reading Whitman, say, or Shelley or Villon.

MH: But this is a very interesting concept. Armand [Schwerner] just sent me a book I haven't had a chance to read much of entitled *The Bachelor Machine*. It's a whole series of essays about twentieth-century modernists—you know, Duchamp, Chirico, the Futurists, mostly in the early part of the century—and their analysis of the machine is two-fold: one, a mechanical application of the word, is that the machine is a functional device, performing a particular task or making something. The other, more radical, use of the word concerns its metaphoric quality, a quality which never can quite fit into a functional definition because in the metaphoric mode, whatever you intend to say, you're bringing a whole world to kind of lean or press against the language you're going to use. And, therefore, you're constrained or opened up to the vast socio-political, philosophical dimensions of the terminology, let's say. As metaphoric pressure, a word like ``machine'' can be effectively used with Whitman or Villon, and probably has been.

Which is what I see in Williams's usage. You know, Williams had situated himself in opposition to the nineteenth-century kind of genteel poetry that was common in his time, a garden party poetry sentimentally removed from the industrial-based society around it. So Williams, in suggesting a different aesthetic with respect to the machine, provides a useful valorization of the term's hardness.

EF: You don't see language poetry as constrained by socio-political factors beyond the formal intention?

MH: Well, I do, as all writing is so constrained. It's what is done with those constraints, picked, valued or opposed, which makes all the difference. The present day fashionableness of the machine aesthetic, its cliche-value, is possibly something to be resisted, certainly with respect to making easy equations or identities. Among some of the poets and writers we are now talking about, their chosen constraints are the ones that least attract me. They seem to me to be mostly art-historical, if you know what I mean. That is, their model is the notion, as I say in that piece, of some kind of planned obsolescence about poetry. My main thrust, which went well beyond language poetry and its practices, concerned what I thought was being missed. And that's why I proposed another thinking about poetry, I guess it would be, and that would be, as I called it, a sort of counter continuity—that is, a notion of poetry in which one sought to bring a meaning to a poem that could directly war with other existing meanings, not procedures that out-foxed meanings or went somewhere else or even invented their meaning, but rather one that was always in relationship to a kind of prior order of experience.

EF: So language poetry is by nature predisposed to say whatever it says?

MH: Not so much that. It seems to me it's predisposed to avoid certain kinds of sayings, ones that deal with embodiment, with a person in history, with voice, for instance. And voice—when I use the word voice I don't simply mean finding the way you sound. I mean everything that is individual to a poet.

EF: Or eccentric?

MH: Yes, eccentric or whatever. I would use that. So my reading of the language poets and their kind of polemical address was the way into the thrust of my essay. Primarily, I was looking for a dialogue on these matters. Now maybe I don't know whether I'm an older generation reacting to the new or simply someone who is still alive, unfinished and so trying to find something yet even newer to perceiving. And, too, I may have been reacting to something that's becoming passé already. Language poetry is already becoming a kind of old-fashioned mode, and the younger poets in their thirties, for instance, who I know, are already resisting some aspects of the movement. Perhaps what is being recognized is the narrow band width of the metapoem, even as it contains appealing transmittals to the critical establishment.

EF: You're one of the few poets I've ever known who is trained as an engineer—trained, I mean, in that way that sees a construction, whether a road or a space station, as a manifestation or an elaboration of formal procedures. That seems particularly interesting, given your challenge to language poets, who after all at one very fundamental level might be seen in some of their procedures as linguistic engineers.

MH: Well, even though I was trained as an engineer, mechanical engineer, I might say that was a falling off from a kind of higher calling, to a certain extent. What had always interested me was science and what I suspect aroused that interest was the wonder aspect or the kind of intuitive aspect of scientific inquiry. I wasn't up to the math of that calling, but, as I've said before in print in a number of places, at some point I saw—and this comes up in my memoir as well—I saw a certain sort of similarity between what goes on at the edges, the frontiers of science, and what goes on at the edges of poetry, at least in my reading of it and my attempt to do it, and that is a kind of process of feeling one's way into connection with the world associated with language and naming—a feeling of risk, of not knowing quite where one is, that particular uncertainty which is on the horizon of all human activity (and I mark that off from something like indeterminacy). I am drawn deeply to the sense that science and poetry have as their habit the deconstructing of their own closures. For that, one needs closure of a sort, something we have barely studied.

EF: Closure?

MH: Yes, not as an effect, but as a cause. What I'm really interested in, in someone like Oppen, is the idea of knowing where you are and finding, as he puts it in a line—where the known and the unknown touch. It strikes me as the kind of thing that was attracting me in the scientific as well as the poetic realm. Of course, I came to poetry much later than I did to science, many years after.

Now the other thing that is key here, at least in my own background, relates to the tremendous precision about science and engineering. There's a certain love of that precision that can be deadly in some ways, you know. All too right brain, we might say, too rational, using the right side of the brain—too constantly bent on order. And so the scientists whom one most admires like Einstein or Feynman, or any of those people, are the ones who make precision work, who seem to be precise but at the same time are also willing to break with—to use the Kuhnian kind of thing—break with the paradigms of their time. One names—to use my personal theory of onomastics—to unname. And the poetry that has always interested me has been poetry which embraced this attitude or activity. I was always drawn to Oppen, who I thought in his poetry emulated this scientific vigor, and to Zukofsky, in any number of places, and to Williams in many, many poems—in the later poems even more than in the earlier poems. The earlier poems have a kind of dazzle and fusion of European avant-garde motifs such as in *Kora in Hell* and so on, *Spring and All*, beautiful poetry, but in the later poems, in ``Asphodel'' or in ``The Desert Music'' or in ``Tribute to the Painters'' and other parts of the *Brueghel* book, there are for me these kinds of significant moments where you feel a true discovery is being made—a true capture of reality.

EF: That's a startling thing to hear these days—``capturing reality.'' Newton's reality? Amy Fisher's? Charles Olson's? What does it mean? Seriously, I suspect that the whole issue of poetry, at least in matters of communication, turns on that question, however it's phrased.

MH: Well, the best way of putting it is that one feels that what is being said has some curious kind of truth to it. You have given something an articulation or a name. Stevens says in *The Necessary Angel* that poetry gives ``the sense that we can touch and feel a solid reality which does not wholly dissolve itself into the conceptions of our mind.'' That capture.

EF: And what does that mean?

MH: It doesn't *mean* anything. Or it means something only in a contrastive sense. Once inarticulate, now articulate, and, hence, available for use or knowledge. It's really a feeling, and it doesn't last. My thinking here goes back to Oppen in a way, or to Merleau-Ponty even. There's a kind of upsurge of the world, and for an instant it seems believable, and you believe it because your craft has led you there. And your attempt at being open toward the world has led you there. And there's some sort of magic to it, a feeling. I associate all this to naming rather than to a word like "process," because my instincts tell me, not that I live *in* language, but *with* it. As I wrote in "Journey to the Exterior of the Symbol," we circumambulate our linguistic structures. Poems, writings, are names to me, and have that otherness or externality appropriate to objects and people. I see great value in this recognition, the "classic" dimension of a work. Now, if I were to fall into my Buddhist lingo, because, you know, I've been a student of Buddhism for many years. In Buddhism, you have a somewhat similar way of talking about the experience, realization, suchness, etc., not satori or anything like that, not that sort of illumination perhaps, but a certain feeling of both the conditioned and unconditioned aspects of reality simultaneously—your sense of that.

EF: Thereby making individual perception highly relativistic and eccentric—relativistic at least to occasion and certain individuals or audience.

MH: Not making. Perception is already singular, individualistic.

EF: Solipsistic? You mentioned Thomas Kuhn earlier, and his position might be effective here, at least in terms of language poets and eccentric perception. It would seem that the writer who adopts formal propositions, who self-consciously gears his or her language to, say, political positions, limits the possibility for Kuhn's paradigmatic shifts. The radical, it may be, becomes a true conservative. Whereas you seem to propose a new formal awareness, if there are no rules.

MH: Yes, awareness is the word. And I would add this to it: I would say that this is very much more than an intellectual thing. I mean that this thing happening, for me anyway, has its validity in its carnality, in its embodiment within a human being. In other words, it's the oldest notion in writing of individual witness—which I keep going back to. And even though such ideas are somewhat culturally declassé and historical, I refuse to buy into that. I've read the same thinkers all of the other people have read in this regard. I've read a great many of the deconstructionists and post-thises and thats. Of course, my reading of someone like Derrida or other post-structuralists will very often be at odds with what I've seen in the pages of *Poetics Journal* or any other place. The problem may be a matter of my feeling that some writers are not going far enough with those thinkers, or with my own overdosing on Walter Benjamin who sits next to Merleau-Ponty and Oppen on my left-shoulder pantheon.

EF: What about Hayden White's work on historiography? I'd expect that to have some interest for you.

MH: Oh, very interesting to me. In fact I had his writings in mind as I was working on my memoir project. I'm thinking here of his collection of essays, *The Content of the Form*. I'm rather taken with White's study of history, his attempt to get under certain forms of history making. In White, I found the study of history as one in which you keep looking for almost heretical testimony rather than official testimony. And this idea led me back to Gershom Sholem's notion of counter-history, which goes back even further to Gottfried Arnold's ideas that, for instance, the history of the Christian church is not in the institution but in its heretics. And these are very appealing considerations to me because constantly it is in just those oppositional figures one finds workability, useability, human room—I don't pose myself as an oppositional figure per se except as I'm able to sense it as I write, but it is in these histories of oppositions that the true nature of, let's say, a Christian ideal or a Judaic ideal seems to work out. Buddhistic awareness practice, by the way, has a supremely heretical or undermining bent. In particular, I'm fascinated by the insights given at the end of *The Content of the Form*. The book has had some powerful influence on me. Have you read it?

EF: Yes.

MH: Well, I can't say I've spent a lot of time on other work of White's because first of all I'm a bit of a magpie-type of reader. But there where he talks about Dante, as God's historian is it? and the allegorical mode and so on, these ideas were important to me. And I was really surprised in some way by his getting back to an almost phenomenological version of history via representation, which White restores to some dignity. I think he gets into Ricoeur here who defines history as ``humanity at grips with the 'experience of temporality,' a definition applicable to poetry as well.

You know, phenomenology has been the one philosophical tradition that I've kind of been carried by. I've sat in that boat. Merleau-Ponty has been one of the more important thinkers to me—particularly in the later work, *The Visible and the Invisible* and some of the other books. All of it, really. Speaking of history, a recent book which I found provocative and useful is Jonathan Morse's *Word by Word*, a very interesting study of the problems of historical retrieval and the misuses of history. Morse deals a lot with the literature of the Holocaust, for instance, and he also manages to touch on significant aspects of Dickinson and Eliot and on a number of different films. He depicts words as ``entrained'' in history, carrying enormous psychic and social baggage with them. In my *Conviction's Net of Branches*, I tried to show how an objectivist poetics worked with those historical thicknesses or quagmires, if you like.

Now it's very hard to simplify the arguments of these people, but all of them seem to me to be investigating that area, that argument between the conception and the lived experience, you know, as the dimension of our existence that is generally overridden by theory. Theory tends to override lived experience because it is a machine of a certain kind which has its own generating principles usually in further and further cerebration and conceptualized ideas. Given its capacity to shroud thought in endless rings of certainty, you end up with a jargon machine, basically.

EF: In the piece I wrote on *In the Builded Place* for *Sagetrieb*, I mentioned that you begin the book by quoting Thomas Browne's somber recognition, ``the mortall right-lined circle ($\ominus$ The Character of Death) must conclude and shut up all'' and that Browne's elegant phrasing was somewhat easier for him as there was still something beyond that ``all.'' There was something beyond doubt and mortality, and he could make do with belief and the concepts aligned with it.

MH: Pound notes the loss of those belief systems when he cries out, ``But I have no Aquinas map!''

EH: It seemed that in *In the Builded Place*, as in what you are saying here, that for you conceptualization ends in self-generated fantasies, the jargon machine.

MH: The mechanistic logic or machinery of conceptualization.

EF: For you, then, the world has narrowed—perhaps intensified, but narrowed—in enormous ways.

MH: But our experience is our experience of everything. I mean I'm not rejecting anything. Certainly I'm not rejecting anything intellectual in one sense if that is the thrust of your comment.

EF: You're not?

MH: No. What I'm saying is that it's all to be tested under something like time or love. Categories somewhat foreign to the metapoetic mode. One of the beautiful things for me about Oppen was that he was a poet who had come out of Imagism and was using rhetoric in his poetry—I mean philosophical ideas and so on strung throughout that poetry, but you felt that they had been tested within him in some way within his experience and against his experience. It is hard to talk about this, and perhaps one can really fall into naive ways of trying to formulate it, but Oppen struck me as someone who was earning through some experience, if one wants to call it that, or learning through some experience the rhetoric that he was using, so that it has its music, its tensions. It wasn't, you know, simply a structure of ideas. It was a structure of idea-emotion which permeated the work, which showed a rare skill close to the prose virtues of late Stevens. An astonishing ``aboutness,'' a hovering and wavering commentary made poetic by objectification.

EF: But if the confirmation in a poem depends on private experience, something not in the poem as such, then isn't it in some way solipsistic experience that Oppen gives us?

MH: Not a private experience but a language experience. There's a certain danger to that, one inherent to the use of language. But I don't think I've ever sensed this as a reader's problem, and I certainly don't know if it's more solipsistic than any other writer. I mean we're all, each and every writer, guilty of the misplaced concreteness of our solipsism if you want to say so.

EF: But here you'd have an argument for language writing, wouldn't you? And it's a classical argument by now, I guess: if you write according to certain procedures then you are diverted from trying to authenticate what you think is being said, in the strictly personal.

MH: But you replace what might be said with the theory and practice of the frisson to a certain extent, and that strikes me, while looking ``scientific'' or beyond the personal, to be as solipsistic in its own way. We are never ``beyond'' the personal, and there is nothing but a personal reception to whatever we write. This fake scientism only leaves you totally unaware that you're being solipsistic. Have you read Bakhtin's *The Formal Method in Literary Scholarship*? He covers this ground about as effectively as anyone in his saying that a practice like Russian formalism, which is very close to many kinds of language writing, as I mentioned here, tends to turn the reader into a kind of psychological apparatus who is simply catching and receiving a number of blips on a screen. One misses the dynamics, the clash or wrestling with, in and between meanings. So yes, let's say for purposes of argument that all con-structed meanings ultimately must be solipsistic because they have an envelope. They create an envelope, you know, in which the writer has locked himself through the trick, as Eliot said, of the box, the music box or whatever, the little metaphor he chooses. To my mind this is a very good thing as long as we recognize that envelopes burst and that closures initiate new insights and new poems.

EF: What a computer does is box or limit knowing in very rigid ways, but it is not solipsistic. And a procedure, whether it's a matter of a computer or a strategy for writing, can help to circumvent the merely personal or solipsistic. The possibility is real to me, though right now, obviously, I'm only trying to be a good interviewer and play the devil's advocate.

MH: Obviously. On the other hand, what is . . . First of all, I would argue, under the meaning of solipsism as we know it, whether a computer is solipsistic or not, whether you can use such a term.

EF: But it does devise commonly apprehended, as opposed to strictly private, meaning, and the meaning need be esoteric only to those who have not studied whatever computer language is in use.

MH: Does it devise any meaning at all? This is my challenge.

EF: Sure. I'm not talking about word processors but computers. They do devise meaning. That's exactly what they were created to do.

MH: You mean the computer machine. Well, I'm certainly no Luddite on this. I've written in favor of everybody having a computer as a matter of fact, but I'm not so sure that the way a computer handles information has anything to do with how we process that information. You see what I mean. I would make that distinction, and so I would say we're receiving certain kinds of information, and, true, it will solve a problem for us. It will perform a kind of instrumental or utilitarian function for us, and there could be no ambiguity about it, but it doesn't mean that we are not somehow incorporating that into another system, which ultimately resides, as I've tried to say, on what we perceive to be the nature of our minds.

EF: So you are saying in effect that the computer provides data, not meaning.

MH: Yes. Right. And the fact that meanings are only constructed. Or let's say we can get appearances of meaning from computers. I mean with some of the computer-generated poetry. Because we have such a desire to connect the two discrete dots into a line, to make a line between them. Whether these meanings then turn out to be useful for us, experientially, is another question and also whether we aren't already involved in a process of discounting that meaning and looking at it from a purely structural or utilitarian way. That's why I invoke the notion of the *frisson* or the ʻping' of sensation to describe some procedural language handling because it seems to me that is the way we get off the hook of those created meanings as well. That is, they become a bit like the editing of an ad or of MTV. Very nicely redone, but their imports are from other realms.

EF: Well, the reader takes data both from the computer and from the poem. Is the difference in expectation? Or is there actually a difference in the language, in its texture or dimension?

MH: Well, certainly there is a difference in expectation. I think that expectation is one that involves us in the notion of personhood, authorship, tradition and so on. If a computer said to me it's all right to jump off a cliff, I immediately discount it. If a poem by X says that, I have to think hard about taking that advice and jumping. My bank balance, I'll take the computer's word, but a word leading to the state of one's mind? That is, the so-called meanings, objective meanings, whatever you want to use, might be the same, but I would take the advice of an individual over a computer any day of the week on that particular sort of risk business. Not to mention the different sorts of aesthetic pleasures associated with the source.

EF: Earlier in this conversation you said that the poem was responding to socio-economic pressures, and I'd like to pursue that, if we could. It's a way perhaps of seeing the poem as outside the self, outside the strictly personal.

MH: I would use Oppen's definition of why he called himself a realist when he said, I am a realist in the sense that I am concerned with something that lies outside the poem. I would say that words, constructed in a poem, ultimately have some point at which they are both real and unreal. Like Blanchot's notion of the way the writer is caught up—and I believe I've even mentioned this in my new essay on uncertainty and poetry—Blanchot dramatizes this very powerfully in *The Gaze of Orpheus*. Anybody who works with words is caught between dread and anxiety about the use of a word. I'm not getting this exactly right, I know. But we know that for us a word has a meaning, a meaning that for someone else need not or will not or quite likely will not exist, and we're caught on this dilemma all the time. This is the creative dilemma that makes us do the things we do in craft—makes us tune words, to use Williams's term, and that's what poetry is essentially. It's not creating a string of brilliant words but of tuning words so that we feel we're communicating.

EF: Communicating the words as such?

MH: No, we're communicating via the words. Williams, in a letter to Pound, about the music of verse, writes that the ''words have become the music itself, and the *understanding* (my emphasis) of the individual is now that which used to be words.'' Benjamin says that what ''has meaning—sense and form—is not the word itself, but the tradition behind this word, its communication and reflection in time.'' Somehow we're doing something other than giving data, whatever that is. And that seems to me to be socio-political or larger—if one could imagine it, a cosmological construct, as in the very large language of Robert Duncan or in the moving pathos of the archaic in Schwerner's *Tablets*.

EF: So the poem in this context is not solipsistic in that here it is a tuning of what you call a socio-political or cosmological. . . .

MH: Well, certainly it is a voicing of it and a tuning of it. But this is true of any poetry, including even language poetry. I mean it's kind of taken for granted that there's a thing called a language construct. Well, what does that mean? Frankly, the earth does not seem to dramatically gape open over the fact that language constructs. On the other hand, the history of the last seventy years or maybe even more, let's say the history of modernism, was first of all an attempt not to talk a certain way. You know, I don't want to talk that way anymore. I don't want to talk as though God exists. I don't want to talk as though all the traditions led me to write in iambic pentameter, whatever way one wants to look at that, and so there was this great overthrow via Pound—heaving the pentameter and all that—and where has he left poets? He's left poets with some greater responsibility for their own form, as I say in my piece, and that is the key issue. And that has nothing to do with 'schools.' It does have to do with the possibility of being a kind of clearinghouse, as I say in the objectivist book, of everything that's going on.

EF: Given that personal responsibility for form, what then, for you, is the experience of making the poem?

MH: Oh, well, that's hard to say. Do you mean my methods?

EF: No, I mean the actual experience of realizing the poem. The experience of finding it. Where do the words begin?

MH: A number of different places. I might overhear something. Or I'll be looking at a book, or I'll be walking around the streets, and I'll see something and write down a note in a notebook. And I'll gather these, and they'll gather dust on them or whatever for months and so on, or I will sometimes hear a rhythm in language and write it down in my book, or I'll make one up. Then I'll be trying to . . . it becomes almost like kind of a seed syllable, and I try to find out why is this meaningful to me in some way. What is the sense of this? What am I hearing? And then from that will perhaps emerge something. I don't know what it will be. It is usually a long process. There are poems I've done just sitting down, feeling moved or inspired, if you want to use those terms, by something, and I write it down quickly. A lot of the stuff, particularly the longer pieces, are usually these constructs of notes, hearings. And then, of course, there's the whole feeling that some bits of language lead to other bits of language. There's a kind of intertexuality going on in your own poem, you know, because you're moving from one jot of experience, let's say language-experience, to another language-experience. Somehow they come together. And for me there are no particular hard and fast rules about any of this, and as I say, I'm willing to let anything happen in terms of writing, but finally by the time I've gotten to an area where a poem is a finished one—finished thing or abandoned thing (you'd think there'd be a better way of talking about it), you just give up working on it. It's achieved some coherence whether it's a psychic or psychological coherence or some mixture of coherences.

I'm interested in things like Elaine Scarry's writings on the body—the body in pain. I'm interested in such things. Or in Meister Eckhardt's famous remark, ``The swiftest beast to carry you to your understanding is your suffering.'' My translation may not be accurate. So as a writer I'm looking always for that discomfort, how to be in that.

EF: So that poetic meaning in the work of a given writer is beyond, or more than, a discrete set of ideas—a point that one shouldn't have to argue, although given the way poems are used in classrooms and among critics, I supposed it has to be repeated over and over.

MH: Yes, but saying that—which cracks open the current vessels of the critical shibboleths—one must return to coherence, history, voice, the art, the pleasure or beauty of those. That is what Eliot was saying when he said, or Hölderlin as well, that the intelligence of a writer is everywhere present. It isn't the abstractable truth in individual lines or phrases particularly, but it's a manifestation of an intelligence which has the power to project itself against another intelligence—the reader's intelligence, let us say—and the reader's intelligence meets it and is affected by it, seduced by it, or it forces a change in that intelligence. ``Alteration of consciousness'' is the old phrase. That strikes me as what makes a writer a serious writer, one who really looks at things in that way and one whom you experience that way. So one experiences Stevens or Williams in that way, as an all-pervading intelligence whether there's a bum poem or a poem that blows your head off or whatever. You experience the writer that way. And that's rare, I mean, because it's also a matter in some way of your whole psycho-social makeup. ``Taste'' is not exactly the word I'm reaching for, but there will be certain writers that reach you because of certain propensities—like you're not immune to them might be the way of looking at it. We're probably immune to a lot of writers. We read them for a minor pleasure, or we say, wasn't that brilliant, and wow, and wasn't that a good read, though I find myself less and less able to do that. I can read junk, but I can't read a lot of serious writing.

EF: Earlier you said that the poem came out of some sort of discomfort. I'm wondering, given what you've just said about some readers being immune to certain writers, if you feel that discomfort is something a reader would have to share in order to feel the pressure of a given work.

MH: Well, I think a reader will have his or her own way of recognizing the feeling. That is, I wouldn't expect my particular sense of discomfort or irritability to be the same as anyone else's. Otherwise we'd have a kind of entropic world at work. Rather it's where one is comfortable or in a state of mental stasis, and the writer presses against that feeling of comfort and induces discomfort. That would be the kind of thing I'm talking about. And there's not necessarily any meeting of the minds there or meeting of discomforts per se. It's that you feel that you're encountering something obdurate, and that's what causes, you know . . . Bloom, in his way, has really touched upon this in his notion of misreading in Agon, and some of those tropological figures which he deploys seem to me to very accurately, at least on a psychological level, portray what might occur there. That is, your encounter with another writer is not sanctifying your view basically. It's kind of desanctifying. I mean, making you think again and feel again. Otherwise, there's no hope, the way I see it. The great hope of writing to me is (a) that a writer has freedom to do what he or she wants, and (b) out of that freedom, particular freedom, and I mean freedom with awareness of the whole historical, social tradition, matrix that one is in, one can try to learn as much about that as is possible as one goes along. Out of that freedom there might be produced a coherence that would push against another's coherence. One could look at the naked 'you' or make it rethink or something, and in that kind of dynamic is, as I say, any culture's hope. Now that idea is opposed somewhat to our reception of traditional art or the art of more traditional societies which appear to replicate their world views or reinforce moral or social status quos. Note I use the word "appear," please.

EF: An art that affirms?

MH: Yes, which does that perhaps unreflectively, as opposed to what seems to me to be a particularly Western thing running through our unofficial poets and unofficial critics. You know, God forgive us for having dead white males and all that, but it does seem that opposition or skeptical irony has usefully been one of the projects of Western poetics. And with the global village effect of the media and the anthropological sciences and so on, the techniques of Western oppositional poetics are on the increase. I mean now we're not only encountering discrete Western obduracies in our local conflicts, but we're getting them everywhere else too. I teach English to foreign students, and I'm very much aware of how they and we are the sites of such struggles and encounters. How their logic is different and not different. What verbal gestures or physical gestures I as a teacher might make in a classroom which will not be read by them the way an American student would read them.

EF: What do you think of the notion that poetry quite strictly is culturally defined, that it has in this instance been defined by men, particularly white, usually well-educated, affluent men, for their own kind?

MH: Well, this is a vexed issue, one that one enters on with trepidation, but I would say two things at once. Certainly the traditions of contemporary poetry have been, as you say, primarily created by mostly white, European-leaning or -influenced males replete with the blindnesses, sexisms, racisms of this inheritance. In one sense, as you say, there is this sort of solipsistic, if one could go back to that, self-affirming structure which has been created. At the same time, out of this culture, and poets have played some part in this, an antithesis has been created—that is, in the notion of the radical or resister and so on. So this damnable culture has created both things at once, and this strikes me as a dynamic that has occurred less frequently in other cultures. I wouldn't say that universally because, you know, other major cultures—say the Chinese or Japanese cultures, which I know a little about, or certainly Latin American cultures or whatnot or, let's say, if you had to switch it around 50% and look at gender issues close to home—it seems to me that a tradition of resistance or change exists, and its vocabulary, its world-shaping words, often come from the resistant strains of our traditions, and so one has to sort that out in individual cases. The blanket judgment seems to me to be absurd—you know, crude negative judgment against Western or Western white, male civilization since it in effect has created the very tools by which to be critical about it. Which is to be politically incorrect, I know.

EF: Well, let me phrase it this way: is there a place where the poem is not culturally defined, whether by, say, an Alexandrian body of critics or by any other social or cultural instance one could cite, and at the same time is not defined by the strictly personal or the solipsistic?

MH: I'm not sure I understand the thrust of this question.

EF: Well, then, going back a while, you indicated that the poem has a very personal, essentially solipsistic, dimension. Or a similar conclusion of that nature—the private judgment, in other words, which others may acknowledge and experience themselves but which always remains in the realm of the personal. In that case, poetry may be highly relativistic, a Tower of Babel, and the poem is then essentially self-assertion, an assault on others. The second thing is that the poem has its occasion in sociopolitical matters as defined, for example, by religious practices, ethnicity, gender, economic status. Since these are matters not only of difference but also, in our culture, of hierarchy and dominance, the poem may then become, indeed among some critics does become, a pawn in one person's effort to assert dominance, moral or otherwise, over another. So then one is confronted with the spectacle of Pound asserting this is the pattern, this is the code, this is the way to write, this is the hierarchy, this is the tradition, this is the way it has to be done. What it comes down to, it seems to me, is dominance: I know, and you don't. That kind of authoritative mode seems inherent to cultural critiques—including, alas, mine right now. So, I think Rilke and Spicer, for instance, elicit, or at least desire, a poetry of dictation—a poetry outside the personal and that version of the personal we understand as the cultural or social.

MH: But we should be under no illusion here. Spicer's counterpunching radio dictates a highly personal, highly individualistic account of pain, outsiderness, loss. And isn't Rilke's ``I'' in ``Who, if *I* cried out among the angels,'' his ``I''? Furthermore, your account of our domination by a poem strikes me as starting from the wrong end of the stick. A cultural or political environment dominates, and poems which buy into or reflect that environment reinforce the domination. The poem which is uncertain about or resists the *zeitgeist*, the fashion, it is this poem which may tend to set a few bonnets buzzing. Canetti grasps the psychology of the resistance I'm talking about when he writes ``no man today can be a writer if he does not seriously doubt his right to be one.''

EF: I'm wondering if you see a way out of that poetic entrapment in the personal and the cultural.

MH: Well, there's always a world. There's always other people, and I mean there's negotiations between them—us and other people in the world. And there are, to joke and be serious, recent articles about all those negotiations. That may be where our poetry arises as opposed to simply perceiving that within us is a purely socially constructed kind of deterministic little box that's making our language, making our poetry, making our practices.

EF: Bakhtin talked about that kind of social construction of one's language. And you don't accept that?

MH: I agree with Bakhtin. He'd say it's socially constructed, but he also has a tremendous sense of the notion of how it's socially constructed between people, the fluidity of social occasion. And as long as there's the between, then you have the possibility of it not being a purely subjective little thing. You have the possibility of being open and affected by otherness at all points.

EF: So you would see poetry as a kind of negotiation between the poet and her or his audience.

MH: A mediation. Yes, a negotiation, a mediation, I guess also you'd say in some ways between the poet and all the poets before and after. That's why I've always resisted the notion of the poem being something like a pure expressiveness. There's always an audience, and there's always a communication between you and another social creature. And maybe in the eighteenth and seventeenth centuries it was God. And now we're talking to ourselves with . . . I mean, we're talking with each other in a kind of new ballgame, so to speak.

EF: Is the objective of this kind of negotiation or mediation to eliminate difference?

MH: I don't know if there's a purpose to it in that way. In other words, to say, Hey you're like me. Quite the opposite perhaps, unless the way we are alike is in our mutual aloneness, about which we could speak.

EF: No, but you're saying the poem grows out of discomfort, and the kind of mediation you're talking about might well be tied to the prevailing kinds of discomfort these days.

MH: Now you're talking as the poetry editor of *MultiCultural Review*.

EF: Simply canceling difference by way of some great leveling process is no way to resolve the discomfort and the guilt. The discomfort is there for good reason—it does not go away. Or shouldn't. Germany should never forget. Nor, for that matter, should white Americans. Or, to cite the present, the people of Serbia.

MH: Oh, no, the discomfort is there. You mean to kind of reduce it? No, I think the discomfort is an absolute condition of existence and can't be rationalized away whether it involves someone of a different ethnic group or social standing or the person you're closest to. I mean that's what love seems to me to be all about. Is the otherness.

There's one sense in which poetry is about subjects that you can't do anything about—you know, death, grief, the natural world, and those are the moments in which a certain kind of otherness is encountered that is not yielding. It cannot yield, and your only thing to do then is to say something, and that's another dimension of what we're talking about which perhaps we haven't really emphasized very much. It strikes me that the root of this discomfort has a communicative dimension, where Hölderlin, for instance, says man is a conversation, man is a witness. Maybe that's where that source of poetry is. I mean that sort of inability to do anything but write or talk or something or even scream.

EF: You're an admirer of William Bronk.

MH: Bronk, yes, one of my favorite poets.

EF: And he seems, in terms of what you just said . . .

MH: Bronk is one of those poets who seems to me to be talking about these matters most eloquently and most forcefully. You've seen the piece I've written on Bronk in *Sagetrieb*. I'd written another thing, too, about his essays way back in the *Times*.

EF: The piece in the book review section.

MH: Yes. Bronk is part of the lineage that I feel I'm in. Bronk is right there.

EF: A lineage including Bronk, Oppen. Also Reznikoff, Zukofsky?

MH: The Objectivists. Williams, some of Pound, although not much. Some.

EF: Which?

MH: Earlier Pound. And portions of the very late Pound.

EF: And Rakosi.

MH: Yes.

EF: The Western tradition, outside poets such as these, seems to me repeatedly drawn to authority or is at least in search of it. Emerson in his Platonic self needed the Oversoul for spiritual certification, but he also told us that everything is always changing, and nothing is really authoritative except the moment and the fact of change. And that seems the basic recognition of the American poetic tradition.

MH: Oh, yes. That's the tradition I would identify myself with. Certainly the tradition which recognizes that everything is fluxional, including the nature of your mind and your perceptions and world and so on. That ultimately leads to a kind of poetic practice which involves change. This is an American, totally American kind of thing which Europe perhaps has only recently become involved in. Our writers (and Susan Howe beautifully articulates this territory) have encountered, in a highly compressed period of time, major doses of change. This certainly seems to be the case.

EF: To bring things together, I'd like to go back to where we began, that is, and ask what role a poetry dependent on procedures has in a culture that resists authority. Is there a conflict, or are procedures simply a way of encouraging change? I don't mean programmatic change—but a more natural process? You initially said some language poets were formalists in that the work involved certain prescriptions, ways of doing things, and I was wondering if in one sense that set them in a more European context. I don't know myself as that's so, but I've heard the point argued strongly both ways. I'm just asking where in that discussion you would place yourself.

MH: First, I would say my own work, the poetry, the critical writings, my memoir writing, these are deeply indebted to such European thinkers as Benjamin, Merleau-Ponty and Canetti. And Baudelaire figures with great importance—I've just begun a prose meditation on how my reading of the objectivists became preparation for going more deeply into Baudelaire.

As to language poets or any other poets? Well, by our bibliographies you shall know us. To a certain extent post-structuralist Europe informs them, informs me—certainly European-inflections-in-America. The main authority for some language poetry, though not all, it strikes me, is the avant-garde tradition, an overwhelmingly European one in origin. This tradition has done more than just survive; it has, with rare exception, survived unquestioned, or at least been bracketed separately, since the nineteen twenties. In America, as Jackson MacLow has pointed out in *Talisman*, ``avant-garde'' always threatens to become a commodity or commodity label. In saying this, I would seek to amplify. I'd like to go back to sources, including, certainly, some Europeans who are rather resistant to a commodified avant-garde. But that tradition, that art-historical tradition which in this country has become virtually a market force, has been, I think, a deep source of authority for some language practice work. And, as I tried to say in that essay, I wonder if the work that I discussed there is not only aligned with our current market forces but also, interestingly, if it doesn't at times embody, among its general configurations, something antithetical to its own political project. But in general, I mean, the invitation is more basic for all of us, for every poet, every writer, and that is how to overcome the seductions of authority, our self-made structures of authority, how to find ways of questioning these, as Henry James said, how to get yourself back in a tight corner, and that's generally the difficulty. Ideologies and even so-called ``natural'' linguistic manners (which are just other ideologies in disguise) threaten to place our lives at a remove or to reduce us to spiritual dwarves. Groping with our uncertainties, experiencing the close textures of our pleasures and pains, these will, of course, have an inevitable crudity to them. Which makes them both honorable and delightful. Or, as Williams said, strike out what you write well. Oh, I don't know, to me those are the real challenges.

EILEEN MYLES

EF: How does it feel living across the street from the Hell's Angels?

EM: It's a problem less and less. I moved here in '77, and in May I'll have lived in this apartment twenty years. Even in the last two months, I went through about umpteen phases about what that means. And now I think it's sort of funny and great, you know, but all of these things happened here; for instance, immediately upon my living in this apartment, I came out. My life began. And the Hell's Angels were, like, big and hairy and young. They were really pierced, and there were these kind of women that hung out with them, and all the stories of them throwing people off roofs and beating black men with pipes seemed to be true at that moment.

EF: And now they're big, flabby, and old?

EM: Yeah, they're old. A few new recruits, but they're basically . . . Their energy is sort of . . . I mean they got busted around ten years ago. They've never really been the same since then. The women are much meaner than the men.

EF: Why?

EM: They're really homophobic. I've gotten shit on several occasions for kissing a girl on the street. "My kid is here; my kid doesn't want to see that, you cunt." Yeah, they're the hard-ass ones.

EF: But there's nothing personal in all that, nothing beyond name-calling, is there?

EM: Not unless you've got a car. You notice they put out those orange witches' hats saving half the street. Don't get any idea about parking when they've already claimed the space. You get into all kinds of discussions around that.

EF: Do they do real damage to things?

EM: Oh, they would. They absolutely would. You wouldn't fuck with them at all.

EF: It's easy to find you, living here.

EM: It still helps to identify the block. People say, 'Oh, you live in the East Village.' I say, 'Yeah, Third Street. The Hell's Angels' block,' and they say 'Oh, *that* block.'

EF: Having them across the street must at least make the block safer.

EM: Yeah, we haven't been robbed in years.

EF: Does being here have any effect on your work?

EM: Yeah, completely. I was walking around this year thinking, I'm like Charles Olson, because I feel as if I've just used the inside of my apartment, the street, the neighborhood again and again and again. It seems it's right in front of me; why not use it? The trees, for instance [pointing to some in the cemetery]: I have a poem that just ends immediately, but it says something like 'Fourteen hundred poems begin with these trees.' You know, over twenty years I've been up here in the trees.

EF: That sounds like something from Schuyler. You were close to him, weren't you?

EM: Yes, that was great and accidental. I came to New York in 1974. I came to get an M.F.A. in writing from Queens College. I applied to a bunch of graduate schools. I was at Little, Brown in the subscription department of a medical magazine called

The Lancet in Boston, and my goal was sort of to be in publishing, but I hadn't gone to an Ivy League school, and I couldn't get any place at Little, Brown, or that's the way I felt anyway. So there was a bunch of us, kind of confused deadbeats at the medical magazine, who were all writers, of course, as anyone who worked there was. And they were all going to graduate school, so I was, too. So I applied to a bunch of schools, and the only one that took me was Queens College. So I went there for two months, something like that. And the guy who taught the poetry workshop was named Stephen Stepanchev—he's still around—and he showed us a few poems. He showed us one, "The Harbormaster" by O'Hara and then he showed us two by Jimmy, one which continues to be my favorite poem—the poem called "Poem." And another one—one of those quick picture poems of his. And I just thought I'd never seen anything like this before. And he went on to say that Jimmy and Frank O'Hara were members of the so-called New York School and denizens of St. Mark's Church. And he sort of said it with a bit of a sneer, I thought. And, you know, I thought that's where I'm going to go, then. And pretty soon I got the E train and got to Manhattan and dropped out of school and headed to St. Mark's, where the people knew who Jimmy were. And I was told I would never meet this guy, ever, because he was unreachable. And then one night at St. Mark's at a reading, I was talking to Charles North about how poor I was and I needed a job or something, and he said, 'There's a job—I don't know if you'd want it, but you could have it.' And I said, 'What's that?' And he said, 'They need someone to take care of Jimmy.' And so I met him, and he was just out of Payne-Whitney, I guess. So it was kind of weird. It was not clear who was who's pet. We were, like, two people in the Chelsea; it was one of those serendipitous things that happen.

EF: You were with him a while?

EM: No, it was like five months. We just became friends. The way the job was structured initially was really like a companion, so I worked with him seven days a week, five hours a day. It was like living with Jimmy half the day, and we got to know each other pretty well. But it was hard, and he was still not over having nervous breakdowns, and he was having one toward the end of when I worked for him. And I actually think I was too self-centered. I mean I could go through one with him, but I couldn't go through another one, and so I passed the job on to Tom [Carey] and Helena [Hughes]. And after that I was just one of a crew of pinch-hitters, sort of filling in when they couldn't. And then slowly over a long period of time we became friends. It was sort of, you know, 'How's Eileen,' or I'd come over and hang out with Tom and him a bit. But he was always generous both with his own poems and with mine. You know, it was heaven to have Jimmy pull a poem right out of the typewriter and say, 'See what you think of this, Babe.' And then he was always there for me to show him my poems, and he was great and a lot of fun—not really helpful, but clear about which ones he liked, you know, and I would usually give him too damn many, and he would seem bugged, and he would pick out one or two that he thought were really good. That's how he dealt with me as a poet.

EF: I'd guess that you got from him not only those trees—the sense, I mean, of having a poem be there immediately, a strong place—but also the way you construct your lines.

EM: Skinniness. Yeah, and it seemed almost as if it was simultaneous. You know, I had read his work a lot before. . . . But it was also accidental, too, because I was . . . You know, I have file cabinets full of these . . . .

EF: Notebooks? Skinny ones.

EM: Yeah, and that's actually why Jimmy's poems look like that, too.

EF: He used the same kind of notebook?

EM: Yeah, when he was an art writer he used small books, and when I was only a poet and nothing else, it seemed like a poet carried her notebook everywhere and was ready. And so, besides seeing that he did that and imitating him, which I certainly wouldn't disclaim, there was always a peripatetic link. I think we were both people who would just do that. I mean he said that when he wrote about art, he wrote it in poems first and put the prose thing in later. And that's why I started writing art reviews, because it's like a response to a painting is a way to get a poem.

EF: Using a notebook that small must be good discipline.

EM: Yes. When I get home the legal pad becomes my material of choice, and the poems get fatter. Actually I could make the distinction between the ones I wrote at home and the ones I wrote outside; they look totally different.

EF: When did you meet Ted Berrigan?

EM: Pretty early. Alice taught a workshop at St. Mark's in '76. I'd heard about this pair but particularly about Ted—that he was sort of this bad guy, that he was older than other younger poets, and that he was this maniac who had sex with other people's girlfriends. It was, like, I'd gotten the gossip on Ted before he moved to New York, and I had this picture of this guy. And I'll never forget being at Cooper Union, I guess, for a reading he was doing, and this guy came up the staircase, and he had this tan cardigan on and a big belly, and it was just not what I had expected this mean guy to look like, you know, with this beard. He just looked like this old hippy, but tall. And I was, like, *that's* Ted Berrigan? And I took Alice's workshop, and I had a crush on her like everyone else in the room, and eventually she suggested that I, young acolyte, come and visit. And I'll never forget that night, armed with pills and beers and poems, and circling the block and circling the block. It was like the date of a lifetime. I was very nervous about going over to visit these guys. And, you know, they were great. I was sitting nervously with Alice—she was a different character in terms of trusting you and giving you whatever—but Ted was yelling things from the bed. And I guess I felt like he always felt not like a parent figure but sort of an older brother. I had a very strong family feeling with him, but then Ted and I had a lot of links—like being from New England, being from a working-class background.

EF: And being Irish?

EM: Yeah.

EF: Not many poets then came from working-class backgrounds, even at St. Mark's.

EM: I went to UMass Boston, which was a state university but also the commuter branch, so it was like going to City in New York or like a kid going to Brooklyn College. I lived with my family, and there was all that about being a townee. But I had friends who were all workingclass from Cambridge. And I was a lesbian, even though I didn't know it yet, so I was disrupted in a variety of ways because the girls that I knew who wanted really great boyfriends and who went to better schools were really trying to lose their accents, and I always felt that my accent was my charm or something. I think I sort of had a feeling that I was going somewhere else, and what would make me different in that other place was who I was, and so to lose it . . . And also there was something wrong in being ashamed of who you were and where you were from.

The reason I mention my school is that when I came to New York, I remember I told Charles Bernstein what college I went to, and he got very excited and said, 'Ah, UMass, the children of the working class.' Now Charles and I are of the same age. He said, 'All my friends in SDS at Harvard knew you guys were really the ones to get to—not the workers, the children of the workers.' Can you imagine some . . . character from Harvard coming to UMass to talk to us about our politics? And, again, it was very clear: I remember UMass was situated right in the South End, and so when we did do our faintly political actions . . . We all were working part-time jobs, we all were working in Filene's Basement. There was no time to demonstrate, or you would demonstrate tiredly between classes and your part-time job. But I remember deciding to pass out flyers on some street, you know, behind the school, and I remember I had this girlfriend who was always on her way to losing her accent, and she took one side of the street and I took the other. And she took the side with brownstones, and I took the side with small factories. So she got all these touchy-feely people who invited her in for a cup of herbal tea, and I get all these guys in box companies who would talk about 'these fucking niggers with Cadillacs on welfare.' And so we both gave away our flyers, and at the end I decided I would never do anything like that again, and she felt really good about it. It was just real estate, everything, depending on what side of the street you decided to go to.

EF: If someone from around here heard your accent, I think they'd think you come from an a upper-class background. Boston, but the Boston of the Kennedys.

EM: Well, I think that's the thing that's funny about being outside of Boston. Some people hear a Boston accent, and read it as that.

EF: But there are great differences, of course, and they seem important in your work.

EM: And in Ted's. There's a New England ear.

EF: So that even after having been here for twenty years, there is something of New

England in what you do, as in his.

EM: Yeah, I believe that.

EF: It's another way place or location gets into the work—as in Schuyler's.

EM: Do you mean the ear or what he looks at?

EF: Both.

EM: Though really Jimmy's in his own world, I think. I think it was Joe LeSueur who was saying that when Jimmy started going crazy was when the poetry started really getting great. Before, he was kind of a handsome, witty man-about-town and really funny. It seems that what everybody loves is really that sharpness, and it seems to me that his personality went into poems. I never walked away from Jimmy and wrote down what he said, which was dumb because he was always dropping little anecdotes and remarks, and I think he was much more like that when he was younger.

EF: Speaking of witty poets, what about Paul Violi? You studied with him, didn't you?

EM: My first and in some ways only teacher, in the sense that I just knew nothing when I met Paul. I mean that there were the poets that I loved in college. Like Stevens. I had a writing teacher, and I had writing classes, but it was more fiction than poetry. I think I already knew that the poetry was more important to me and much more was at stake. Actually I got quite a good education; the teachers were great, but I remember this one writing professor saying to me, 'I don't know much about poetry, but Williams and Stevens are the people that everyone talks about,' so I looked at them both a little bit, and picked Stevens.

EF: You loved Stevens?

EM: Yeah, a lot. And then you know, some Baudelaire and Sylvia Plath and Pound and Wordsworth for nature and Dylan Thomas for sound. So that's what I came to New York with. And then Frank O'Hara, just as I was leaving Boston. I saw again "The Harbormaster" at a workshop. But when I came to New York, I was basically a cute girl in her twenties wanting to be a poet that all the guys would then try to fuck. I mean that was just the lay of the land. And be advised not to be a feminist, you know. And so I just sort of caroused around, and I drank a lot, too, so it was just sort of I came to New York to be a poet. I was out there, and who I met tended to be guys who wanted to date me or fuck me or something, and along the way they would all say, 'You've got to read Paul Blackburn.' Or, 'Don't read Paul Blackburn; read Ashbery.' Or 'Don't read Ashbery; don't read at St. Mark's.' And everybody told me something different, so finally when I went toward St. Mark's and met Paul [Violi] and was in his workshop, I mean I just decided to believe this guy. And he really said, 'This is Black Mountain, this is New York School.' He told me who these groups were, and kind of told me what was what. And then I showed him piles of poems, and he did that thing quickly of, 'This is good, that's not good, this is good, that's not good,' without really showing me why, so I could only guess why this was good and that was not good. And somehow I think I learned line breaks from him; I think he did sort of Ashbery line breaks, and I imitated his. I loved what they did. I could see that they were doing something. I thought that that was exciting. Later on I got it with Ashbery. It seemed to me with both there were sort of vanishing line breaks going on. And something about the end of a poem that I learned from him, too. I think that he was and is a really good poet, and I did that thing with him once where I just decided to let this person's word be *it*. And I think that it's important to get that, once..

EF: But your work is not really much like his.

EM: It's interesting that what he did and helped me a lot was that he totally discouraged me from writing personally. My first impulse at the time, of course, was to pour my guts out. Which, again, I think is sort of a class thing, because it was sort of like the fact that I could be here at all, not just as a writer, but as a person. You know, you're really taught in the kind of Catholic school education I had that you're not something special: 'We don't want to hear from you.' So I came to New York glad to be in the phone book. So there was just a lot to say. And you know, like many others, I had this massively damaged, fucked-up childhood, a crazy family, the whole nine yards. So Paul was having none of that. I mean his work rarely is personal, or what is personal gets played through a whole lot of special effects. And so, again, I imitated that, too, and started to just take things on. I read Michael Brownstein's prose poems, a little book called *Brainstorms*; that really knocked me out. I mean I read all the New York School poets and stuff. And when I moved to this apartment, there was a pile of . . . Someone who went to workshops at St. Mark's had lived here before me, so there was a pile of mimeographed books including Patti Smith, including *The Sonnets*, including Peter Schjeldahl, whose early work I loved and still love, really great poems. He's one of the second-generation New York School poets. Tom Veitch. You know, when I came, they were all in my apartment . . . I was doing this really imitative thing, but I really got the message for quite a while, I mean two or three years, that personal poems were not really where it was at, and it was kind of, like, it had been done by Frank O'Hara—like, that had already been done. And I remember very particularly there was a poem I wrote, like, '76 or '77, "The Nude Bombadier," which is in an anthology called *Fresh Paint*, edited by Yuki Hartman and Michael Slater; it was about waking up with a horrible hangover and just going through the motions of feeling your tongue and having a cup of coffee and remembering what you did last night and stuff. And it was a personal poem, and I remember I just got something. Because not being personal gave me an opportunity to gain other kinds of control. And so I think I had a sense of what a poem was by then, but that morning it just seemed that waking was, like, synonymous with being this person who was collecting herself as she was waking up and stuff, and I wrote a personal poem. And it seemed to me that even though it was personal it was good. And I can't remember whether I still showed my poems to Paul at that point, but it was an important poem, and maybe the next year I did that again, because Alice, when she first saw my poems, we had some sort of argument about form, and she was writing sonnets, and she was looking for form, and I think she was already going toward long poems. But I somehow was getting a message from her, whether she was saying it or not, that I wasn't writing formal poems, and that I had to deal with form in some way. And I was thinking about what that meant. And, of course, I liked Alice and I also wanted to nudge her in some way and say that wasn't true, and so I wrote another poem that was important, which is this poem called "The Irony of the Leash." And when I wrote that I thought in some other way, 'Well, this is my first real poem.' But that was '77. It was about, 'This is the form.' And it was good. I felt like what I was saying was 'I' was a substance and somehow the form was outside of me. So I think it was both nonliterary and, I think, abstract in terms of personal identity. Because I am plagued with personal identity, and I think in some interview with Bernadette, she said something like 'the pronoun *I* can be like the mast of a ship,' and I loved that. Like the wind is just blowing through the *I*. And, nonetheless, it's what moves you. What enables you.

EF: Your fiction, on the other hand, seems very personal.

EM: Yeah, somehow more and more I find that's where the narrative gets to go. But it's always this thing where I feel like I have to. . . . I hate the phrase 'pay my dues.' I feel a burden, a necessity to make some kind of exchange which then gives me permission to have the guilty pleasure (which I must have) of writing about someone very much like myself, if not myself.

EF: The fact that it's fiction, does that make it all right?

EM: Yeah. It's a new form. One that gets to tell stories.

EF: But writing that way cuts off all sorts of moves you could make. You name another person in the work, and then you're limited in what you can do.

EM: Oh, no, because I still think it's the telling that's the fiction, not the subject matter . . . . I mean you say, 'This is the white painting on the wall': I could describe that very precisely, and that would be fiction, but 'Ted Berrigan' would supposedly not be, because that's a real person's name. It's just the name of a total entity.

EF: But what will people imagine or think when they see the name? They won't know there's a white painting on your wall, but they'll know the name and come to the story assuming certain things.

EM: Except that we're all inventing. I mean, as well as inventing 'I', I'm inventing 'you.' The 'Ed Foster' that I'd write would be assemblage; it would be total language. I mean, it's a novel because I say it's a novel. But actually I hate the term 'fiction,' but I think the reason I hate it is that it's niche in the market place.

EF: It sells. Call it 'poetic prose,' and it won't. Call it 'fiction,' and it will.

EM: Right, it's lame. I mean, poetry's fiction. It's all fiction, because the moment you with your faulty perceptions sit down to write something, you start fictionalizing.

EF: But in the novel that you're working on and that you read from the other night at St. Mark's, the episodes themselves are factual. [A few nights before, Myles had given a reading from a work-in-progress in which a older girl at a summer camp falls in love with one of the younger campers.]

EM: Yeah, utterly.

EF: And that business about your gaining weight, that part of the story is all true, isn't it?

EM: Oh, *that*, absolutely. And it was really fun, because I feel I've never written about *not* having sex and eating—unbelievable. I mean it's like here's a whole kind of pastime. . . .

EF: So at what point does something that happened become fiction?

EM: It's so weird, writing about an eighteen-year-old deeply confused girl by an almost forty-seven-year-old lesbian who's been writing about herself and her life for years and has a whole idea about what identity means. So I'm imposing so many of my fictions on what was really going on inside of that girl's head. I knew something happened at the time; I knew when this girl left in the middle of the summer, I just went back to my cabin and cried. But what that meant, or what was going on inside . . . My particular pride in that piece is that there's a fiction. The counselor writes a report about the girl she gives to the girl's parents. They're astonished. There was such a report, but who knows if it exists. There's a number of speeches in that story and other ones in the book that are pure imagination. It was like turning a key and letting it go, the speech. That was fun. I mean I don't make things up. More and more I'm thinking the fun is making things up and figuring out . . . I mean you do it all the time in art writing. You go and see somebody's show and you take notes or you write a lot of it and then you forget or you just start trying to turn it into a review. And all you're trying to do is make it look like an art review, and things are getting lost, but if it sounds good. . . . You know, it's just all art; it's all fiction.

EF: Why did you start writing that particular story, making use of things from years ago?

EM: The way I started it was . . . *Chelsea Girls* had just come out, like, two months before, and I was thinking, God, can I still write stories? You know, that way you feel after a book or something. And I thought, ok, I'll make a list. I mean I always do this, and I do this with prose, not poetry. I made a list of the stories I *would* write if I could write stories, and so I did that, and then I took just one name off the list and saw what it's like to write that one, and it was the name of the school for the mentally retarded in Waltham where I worked just a few months after college. They were doing a behavior-modification program on severely retarded adult males, and it was buzzers and charts and nudity and penises exposed and pee and shit everywhere and stench. It was fascinating. It was real *Titticut Follies*. And it was just perfect for someone right out of college, but also I was just into looking. I was just into sniffing around. I didn't really care. I couldn't really be active. I wasn't going to be a person who was going to have a career in mental health or an institution. So I was young, I was an alcoholic, I was hungover, I was confused about my identity, the whole thing. So there was that, so I started writing that story, and some place in the midst of the story I thought, 'Oh, a novel is just like if you decided to shuffle all the stories into each other.' And I thought that a commonality that all the stories on the list that I had made was that they were all in some way involved in an institution like camp, you know. Even the long piece about the Poetry Project that might not go into this novel. And writing about institutions from the perspective of an insider . . . Because I thought that so much transgressive fiction is about being outsiders, and you know, there are a multitude of ways I felt like an outsider, but I'm much more an insider. And maybe that's a female perspective. There are so many places I've been in, incarcerated in a way in that I didn't understand my true condition. I didn't know who I was or how I was being used or the truth of the place I was in.

EF: What do you mean a female perspective? In fact there's a lot in what you read the other night that seemed to me somehow very male. Even the account of your character's relation to the young girl: it was all images, almost like cruising, the way that some men see each other or that women claim they're seen by men.

EM: Well, it is and it isn't.

EF: Isn't there a theory that men are interested in images and women are more likely to tell stories or narratives, to gossip?

EM: That's interesting. Yeah, I think there's a lot of truth in that. It's stories.

EF: Men look and women gossip.

EM: I've never had a relationship with a woman that didn't instantly . . . I mean as soon as we had sex and *any* sort of week or two of romance, then the stories began. I don't know if men do this, but we, my girlfriend and I start doing this . . . saying 'And when I was at this place and you turned and you said . . .' We're instantly building a history, a story and that's what turns us on. We fuck in it, basically.

EF: I think of pornography as being male. I don't mean the stories; I mean the images.

EM: Well, some women love pornography. Lesbians do, certainly. Most lesbians I know love it and have it. The book I read recently and loved is called *Dirty Pictures*. By Red Jordan Arobateau. You know it's dyke porn. And the porn is about this lonely butch who reads girlie magazines and jerks off to it and goes off and finds a girl.

EF: I've certainly known women who can be self-righteous about these things.

EM: I was someplace last night where I heard a woman talk about her boss and what a sleaze he was. And what a sleaze he was was that he had porn in his desk. My dad had porn in his bureau, and that made him interesting.

EF: Much of your work, both prose and poetry, seems particularly visual, clear.

EM: My first impulse when I was a kid was what I was supposed to do when I grew up was to be a visual artist. That was how I got through grade school: I could draw. That was my claim to fame. It was, like, they knew I was smart, but I was spaced, and one teacher thought I was mentally retarded. And I was just in a state of daydreaming all day long, and I would just sit there and draw, so the nuns would loan me to other nuns to draw gladiators and Christs for the wall. And they would give me candy, and I would get out of school. And that's what I was really good at. And I think that they just expected me to go to art school. And I was so stupid; I should have gone to Mass Art, that whole other world. You know, but I thought it was the dumb part of the state college system in Massachusetts, but actually people from all over the place came to it, and it was a good school. And I would have met Bill Wegman and all these people. But I had an older brother who was supposedly the smart one, and he was always held up to me like I was stupid and creative, and he was smart. So I just had that competitive streak, and I just had to show that I was smarter than my brother, and so I said, 'Damn it, I'm going to college.' And I wound up in college, and instead of drawing pictures in the margins, I started writing poems. But I think it's not for nothing that those things happen; you know. You know, I walk down the street thinking, 'Shit, if I were an artist, I'd have money today,' and that kind of whiney stuff. But I think there are real reasons people do things because they really. . . . I mean *desire* is the thing. People survive because of desire, and people make choices. And I don't think I wanted to do *that* enough. But what's interesting to me is that what people always say is that the visual thing is in there so strong.

EF: Do you think that being a lesbian makes you see things more clearly?

EM: Differently.

EF: How?

EM: Well, I think in terms of heterosexuality, with patriarchy and all that . . . I think, even before I knew, I was responding to a whole different system of desire, attractions. I mean I did always conceive of myself differently. I used to pray to be a boy. I used to pray to God to make me be a boy. And I don't know if that was because I thought I was masculine or because I liked what masculine people got or that I wanted women. But because of that, you know, I think that the business about my accent, for example, I didn't have the same desire to gain approval from men, because on some level I knew I wasn't going to get in anyhow. There were so many places that I didn't gain access to, not just because I couldn't gain access but because on some level I just knew I didn't belong. I could only be a tourist.

EF: But being a man wouldn't have meant doing the things expected of men, would it? I mean the desire wasn't to have an office, obedient children, and a retirement policy—or was it? I mean the issue in maleness wasn't fatherhood, for example.

EM: Well, weirdly, now that I'm in my forties fatherhood starts to sound appealing. I met a woman in Russia who was doing what lots of lesbians are doing—you know, donor insemination. That's so funny, because when I came out, I thought part of what I was rejecting was this and not having a part in this. And, of course, by now it's so popular to all serious dyke couples who have more than three cents. They're on their way to buying some sperm and stuff. And it's a few years since I've given up the idea that *my* body would do this. And since I came out, I've never spent more than a few moments seriously thinking that's something I might want to do. But I met this woman in Russia who was going to do it with her girlfriend, using her brother's sperm, and she just sort of gleamed and said, 'What I'm really interested in is fatherhood.' And, of course, when you put it that way, I thought, 'Oh, me too.'

EF: But you don't really want to see the world, do you, in the way a man does, I mean one who is conventional and married and a father?

EM: Well, I think men's lives are interrupted. . . . Men are distracted and disturbed, too, but there's something about being female and walking down the street. . . . There's a privacy in public that women do not have, and I think a lot of my desires to be masculine are desires to be . . . In fact the vast majority of my poetic models are men, and I'm really interested in public poetry and a private person's public nature. And I haven't found that a lot in women's work because it's not a lot in women's lives. I mean it's kind of a fool's journey in a way, too, because I have the fate of a woman, that destiny. And so, much as I might like to move it over there, a lot of the reason my privacy will always be disturbed is that I am female. Yet, for instance, when I was in India, I went as me, but in a culture that doesn't read me the way this culture reads me. I read *male*, and I was constantly either corrected and told to get out of the women's section when I did obediently go into the women's section, or was just taken to be a man and had a lot more freedom than most women would have travelling alone. And I relished that. And I think as I get older, I'm getting more frank about the nature of my attraction. Like, when I came out, it was the seventies, and it was the heyday of lesbian feminism. And everybody was looking kind of butch and wearing sloppy clothes. Being a conventional-looking woman wasn't considered politically correct in the old-fashioned lesbian sense of the word. And that was a correction of an earlier butch-femme reality, which was more lower class and stuff. And the same thing seems to be happening among gay men and gay women, refinding a lot of stuff that was considered lower class and putting that into the center of a gay discourse. I'm much more interested in being a butch than a femme, but we're all sort of all over the place. I am in a variety of ways, but I like women who look conventionally feminine. That's really attractive to me. It seems that it gets clearer as you go along what you were so embarrassed by. On some sexual level, I see myself as really masculine, and I love women who look really feminine. And I'm much less guilty about that now. But also the times have changed, and that's more fashionable. And it's great when your own desires line up with what's permissible. It's easier.

EF: One stereotype about women's writings—like Virginia Woolf's—is that it's more interior, more personal. It's as if a woman could do in writing what, as you said, she couldn't in public.

EM: You mean, take a lot of space? I've actually been criticized in my writing for being 'personal.' Like that's not so important. Whereas I don't think we have yet much of a female personal in the public sector. I mean in some reviews I got for *Chelsea Girls*, the reviewer was saying that what was trivial and unimportant about my work was how personal it was. It's a funny way of making their objections to my writing sound abstract. They basically just didn't like hearing about a woman, a lesbian.

EF: What's the difference between the poetry, *as* poetry, in *The New Fuck You* and poetry by heterosexual women poets? More personal?

EM: That's a good question. The first thing is that just formally we did something really great, which is that there's poetry, there's fiction, there's performance texts, there's plays. We didn't make any genre distinction at all. We didn't suggest that these kinds of writings can't be next to each other and not gratify each other by being where they are. And we mixed up mainstream writers with girls who were in my workshop last year. I think that's the challenge in publishing, to put together those who shouldn't be together or to insure that they are together. I think that culturally we're at this moment where the worst part of mainstreaming is that you have businesspeople making very one-dimensional calls on what is literature. And this whole wealth gets lost. And it's freedom of speech, because they're really getting to say who talks to each other finally. Because someone says this is what counts, and everyone looks that way. So much is erased.

EF: But is the work itself different from heterosexual writing in quality or the nature of . . .

EM: It's not different from heterosexual writing, but it's different in the quality. I think it's really different. The work is really good.

EF: But is the work itself different?

EM: Different from what?

EF: Work by women who see themselves as heterosexual.

EM: So we're comparing . . . Maybe a little darker and little stronger, a little riskier, a little funkier. Just in terms of being willing to get dark. But that business of just positioning yourself oppositionally is not exactly what I was interested in. Except maybe positioning yourself in opposition to the opposition. I mean there's not just one stance. In the same way that there're a lot of genres, a lot of age groups, a lot of wings of the poetry, literary world, a lot of different ways of looking at even transgression.

EF: Well, I'm wondering what some women writers outside the mainstream but not as dark or funky or risky might have thought of what you put together. Women, say, in the group Anne calls the Outriders.

EM: They liked it. I would say that among bad girls this was considered a great book. And among other people it was considered another bad girls' book. But I think bad girls liked it because it was bad *and* the writing was good.

EF: And it sold?

EM: Yeah. It just kept selling out and selling out.

EF: No problem with bookstores stocking it?

EM: Not to the extent that I know.

EF: What about a sequel, a second volume?

EM: I'm not going to do another one. I decided to bow out.

EF: I have a sense that editing is a kind of writing, that editing, writing, and reading are all bound together.

EM: For me the act of writing is really reading. And even with all the neighborhoodism and the localism and the East Villageism, I'm just reading who I am. And I've always felt that writing is to a very large extent the work of a scribe. And to be a good reader is to be a good writer, to be open to what is really there to be read. And I do think lesbians read differently, and the book was for the benefit of their reading.

EF: But how is it different?

EM: Oh, I think there's no one answer, but I think we read power differently. Because it's sort of like you're a woman on the outside on the inside. For instance, if I have a girlfriend who betrays me with a man, there's a ton of rage involved, and the rage is that it's sort of like privilege is still assembled around male power. You know in a way it's weird because as a dyke I feel perfectly comfortable with guys, I mean, I always had lots of boyfriends, relatively speaking, I came out late, twenty-seven, when I moved here. I read guys. I feel comfortable with male ideas, I've always gotten along with men, and sometimes I have more male friends than female friends, and to be totally frank, to have a career you have to have relations with men. You can't be drawing these lines. You can't live in a lesbian or a gay world exclusively, I wouldn't want to and finally I think it would be unsafe if you could. The strength of a culture relies on its interrelations. *The New Fuck You* was not all dykes, it even contained a man. To do that around the word *lesbian* makes everyone safe.

I'm probably not answering your question anymore, but let me talk. I had an experience with violence last year. I had a relationship end, and the person I was involved with was violent towards me. And it was bad, and I pressed charges ultimately, and I got her arrested.

And everybody supported me but lesbians. It was so weird. Lesbians thought there was something wrong with putting a woman in the hands of the law. It was an isolated position. 'Cause straight men could understand that violence was bad. Straight women could understand that violence was bad. Gay men could understand that violence was bad. Lesbians could, but it really made them embarrassed. And the police were *other*. And there was a lot going on that was class: you know, having to even *think* about violence was lower class. You know, let's pretend it didn't happen. And I thought it was a bad example of where lesbians are at. I thought we're so alienated that we can't even take care of ourselves. You know, I'm a citizen, and as a citizen, I'm no less entitled to go to the law and gain protection because my assailant was a female and even a lesbian. But lesbians in some strong and profound way . . . The thing I was trying to say about betrayal, it's sort of like your lover means so much to you, because you have a place you're at home in the world, between two women. Because there's still such a sense that the world is not a woman's world, that we are sort of chattel in a way, and to walk in the street like a man is in many ways like waiting to get punched. And I have been punched many times. I don't mean literally, but I think one is a target. It's a gay man's joke (Frank Maya, performance artist, died of aids 1995) that the only cure for homosexuality is fame. Men are out, though. And you know, with exceptions, the biggest women in media and writing today are lesbians. And they would never come out because, you know, it's not so important that they're dykes, but who doesn't know that Virgil Thompson was a fairy? There's such a tradition for gay men in power being out, and gay women are not. And I think the bottom line is fear. We're not safe here. So there's just an inside of the world place where lesbians live, and the world looks different there.

ALICE NOTLEY (1)

EF: You lived in Needles, California, out in the Mohave Desert most of your life until you were eighteen or so, and after you moved east you once said it was still your "official hometown." Do you still think of it that way?

AN: Yes, yes it is. It remains that. In my legend.

EF: Not New York?

AN: I guess I resist thinking of myself as a New York poet. For some reason, it's really important to me that I come from the Southwest. It has to do with the way that I speak. Living in New York has made the way that I speak faster, but I think that I still articulate in a lot of ways that Southwesterners do and make sentences the way Southwesterners do.

EF: And you never stopped thinking of yourself as a Southwesterner.

AN: If you're from a place like Needles, you're always from a place like Needles. That landscape, that desert landscape is very powerful, and if that's in your story, you're going to have to keep it there. There's no way you can take it out of your story.

EF: How does it get into the poem—the landscape?

AN: It's only in my poems now, it seems to me, when I call on it, but you could correct me and tell me that you perceived it in my poetry. But most of the time that I am conscious of it as being in my poems, I have started out to summon it up for one reason or another—like when I got interested in John Ford's movies again last year and wrote the poem "Horn, Candle, Paper, Roses." I was interested in them from the point of view of someone from the Southwest.

EF: To what extent is your view of the Southwest shaped by the movies?

AN: Probably a lot. Probably those movies have a lot to do with my idea of the Southwest, but really it has to do with my relations and growing up in that terribly lonely landscape—in a very small town very far away from other towns. My relatives are kind of like people who are in those movies. There's no way around it.

EF: Did the Southwest sort of make itself conform to the movies' idea of the Southwest, or is it the other way around—the movies drawn from what the Southwest was or is?

AN: Well, it works both ways. John Ford's movies are these myth movies. I don't know how to talk about this right now, because I'm thinking about it a lot in terms of other cultures, in terms of the Greeks, and reading books about what myth is.

EF: Your poems make frequent use of narratives and images from films. Is there a reason aside from simply an interest in movies, in films?

AN: Well, it was what I had when I was young—when the basic input was the movies, and what you take in when you're very young is what's most important throughout your life. It's always what you read or what you see or what you do in childhood that stays fresh for you forever as an artist.

EF: How about narrative?

AN: I have a hard time with narrative. I once studied to be a storywriter, and the main drawback in my talent as a writer of stories was that I didn't know any stories. I can't tell a story. I'm the world's worst relater of anecdotes. I just have a poor sense of story.

EF: What about your definition of narrative in the introduction to Jeff Wright's *All in All*?

AN: I don't completely remember what I said—something about how a story in a diaristic kind of writing, how a story gets formed. You can trap events from day to day. If you keep a diary, you slowly notice that there is a story formed or being told as you proceed from day to day, but you don't know what it is until you're at the end of a certain number of days. I do write a lot along that kind of line, but that's principally in the back of my mind, because if I keep it in the front of my mind, it won't work.

EF: Is that in any way connected with experiences like growing up in Needles?

AN: I don't think so. I think it's something I discovered from living in New York, from writing a lot out of daily details around here. In Needles, in the Southwest, in that landscape, I had no idea . . . I don't think anything ever happened—there was no daily life, no density to daily life. It was very stark. It was very boring.

EF: Boring?

AN: Yes, for me it was.

EF: You have that poem "After Ts'ang Chih" about wanting to get out.

AN: There weren't any people there, and yet I mean there was a lot of life happening if you were a grown-up. It just wasn't enough going on, for me. New York is very busy, and you can find a story any time you get sucked into it. You just have to go outside and stand on a corner, and if you stand on the same corner for a few minutes every day, you'll probably have a story.

EF: What about religion as a way of alleviating boredom in that type of world?

AN: Well, it's not that religion alleviates the boredom of it; it's that there's a big emptiness there, and the natural thing is to try to fill it with religion. It's a landscape that calls forth religious impulses from people. It's very, very empty and very, very big, and you feel either naturally religious or the opposite of that there—I mean in the way that you do relate to religion. You can't not think about it.

EF: And for you, growing up there, that was important?

AN: There were about twenty churches in Needles. They've only got about four thousand people in town, but they've got all these churches. I went to two or three of them. My mother liked the Church of Christ, but they didn't really have a good branch of the Church of Christ there. First I went to the Methodist church, and then I went to this church called the Christian Church. It's a very fundamentalist-type sect—like the Church of Christ. It's a Campbellite church. My father didn't go to church. He went to the Masons every Monday—which is the same thing. And everyone did something which related to church. The strongest churches in town were the Methodist and the Catholic, of course. They were the biggest churches.

EF: Does that religious background enter the poetry?

AN: Well, I've never dealt with it directly. I hated it, and I tried to forget about it. On the other hand, my mother was an avid Biblereader, and I learned a lot from that. I became an avid Biblereader, too, and I learned a lot about how to read and how to study and hold onto words from that aspect of churchgoing. We studied the text. That's what we did, studied the one text, and we didn't go outside of it. Like the New Criticism. So when I finally went to college and went to Barnard and started reading people like I. A. Richards and so on, it wasn't very different from hearing my mother talk about how to read the Bible. It was all right there on the page.

EF: So the Bible was "the text"—language as authority.

AN: Yes.

EF: How about music? When you were growing up, was music important?

AN: Well, I was a pianist. My father went to Prescott one weekend and got this upright piano for two hundred dollars and brought it to the house. That's when I was ten. And I started taking piano lessons, and I took piano lessons until I was about twenty-one years old, and it was a very important part of my life.

EF: When you were at Barnard . . .

AN: Yes, I studied music at Barnard, too, and a little bit in Iowa. I just always took it along and did it. I wasn't a very good pianist, but it was always important for me to be relating to music.

EF: What type of music?

AN: Classics.

EF: French or German or . . .

AN: I played a lot of Chopin and Bach, Schubert, a little Beethoven. I wasn't very good though. I wasn't very good at playing any of these people. Ravel, Debussy.

EF: Ravel and Debussy?

AN: Yes. Bartok.

EF: And jazz piano?

AN: No, I didn't know how to make any chord changes. I had no ear. No one ever taught me how to have one or let me know that was something you could go after.

EF: Was anyone else in your family interested in music?

AN: Yes, my sister is studying music at Yale, as a matter of fact.

EF: Where did your father work?

AN: Needles Auto Supply. It's this great store—my mom still runs it. I mean it's all full of auto parts, and you walk around inside of it, and it's all full of these strange objects and devices and things—hanging and being in boxes and in the back and front. Everything is all shiny and knobby and colored.

EF: Did he open the store when you moved to Needles?

AN: Yes, he did.

EF: And your father was once mayor of . . .

AN: Yes, he was the mayor of Needles for a couple years.

EF: Your father seems very important to your poetry—*How Spring Comes* and a number of other works, *Alice Ordered Me To Be Made* and so forth.

AN: Well, I wasn't conscious of what my parents were like for a long time. You know, I lived with them, and then I rebelled against them, and I went to college, and I was still quietly rebellious. After I married Ted [Berrigan], I saw them through his eyes, and he thought they were really terrific people, and he saw my father in this really special way. Then my father died kind of young, and when someone dies young, you remake them. I tell my story of him. I tell it in different ways. Whenever I get ready to, I tell it again. I look like him.

EF: You do?

AN: Yes. And my son Edmund looks kind of like him.

EF: Are there other things about Needles that you should mention?

AN: No, I don't know how to tell about Needles.

EF: Why did you choose to go to Barnard?

AN: Because I wanted to get away from Needles, and it was in a big city, and it was as far away as I could go without leaving the country. But I didn't know the name of it, and I went to see my high school counselor, and he said there's a girl's college at Columbia, but I don't know the name of it, and then I went to see him again, and he said, it's named Barnard, and I said oh, and I applied, and then I got in, and I went there.

EF: You went there with the idea of majoring in English or music or didn't you have an objective?

AN: I've never had an objective in my entire life.

EF: Except to get out of Needles.

AN: Yes. I have very, very vague objectives. I have never thought in terms of how you major or what you do or how you be or anything. I can't do it. It's too finite.

EF: But then you wound up majoring in English, right?

AN: I majored in English with an emphasis on creative writing. They had these strange majors there, and if you were an English major, you could either be English literature, English writing, or English, just English speech, and I think that there were two kinds of speech majors, and I did English with emphasis on writing. I took these classes, and I wrote these weird stories. Actually they were straightforward stories. They were all about smalltown events in Needles, and at first when I wrote, they had as their protagonists people like my friend Tony Garcia. He was this friend of mine, and he was later killed in the Vietnam war. But I made up this incredibly melodramatic story about him concentrated on physical details: what it was like to ride around at night in a car in Needles and what the air felt like and what it looked like and what kinds of small things you might sense. It was all about sense data. I think all of my stories I wrote were about sense data. Very contrived melodramatic plots because I thought that every plot must involve a death and so I would write these stories, and there would be a death on page nine or ten—sometimes on the last page.

EF: And after Barnard . . .

AN: Well, I was doing this thing with stories, and then school was over, and I didn't want to get a job. I knew that that was a mistake, and I didn't know quite what direction to put myself in, and I guess I figured I was going to be something like a writer, but I hadn't discovered writing poetry yet. And someone told me about the writing program at Iowa, and I went there as a storywriter.

EF: To study under . . .

AN: No one in particular.

EF: Do you want to talk about that—being at the Iowa . . .

AN: Well . . .

EF: In terms of the poetry, how that happened.

AN: Let's see, what happened? Graduated from Barnard, and I was living with this guy, and I went to work for Radio Free Europe.

EF: Really? In New York?

AN: Yes, in the summer. It was the kind of job that they would get you through Barnard. As a typist. And I just kind of observed the kind of things that went on there. I don't think this has any significance in this story, but that's what I did. And we saved, and he worked at the West End [a bar near Columbia University] or somewhere like that, or he worked as a chauffeur or something, and we saved up money, and we took a trip across the country, one of those important trips that you always make from coast to coast, and we went to Needles, and we went to San Francisco, and then I went to Iowa. And I really didn't know what the hell I was doing. Suddenly I was in Iowa with all these people who were aspiring writers, and they all—their aspirations were so strange, and there were a lot of different kinds of aspirations, and some people just aspired to be short-story writers, and some people were writing novels, and I met some people that were writing poems, and I thought that was really strange because I had never met anyone who wrote poems before. And they were writing poems, and I almost instantly started writing poems. And I was really fascinated by the fact that you could do all your manipulations on a single page, and that the material was right there in this block, and there were terrific kinds of control over words that you didn't have when you were writing stories, and it all came down to the words, and I guess that's when I found out that I was a poet. So it really turned out that I was more interested in words than I was in stories or a kind of narrative flow. I wasn't interested in creating a reality. I was interested in doing something with words and truth. And so somewhere in there I started turning into a poet, and I broke up with that guy, too. And I started becoming a poet, and I went to my first poetry readings, and I went to a first poetry reading by someone whose name I can't remember, and he was truly horrible. He was a really awful person. And I went to a poetry reading by another poet, and he ripped up his book at the end of the poetry reading. He ripped it in half, and I thought he was a complete cornball. And Bob Creeley came to town, and he gave a poetry reading, and I thought he was really wonderful, and I wrote a poem about the fact that he only had one eye. It was my second poem. And then I wrote a lot of poems that were no good like any beginning poet does, and they tended to be in three and four line stanzas, and I guess they had images or something. They had image and metaphor type constructs, but it didn't occur to me that I was making that. I didn't know who I would have been imitating. I had read a lot of Blake and Yeats and Emily Dickinson. Those were the poets I liked, but when I started writing poems, I thought I had to be like the people around me who were writing poems so I read a lot of bad poets of the midwestern, academic sort, and I can't even remember all their names now. And I read a lot of Bob Creeley, and the first year I was writing poems I was kind of handling that material. But I was also pursuing this story-writing line, and I was reading people like John Hawkes, Nabokov, and people like that, because that was what we read in the prose part of the workshop. And then I got really confused at the end of that year, and I didn't know what I was doing there or what was going on or why I was going to school, and everyone was getting assassinated, and Martin Luther King got assassinated, and I felt just slightly freaked out, and I saved up all this money from being an artist's model and went to Canada for one day. I thought I wanted to move there. And I realized I hated Canada so the second day I was in Canada I flew to San Francisco. And I worked in San Francisco. And then I took a trip to Morocco and Spain, and then I came back to the Writers' Workshop. And I met Ted, and after that everything was different, because after that I knew what poets to read, and I suddenly—and it all opened up for me, and I knew who I was as a poet and who my models and peers and so on were going to be. And what language I wanted to live in.

EF: And who was it you began reading?

AN: Well, I began reading Frank O'Hara and Allen Ginsberg and Gregory Corso and Ted's poems. And I read Anne Waldman and Ron Padgett. I read all of Ted's friends. I started seeing into Williams. I had read Williams before, but I began to see Williams in a different way. I began to see Williams in terms of the relationship between Williams and O'Hara, for example. And so I started seeing constellations of poets and what the real tradition was that the university didn't know about yet and wasn't going to know for a long time. And I became aware of who Whitman was and, therefore, who Kenneth Koch was—that kind of thing. And I saw it all. And I started reading Philip Whalen. And I read Keats in a different way. And things became this line—this line of poets—this tradition. And I saw that there was a place for me in it. And I haven't been the same since.

EF: In your "Tribute to Philip Guston" you said that in 1970 you returned to New York to "sort of formally undertake being a poet."

AN: Yes, I came here to be a professional poet. I graduated from Iowa, and I came here, and everything between me and Ted was all mixed up, and I wasn't living with him, and I lived in this apartment on 12th Street, the building that Allen and everyone lives in now, and I just wrote my poems every day. That's all I did, and I went to the readings, and I went to the art galleries and read a lot of books and did that. But I can't remember what I did for money. I must not have done anything as usual. Every once in a while I'd get my mother to send me about seventy-five dollars, or I'd go model for an artist. I modeled for George Segal. He did this incredible sculpture of me which is in this museum in Germany. And I modeled for some other artists, and I finally did . . . That phase only lasted for a few months, and then I did hook up with Ted, and then we traveled around together after that, and sometimes he would have a job, and sometimes he wouldn't, and I rarely had any work that was ongoing, you know, money-making work. And I pretty soon was having the kids anyway so I never provided much financial . . .

EF: 1970-71 you went to Southampton out on Long Island?

AN: Let's see, I came to New York in '70. I lived over on 12th Street until June. Then we went to Buffalo, and Ted taught this course at Buffalo which Charles Olson had started. Then we went to Southampton, and then we went to Bolinas and San Francisco, and then I became pregnant with Anselm, and we went to Chicago, and then we went to England, and I had another baby. Then we came back to Chicago. Then I was the person who had the babies, and then we came to New York and lived inside this little tiny space, and sometimes Ted worked, and sometimes he didn't, and I hung around and wrote poems, and we were always surrounded by these babies, who grew up.

EF: Before, you were talking about this tradition, and an academic might understand there were maybe three parts to the tradition. You have New York poets and you have Beat poets and you have Creeley and Black Mountain poets. Is that kind of distinction artificial, meaningless?

AN: Yes, because those people are all friends. They all know each other, and they're all part of one tradition, which is modern American poetry. And most of those distinctions, those all break down. None of those people think of themselves as being that. They're all friends. They're enemies, too, but they're all friends.

EF: Which poets influenced you most in terms of rhythm?

AN: The ones who are probably most congenial to me are O'Hara and Whalen—offhand.

EF: But there seems to be a kind of nervous texture in your poetry that is not as insistent in theirs.

AN: It's pretty insistent in Phil. It can be. But he has a theory that he writes in the baroque, sixteenth-note pattern—is it?—or eighth notes. I've been pretty influenced by Kerouac's prose rhythms and probably by Gertrude Stein's rhythms, and, I don't know, I could name a lot of people who were some sort of influence on the music, but I would have a hard time thinking of who they are now. I think I was influenced a lot by my misunderstandings of people like Olson and Williams—it's totally misunderstanding.

EF: Of what they were trying to do.

AN: Yes. I've probably been influenced by O'Hara in that respect. And hardly at all by Ted, because his background was different from mine, but I was influenced by the way he spoke, very heavily by his speaking rhythms. I've been influenced by the rhythm of dialogue as perceived in the movies and on the street corner and in my own house. The rhythm—to keep the talking very rapidly to each other back and forth.

EF: Some of your poems are . . .

AN: I think the whole music of that has in an abstract way gotten into my total poetry. And the fastness of fast American poetry, it seems to me, comes out of dialogue, comes out of conversational dialogue, and I mean that's what O'Hara's all about. It's all about talking fast to someone. That's what we do. We talk fast to someone.

EF: What about "workshop poets"? They claim to have learned from Williams, don't they?—and in a superficial way that seems to be true.

AN: There's this factory. You know, there are these factories around the country. They turn out these teacher-poets, and they make factory poems, and they go teach everybody how to make them.

EF: Is there any easy line between their work and the tradition?

AN: Well, I don't think about them. I mean I refuse to think about them. There's nothing to say.

EF: Nothing to say. Anything to say about poets who are political in obvious ways—like feminist poets, for example?

AN: Well, as with anything, it all depends on who's doing it. I mean that's the key to all poetry—is who the poet is.

EF: Ted once told me, "I have gods, and Alice has goddesses."

AN: I'm not sure that's true, but I made a point of calling my deities goddesses for a while because I like to turn everything around anyway, and I like to reverse sexual identities whenever possible—or I used to like to. I spent a number of years doing that in all my poems.

EF: Really?

AN: Well, *Dr. Williams' Heiresses* is about that. It's about my being able to relate to him and identify with him out of sexual reversal. I guess my theory was that it was easier—it was probably easier to be like Williams if you were a woman, because you couldn't be like him because you were a woman—and opposites can be same in spirit, and you could relate to a person like that in this whole opposite way—in a battle of the sexes way. I don't know if that makes any sense to you.

EF: Well, yes, but it's still . . .

AN: I don't do that anymore.

EF: No.

AN: No. But I've noticed I've been able to make use out of Olson. I think I relate to Olson a lot differently than men do, but I don't know how to talk about it.

EF: In any case, there is not a distinct poetry tradition for women and a distinct tradition for men?

AN: There's only one poetic tradition, and it's always changing. You change all of the history that went before you, and the moment I enter this tradition or this history, it ceases to be a male tradition, and its entire nature changes. That's how I see it.

EF: So that the men who follow you . . .

AN: I put back on it all this femininity that it never had—or bring it to light somehow. Suddenly the potential for me was always there, and it isn't a male, macho, sexist tradition. It's a tradition that I can be a part of. That I am a part of. That I always was a part of.

EF: Which is now there for men to use themselves?

AN: Yes. There has to be total give-and-take. You can't create this female tradition and keep it all for yourself. It isn't nice. It doesn't matter if men haven't been nice. You can't repeat their sins.

EF: Some women haven't been nice, too.

AN: Well, poets aren't very nice anyway.

EF: No?

AN: Well, maybe they are. That was just something to say in case you wanted to take it up, take it somewhere. Poets are very nice.

EF: Going back a moment, were you saying that what is "feminine" in poetry doesn't belong exclusively to women?

AN: I used to have this girl theory of poets, that all poets are essentially girls, and especially all the ones I related to, and that was what made all male poets different from other men. I think there's a corollary to it. I think that men who are poets have to be in touch with their girl selves in order to be good poets, and I'm beginning to think it's my responsibility as a woman poet to be in touch with my male aspects in order to work properly. I think that's probably true. The significant dreams that I've had this spring have been about being a father, my being a father. It's as important for me to be a father as it is to be a mother in terms of my poetry.

EF: Yes, androgyny. Maybe one shouldn't be half a person, but maybe that's also one reason people don't like poetry. They don't want that. Women should be women; men should be men.

AN: Well, a poet has to be in touch with the most delicate parts of his nature. He has to have this sense of delicacy. You do these small things with words. That's what you do. You know, almost as if it were with your fingers or something. There's this other part of it, which I can't define—you have to be a good father. You do. You have to be a good father; you have to give people direction. You have to build something.

EF: What about "voice" in poetry? What is it?

AN: The voice is the personality that shapes the sounds that come out of the throat. That's exactly what the voice is. There's no getting away from the personality. Poetry is about personality. It's the writer or the poet giving her whole self, and a self is personality. And even if it's Chaucer, it's that. And I mean even if it incorporates all of these personalities and all of these personalities of the age, it's still Chaucer, and it's Chaucer's personality. Poetry is a display of pure personality.

EF: OK, Chaucer is in a different tradition.

AN: Right.

EF: So the poet works in the tradition, which is then newly shaped by the special nature of the individual voice?

AN: Yes.

EF: That is what continues the tradition? Keeps it alive.

AN: Yes, I like that.

EF: To what extent is the voice not words but rhythm and music in an abstract way?

AN: Well, as I said before, I think voice is organization of sounds, and I mean to a large extent it is that—it's a music. You know, it's pleasure in talking. People really do like to hear the sound of their own voice and the sound of others' voices, and you play with sound, and you play with durations, and you play with opening and closing your throat. And other kinds of play come in. And you're conscious of all sorts of rhythmic patterns and rhythmic organizations that come to you out of speech and out of music and out of jazz and out of classical music and out of babies and out of people screaming and birds, and, you know, all the ways that anything can sound when there's more than one sound. And that's play. You play with that all the time, but then you have your intelligence going, too, and so you make something that goes between, that uses mind and uses sound.

EF: Which is . . .

AN: Well, it's language mind. It's what-words-mean mind.

EF: There's the idea that the poet is the namer, the sayer, but that's very different from what we're talking about now, I think.

AN: Well, it's just another way of saying that. When you're saying that, you're saying that a poem is a name, that the whole poem is the name.

EF: Is the poem its own name or does it name something outside itself?

AN: Well, I think it probably does both. I don't think it would be any use to anyone if it didn't name something outside itself.

EF: Are you interested in linguistics?

AN: I don't know anything about it. I'm not uninterested. I'm just ignorant.

EF: What about the Sapir-Whorf position that language is its own internal coherence, that it's not referential?

AN: Well, I suppose it's useful to say that sometimes, but it is referential. I think that's why we have it.

EF: What about love poems? When you have a love poem does it include the person to whom you're writing?

AN: Well, yes. Actually I think you write love poems out of an impulse to change the mind of the person you love, in some way. In some very specific small-time way, you are doing that, and you are trying to effect a change in the person addressed or show them something. Love poems are very personal, but you give them to the whole world, and at that point, they change. Someone said to me the other day that writing that kind of poem is like masturbation, but it isn't because you give it to everyone finally, and you show something to the whole world about love, and everyone likes it, and it isn't that. It's completely different.

EF: But if you take a seventeenth-century poem like Lovelace's "To Althea from Prison," the person the poem addresses is not in the poem.

AN: Yes, as I was making my answer I was thinking about times when love poetry has become a convention. On the other hand, that's true for that century, but it's not true for Wyatt, and I guess that's more at the beginning of a convention than at the end of a convention. I always believe that Wyatt is as miserable as he says he is, and that there is a real person behind each of those poems. And Wyatt is the one that we Americans like to read the most of all the love poets from the fifteenth, sixteenth, seventeenth centuries. We like Wyatt and we like Donne. And there's certainly no one more real that the person Donne loves. We even know who it is—at least in the case of a lot of the poems.

EF: What is the importance of the way the poem looks visually on the page? Does it make a difference?

AN: Yes, it directs what you hear in your head, and it organizes your thinkingreading about the poem. It organizes your experience of the poem.

EF: What determines a line? In American poetry.

AN: Well, that's very interesting because as poetry has gotten away from being strictly oral, you know, and it's become something that works by combination of sound and by sight off the page, then a line has become a more complicated entity. It's a combination of something that you hear and something that you read. We're very complicated people now with regard to poetry, and we work off an experience that is both a heard experience and a read experience. And a line involves both hearing and reading, I think.

EF: It has to do with both duration of sound and duration of an idea?

AN: Duration of sound and maybe duration of energy. And sometimes you stop a line because the energy has run out and needs to click into a new energy. I say I write until I reach the end of a page, and I do tend to do that. I write in these books, and I write until I reach the end of the page, but when you know you're doing that, you accommodate yourself to that length, and you do things that make it be a line, and it's not just that you've gotten to the end of the page. You make sure that there's enough tension all the way across, and that it's a good place to end that sequence of sounds and a good place to end that sequence of eye information. I don't do tricks at the ends of lines; I consider that to be corny. But a lot of poets do. I don't like to do it, and a lot of my lines will run over into the subsequent lines, like there won't be a clear break in the sound—the line will run over. And when I'm doing the alternately long and short lines, the shorter line half belongs with the long line. I don't like to make things be cut-and-dry. I just don't like that. I'm not that kind of person. I don't like units with brackets around them.

EF: What determines shape in a poem?

AN: I don't know. Different things different times. It might be the form you've decided to use or the form that's taken shape, or it might be a decision to repeat words or a decision to be faithful to an anecdote you're telling or a decision to be relating to your physical setting. All those things give shape to a poem. Or a decision to use a vocabulary or a line length.

EF: So there's no special way of knowing when a poem is over?

AN: Well, you know when it's over when it's over. There's no special way of knowing unless you're writing in a preconceived form or if you tend to be writing a one-page poem nowadays or sometimes you go on long. I guess you have a sense of what length poem you're going to write usually. I always know when I'm about to write a ten-page poem as opposed to when I'm about to write a one-page poem, and there's also a one-and-a-half-page poem, which I don't get too often. And I get an entirely different feeling when I'm about to write that one. "Hurricane Belle" I wrote during Hurricane Belle. Do you remember Hurricane Belle? It was the hurricane in 1976, and I decided to write a poem that would be the shape of the hurricane and the duration of the hurricane, and so I started it at the beginning of the hurricane and finished it at the end of the hurricane, and in the middle of it, John Candelari pitched a no-hitter in Pittsburgh, and so that's in there, too. And it's all about how the shape of a hurricane . . . You know, it's a valid psychic shape. There's a storm, and then the storm goes away.

EF: In your book on Williams you spend a lot of time discussing what he called "the variable foot."

AN: I can never remember what he meant by a "variable foot" unless I read what he said about the variable foot that instant. Variable foot . . . I know I say in my book that the variable foot has to do with tone of voice. In any American poetry, there is a search for a changing measure, not a fixed measure but a changing measure, and I think that's what that was about, and I am about that. We need something that's more than a foot or a line. It needs to be something that's more nebulous than that.

EF: You say in the book, "Variable foot is maybe about dominance of tone of voice over other considerations."

AN: Because you have to be able to change according to how you're speaking. American speech is different from English speech in the ways that it speeds up and slows down, and it has to incorporate more or less syllables at different moments in speaking. It can't have a rigid foot. I think that with the variable foot we are all involved actually in trying to find an American way of going on at length, and that's partly what that had to do with. If you want to write a long work, there isn't a clear way to go on and on and on the way you're supposed to in a long work, and what Americans do is they wind up writing long works that are composed of short works because Americans so far have just had to invent each line and each stanza as they go along, and that's what happened in *The Maximus Poems* and what happened in *The Cantos*. You invented the music of it as you went along so you didn't . . . You weren't going to have a flowing narrative, and I think Williams was working for something that would enable an American to have that, you know, to have a flow—to be able to tell something long and not have to have it be broken up into parts. And no one has . . . The variable foot has not been useful for that really. I mean he got to write "Asphodel," but the fact is there hasn't been a narrative poem, a long narrative poem. There hasn't. And that measure hasn't been found yet. That way of going on hasn't been found and might not get found. There are other problems involved because for one thing no one knows what story there is to tell. And if you're going to go on and on and on, there should be a story to tell, and if people tell these stories that aren't stories . . . What Olson also does in *The Maximus Poems* is that he uncovers data rather than tell it, tell as story.

EF: But the poem moves according to sound, not story.

AN: The poet organizes durations and silences. That's the most basic thing the poet does. And before you have the words, you have the sounds. And Americans like to keep the sound going, I think—Americans like me do, Americans from the West. To see how many sounds, how many buzzes. You try to keep something open as long as possible and shove as much into it as possible. Williams is always trying to get on top of that and organize it, organize it into these threes, you know, but inside each of those threes, you can actually say a lot of sounds. There are actually a lot of sounds inside each variable foot. You try to keep the throat open as Doug Oliver would say and the possibilities open, and it's like he's made a line that's also a stanza. And it's a line that's split in three, and it's a stanza at the same time. You don't know where line ends and stanza begins or however you would say that. It's all one thing. It's all bound up together. The distinctions aren't clear between line and stanza. That's American poetry, I think. And there are lines within the lines, too, obviously.

EF: How about using other people's voices in your poems?

AN: The American way is to be inclusive rather than exclusive, isn't it? You know, you have to find new words and new things to say and new ways to sound. You get tired of your own voice, but the other voices you use, you're still the organizing intelligence, and those people never get to be themselves in your poem. They always end up being projections of you, poor things. Ted used to yell at me about that all the time. "You think that you're using my voice, but it's just you! It's always just you!"

I try to keep myself open to all of the voices inside of me now, and hopefully there can be different ways of speaking inside the same unit—because it will all be organized by me, and I control it, and there won't be so many clashes, and therefore, all the aspects of me can speak and be united.

EF: When you write a play, I would guess basically you write as a poet, but how is that different from what a person who is professionally a playwright would do?

AN: Well, for me the first consideration is language rather than plot, and I know writers who go at playwriting very seriously and follow all the rules, and they will not let language interfere with their stagecraft. And if I'm going to write a play, it's going to be language.

EF: Is it possible to teach a person how to write poetry?

AN: No. It's possible to teach people how to change their poetry. It's just possible to teach people occasions for poetry, to show them occasions for poetry. And it's possible to teach people how to read poetry, and sometimes you have to learn how to read poetry by writing.

EF: And that is what you do in the workshops you teach?

AN: Yes, I think so. That's what I do.

EF: Ted once told me that in order to write a poem, there had to be a risk, that you had to be in some way on the edge.

AN: That's probably true. It's hard to talk about. I guess I'm always on the edge. I live in an on-the-edge way. I never have enough money, and I never have enough space, and I never have enough room or time or anything like that, and that all creates a certain amount of edge. No one wants you to write poems anyway so there's this sort of built-in edge to writing poetry. Anyway it's almost a sort of forbidden activity. People don't mind that you write poetry, but they don't want you to do it all the time and offer it up as a profession or a commodity or something that's equal to all the other things people do. They really don't want that. Do you think people want me to be a poet?

EF: Do you know why?

AN: No, I don't. Sometimes I think I do, but inside me, I suppose . . .

EF: They really don't.

AN: No, they don't. Why do you think they don't?

EF: I don't know.

AN: What you offer with a poem is simply not obvious. It doesn't give any obvious kind of satisfaction. Music gives an immediate obvious satisfaction. But art is now a commodity. It's total commodity, and poetry is neither a commodity nor instant satisfaction of any kind.

EF: Maybe people no longer know what to expect from poems.

AN: Poetry has to do with truth more than anything else. Well, I don't think anyone's interested in truth, frankly. People are interested in the surface of life. They're not interested in truth. They think they are. I don't know. Poetry would interrupt, you know. It would just interrupt you.

ALICE NOTLEY (2)

EF: What kind of poetics were writers you knew thinking about in the early 70s? What does *Phoebe Light* have in common with work being done by other poets in the New York community then?

AN: In the early 70's I got mixed up in Don Allen-anthology and 2nd-Generation-New York-School poetics I guess, sort of on the rebound from Mainstream-Confessional poetics, with which I had a brief encounter at Iowa. Looking at *Phoebe Light*, I see what I thought were imitations, of poets like Schuyler, Creeley, Blackburn, Whalen—but I'm struck by the fact that many other poems in the book were written according to "methods" in use by second-generation New York School, which those poets had gotten from Dada and Surrealism, Cage, and Burroughs. I see found poems, poems written by crossing out words in other poets' poems, cutups, fold-ins, poems made by letting my eyes fall down the page of some book gathering "random" phrases, a poem made by reading across columns in the dictionary (a method I invented myself), use of word lists, etc.

These methods point to an interest in a more unexpected and subconsciously fed language than the Midwestern and Confessional poets were using. But the tonal differences between the two major divisions, and also among the camps in the Allen anthology, are also very much to the point. New York School in particular was against anguish and in favor of humor and the general light of day. This could be very liberating, but got to be a problem if one encountered anguish in one's life and wanted to write about it. You can see towards the end of *Phoebe Light* a little darkness seeping in, and a sense of a woman's problems and of feminist concerns. These felt a little forbidden, unless handled inside a certain tonal range. The message seemed to be Don't have those feelings and thoughts, because our poetics doesn't include them. But all poetics, all poetry schools do this—rule out something or other—and so they're all suspect. Which doesn't mean they can't be useful at some point or other. But a poetics is a lot more transitory than a poem is.

EF: When you wrote the early poems, why did you choose to work outside whatever was happening in the mainstream? In the early 1970s wouldn't it have been usual to take, say, Anne Sexton or someone out of that world as a model?

AN: I realized that my spirit, my mind in flow, didn't sound like Anne Sexton or like anyone in the mainstream. I sounded more like Frank O'Hara and Gregory Corso. I perceived this directly—no explanatory stuff necessary—once I opened their books. My spirit was playful, attracted to both luxuriant and vernacular usages, and sympathetic to others. I also had an extremist instinct in me, and was looking for poems that looked a certain way. I had a feeling that there was probably a new poetry, as I had found out there was a new music, and that I should attempt to discover it and understand it. If Edgard Varèse's music had been composed, then there was probably a poetry equivalent which made its own rules too, word by word. I was very attracted by poetry which covered the whole page, though it was a long time before I understood how to lay out that kind of poem. I was never really attracted by the mainstream at all. At Iowa, before I heard about Corso and O'Hara, I was exposed to Bob Creeley's work at the same time, and with the same emphasis, as that of the mainstream poets, and I seem to have chosen his over theirs but without thinking about it. I think it's very much a question of what you're like to begin with: there will always be people to write and read mainstream poetry. I seem to have given Sylvia Plath's poetry a moment's thought, since I bought her book, but I can't remember what that thought was. I honestly can't remember what reading her was like for me then; I think it was part of an educational process. I don't remember actively judging anything until I had the experience of reading a lot of the New York School poets, Beats, and Black Mountain poets for the first time. Then I began to judge. At which point—and especially a little later, when I was dealing with the problems of being a young mother and an aspiring poet—I decided the poems of Plath and Sexton were a genuinely negative force. I've thought for a long time that the usages people—men and feminist women—have made of them have been quite immoral. It was as if both men and women were showing you those poems and saying, Here, this is what it's like to be a woman. Well no it ain't. It wasn't. But I do wish people would stop showing other people some bunch of poems in some one style and saying Here this is poetry not that—Poetry is so huge and there are so many kinds.

EF: What did you find consistent among Black Mountain, Beat, and New York School poets that set them off from work that poets like Plath and Sexton were doing?

AN: Something like that the shape of the poem wasn't necessarily a rectangle, that its logic wasn't necessarily sonnet-like or traditionally stanzaic. The main thing said was all over the poem instead of, sort of, buildingly towards the end. Humor was possible in all three schools, even required; the sense of how people spoke on the street was required; but the language of the poem could come from any-where—people's mouths, scholarship, the dictionary, science—and could never be anticipated. All three schools were in love with words—even if the diction was plain one felt the poet was in love with plain words. All three schools were also interested in a new metrics, or non-metrics: the sound of it was always interesting. Mainstream poetry has a predictable sound. Mainstream poetry is largely humorless, and some-what lackluster, because it tries to serve too many people, tries to serve a sort of consensus as to what people want. But humor comes out of active particulars, and the insouciance of the poet, and the word "active" brings up the other thing—that the three non-mainstream-schools are about the performance of the poem as it's being written, what happens now while you're writing it that makes this occasion and shape in time unique. These schools are/were much more sophisticated about time, and notions of how time is fed into the present by the past and future, than the mainstream schools. I wasn't conscious of that aspect exactly when I was young, but

I did think that mainstream poetry felt dead, not alive now, and hadn't ever been really alive. There's obviously quite a lot of vividness, even savagery, in Plath's poetry—but I find her sense of form rather undeveloped. She exploited the rectangle quite fully but her poetry might have burst out of it, and pushed itself into the future, if she hadn't been such a careerist. Poets like Plath and Sexton, and even more of course all the men, wanted the mainstream rewards of poetry, it seemed, much more than they wanted a rich satisfaction from the writing of the work; but I've always gotten so much back from writing itself, from being in process with it. It's only since I've become older that the dissemination of it has seemed more urgent, but as much for what you might call political reasons as for a desire for recognition (which it's hard not to have, finally). The mainstream tends not to feel like they enjoy the writing and that therefore you should really enjoy the reading!

EF: I'm very interested in the notion that the poets you admired are or were more concerned with time and process. One criticism that is made of some, I think, is that this can lead to beautiful surfaces but not great depth. Things move too quickly for that. I don't think this is true, at least necessarily true, but I understand where it comes from. Can you comment on that?

AN: I guess it seems to me that the opposite is true, that the continual use of traditional forms tends to block depth in that it makes what gets said the same old thing said. Traditional forms say traditional things, that's what they're for. They can also be used for doing a traditional task in a very updated way—say the way Doug (Oliver) modifies ottava rima, in order to tell a story and to sound like New York, in *Penniless Politics*. But this is not what mainstream poets do. And the mainstream form and sound automatically excludes the really untraditional, the people who can't help but bring another sound to poetry—the woman poet for example, from a small town in the southwest, the voice that hasn't been heard yet. Classical forms imply that they are anyone's voice and truth, but how can that be when not everyone has come along yet? In the early 70s I probably thought I could take it from Horace though I wonder now. I don't kiss the ass of the greats in the way same I used to. I could take it from Ben Jonson in his poems because I knew what his plays were like, specific to his times, and the poems and the plays make a body of work together which is deep and rugged and imbued with the sense of his life lived and suffered. I've always like Auden quite a lot, but he found a way to say whatever came into his head within traditional forms (but not traditional diction. And he really had to ransack the form and metrics books to keep it all going!). I couldn't take it very much from Americans in the early 70s. Depth of course is a funny word. And Frank O'Hara is a very classical poet in a lot of ways. . . . But what is your definition of depth? Mine would probably have to do with taking on the big questions in a very specific way, anchored in one's times and in dialogue with them, without narcissism. Much of mainstream poetry seems more narcissistic than O'Hara's say: he never says Admire my emotion, or as Adrienne Rich often seems to, Admire my emotion which is Our emotion. He's saying Together we will make a little fun of my emotion, which may also be like yours, while I try to demonstrate how emotion is the glue of our existence (an example of a big thing to say) and what the difference between good and bad emotion really is. Of course he would deny that was what he was saying! He might say he was taking a stance this very minute though, the only one to take which is to be right here, as fully as possible, and to go on: Shall we continue Yes we shall continue It's the only thing to do Etc.

EF: Did you feel there were strong differences between New York poet who weren't aligned with the mainstream and west coast poets who also kept their distance from poets like Lowell and Plath?

AN: I heard a lot of stories and bitchy comments about and among the elders—the ones born in the 20s. One felt these people were like a quarreling family—which meant the feeling could get pretty intense. People bitched each other within schools and across (non-mainstream) schools. The Beats and The New York School always seemed very close to each other, even across coasts, because Allen and Gregory and DiPrima etc, frequented both coasts and had bi-coastal sensibilities. They were very mixed up in New York School and you can see their names all over O'Hara's *Collected*—and he and Phil Whalen met and esteemed each other. And everyone in the east had favorite poems of Snyder's. The biggest gulf seemed to have to do with Duncan and Spicer, probably because they were so dogmatic, and so competitive about their *ideas*, which the Beats and New York School tried very hard not to be. But everything was more mixed up in the Second Generation, who would like who couldn't be predicted. When I was young I would give anyone's poetry a try; I found out I couldn't like all of it, but in spite of all the complaining we New Yorkers did about how silly California—San Francisco—was as compared to New York, I don't think that had anything to do with my own preferences. As you know, one of my biggest influences has been Whalen. But I have an East Coast/ Southwest background.

I just realized I've misread your question—I seem to have taken differences to mean disputes. I must still have this flu . . . I felt that the New York School and the Beats were more cosmopolitan than the other schools, that they knew what a city was, not Olson (whom I also deeply admired) and that they knew what it was to feel part of others and responsible to them. The latter without any loss of individuality. Sympathy is actually the primary quality for me of Beat writing, it's what I so admired in Kerouac; but O'Hara had it too though it's harder to describe in him because it has to do with self- portrayal, whereas in Kerouac it has to do with self-effacement. But the Beats are bi-coastal, so I still haven't answered the question. Obviously, Duncan and Spicer seemed different. I am bi-coastal though, as I've said; I didn't think of it so much as an East/West thing. Everything is all mixed together for me—I guess that's why I'm having such a hard time answering such a simple question!

EF: But among poets outside the mainstream in the 70s and 80s, do you see everyone as bi-coastal or were there differing communities and alignments?

AN: I lived in a lot of different places until 1976 and so had the sense of a rather large community-in-the-air which included a lot of different people of different ages and even different countries. I was aware of "schools" in England for example which seemed to share my poetry concerns. I'd lived briefly in Bolinas, and in San Francisco, several years in Chicago, and in England—I had a sense that there was a lot of migratory poetry activity. Ted was, during those years, a migrant poetry teacher, as was Anselm Hollo; one had a sense of people going about delivering a sort of general poetry message, not a factionized one. Then in 1976 we moved to New York and I began to teach at, and be involved in, The Poetry Project; but I never lost my sense of other places and the fact that there was a larger world involved. One would go read in Buffalo or San Francisco or Chicago, and hear about the other poets everyone was interested in. But, there was Second and even Third Generation New York School in New York, but there were New York School-like poets everywhere, and the label ceased to fit anyone except maybe a handful of people who stuck around St. Mark's. I've never quite identified with it. Then the Language Poets arose, and they functioned on two coasts. My sense is that their friendships, their relationships among themselves, function on separate coasts, though the poetics doesn't seem to have a similar split. In the early 70s there was a sort of sub-Black Mountain Group in Buffalo as well, which didn't seem to grow much thereafter. The Bolinas poets were never a school, they were people living in Bolinas. Then back in New York there were the Umbra Poets, who had their own concerns, but they certainly felt "around" and had very strong individual identities. And then the amazing Nuyorican thing sprang up, which must be still going on in a lot of ways. That was continuously energetic, and open, for at least ten or fifteen years—is it still? The Bay Area has always had a corresponding array of scenes, various kinds of 5th Generation Beats, Street Poets, Latinos, Feminists . . . I'm always astonished when I read what's going on in *The Flash*. And then there's what goes on at Naropa—what do you call that? There's always so much more anywhere than any schools, and the kinds of activities flow from coast to coast really. So many people have moved around and have ceased to be identified with their original "places."

EF: Where would you place your early work (the poetry from the 1970s and 1980s) in that context?

AN: It doesn't fit with a school, I never identified with a poetics outside myself really. Partly I had such trouble with the concept of the line—what it came from and what to do with it. As I've said so many times, it seemed so male-owned; but I had no confidence in any particular version of it so I couldn't go with any of the schools I saw around me. I was always rebelling against the line! It was a huge passion. So I invented a lot of eclectic forms in the 70s and 80s, taking hints from writers like Williams and Stein, Olson O'Hara Whalen etc, as well as prose writers like Henry

Green and George V. Higgins, and an array of dramatists. I invented forms like that for *Songs For The Unborn Second Baby*—an exploded odeish form; for "September's Book"—alternating prose and poetry sections of monologue and dialogue for "characters"; for the conversational poems in *Waltzing Matilda* and *Margaret & Dusty*. I also wrote in forms in *When I Was Alive*; and utterly nakedly in *At Night The States*. I consistently stood for "women," for a female voice and consciousness, that possibility—who knows if it exists? But the idea that I would have to stand as a different kind of voice from the ones who'd gone before me. When asked some form of this question, I often ally myself with all the women who were writing in my generation at that time: I have most in common with them as an across-the-board phenomenon, not with any school or poetics. I don't have a poetics, except a need for inclusiveness and change. I am, and have been, engaged in a search for blockages so I can knock them down. Also I was trying to learn how to do anything and everything, in the 70s and 80s, which is why I worked in traditional forms sometimes. I felt as if I had to incorporate a lot of previous literary activity into myself in order to make a body of work, by a woman, which would stand next to all that male work. So I suppose I could be placed with "the women." But anyone wants to be unique. I don't accept any labels or placements even for the "early work."

EF: That, of course, makes it all but impossible to see your work as fundamentally part of an historical continuum. And I guess that's always been a problem poets seeing their work as essentially different from other poets' work. And then, too, there are claims that poetry is prior to history—that it is "the Orphic voice of the earth," for instance. What is it that underlies these claims; or, in other words, what is ithat differentiates, say, a lawyer, who sees his/her language as entirely historical and meaningful only within an historical context, and a poet, who in some part resists that identification?

AN: That is a good question, hard to answer. Poetry can't get at the truth within a historical context because the historical context will close poetry down into its own language and definitions; poetry tries for a bigger truth and has to have the freedom to do what it wants with language. I also think it must have some sort of dialogue with the historical context to be valuable. The trouble with poetry movements, and poetics, is that they work like historical contexts and therefore they tend to close poetry down at the same time as they open it up. It seems to me that most poets feel part of a "movement" mostly in their youth. Movements are constrictive, a poetics is constrictive. A poetics is also—I can't stand to say this again—a male thing, the manifesto is male, the let's-change-everything-into-what-We-want-now is what men have done in poetry. I see most women poets as either clinging to a maleish move-ment (as far as a discussion of poetics goes), or doing a feminist politics but not poetics in some programmatic way, and/or being in some sense independent. I mean were we really part of any of those movements? As far as the men—the most Impor-tant members of course—were concerned? If so, at what point? After how many

years? How many years does it take for a girl to get recognized as part of a movement? (This could be like a lightbulb joke: five years to certify her and five more to screw her in.) The most important overall movement of the last twenty years has been a broad multiculturalism-cum-feminism, which implies a broad change of consciousness for poetry, which feeds in subtle ways into the language of poetry, the connections and syntax, and so forth. I think the door really finally opened. What's interesting about the new young poets, as in the Talisman anthology*, is that their consciousness is different, a lot of these changes are built into them. So far they don't seem to need manifestos or movements or organized poetics.

The biggest driving force across my life has been the desire to know things directly for myself, without interference of opinion of others. This has never seemed something one can do in conjunction with others, they do things like try to reformulate what they think you're saying into some received language or they imply you're stupid when you're not. Stupidity means haven't read enough in the area as staked out by the experts, them. I've been led astray from time to time, into accepting someone else's ideas, but in general I have to find out for myself. I've increasingly come to distrust almost all of society's formulations of the truth, almost all of the language of "the historical context," and pretty much all the language of current philosophies and poetics. I want to stand face to face with whatever reality is and I feel that all the friendly theoreticians in my neighborhood are keeping me from doing this by proclaiming that there is no such reality as is made evident in the works of so and so philosopher or poet. I've consistently used dreams and myth-making techniques in my poetry—there are dream poems even in *Phoebe Light*, because the truth lies somewhere in there for me. But when I make myths, I don't make them out of preexisting myths or already known materials and stories. I try to build from scratch, psychic scratch. After a reading during which I'd read the "Headless Woman" section of Book III of *Alette*, a well known poet whom I respect asked me, "Where did you get all that?" "Out of myself," I said. He didn't believe me, and was only satisfied when I said I'd been reading a lot of anthropology, because that indicated to him that I probably really had a source. But I didn't, it all came out of my own dreams and visions. When I think of my poetry in this way, the idea of poetry movements and poetics and so on seems to become so irrelevant. Making a poem is a large act, hugely real and involving; it's like living a second life in the midst of this one. Having piddly conversations with so-and-so about what poetry Ought to be doing, or what those guys over there think, is just, nothing.

EF: Do you mean that there is something profoundly different about women as poets—or at least poetry by women? And if so, is that the result of history, or is it an essential difference—something outside historical consideration? To approach this problem from another angle: do you agree with Mary Margaret Sloan whne she says,

*Lisa Jarnot, Leonard Schwartz, and Christopher Stroffolino, *An Anthology of New (American) Poets* (Jersey City, NJ: Talisman House, Publishers, 1998).

in her introduction to *Moving Borders* that a book like hers, "marks the occasion when, at the end of a period of historical transition, such a book is no longer necessary. A barrier has been crossed. . . ."

AN: I mean that men own the ways poetry has been done as a "public phenomenon"—the existence of movements, of schools, of ways of talking about poetry, of literary criticism as both an academic and popular (as in newspapers) phenomenon; also, when I was young they seemed to own the secret of the line. That is, what it had to do with oneself personally, where it came from inside one (psychically), how you chose one (just one! which everyone seemed to do) and remained loyal to it. This is a simple fact and has nothing to do with whether men or women are different from each other, it has to do with ownership of history and art. I don't know if I agree with Margy or not, although I guess I think a lot of barriers have been crossed recently. My point is not that women are approaching the poem or the line differently and making a radically different poetry. I don't know if I can tell a great deal of difference between men's and women's poetry, in general. Maybe in tone. My point is that women are not constructing poetics (plural) exactly or theorizing about the future of poetry, they're not trying to take it over and and reorganize it into some new kind of map as men have been doing throughout the last two centuries—they would probably have to organize men as well as each other in order to do this and there's no way anyone's going to stand for that! The men who participate in movements are very aggressive. My sense is that women don't necessarily want to do things that way—although I'm not sure they're thinking about it very much. But if you undertake to interview a woman on the poetry movements and so forth of the last thirty years . . . at a certain point, the concept breaks down because we did what we did most markedly, the women of my generation, across the lines of the movements. Our achievement has probably been to become ourselves in spite of the movements. I think we are now less known through our alliances with specific groups than as members of that sudden generation of strong women poets. I take that to be what Margy's anthology demonstrates.

EF: *Mysteries of Small Houses* seems, to some people, very historical and biographical, and they read it as such. Can you comment on the legitimacy or illegitimacy of reading a poetry as history or as biography? That question in turn circles around to others: is there anything in poetry that is not "essentially" historical; what (if anything) in poetry can not be appropriated as a "subject" by the historian?

AN: *Mysteries of Small Houses* is meant to be an investigation into what isn't biographical or historical; it conducts its investigation using the shape of chronology in a specific time period but repeatedly researching the depths of the self and asking the question What is constant in oneself throughout historical and biographical change? What in the self, if anything, transcends this ephemera? What is the self if it isn't history? I'm convinced that I am a self or soul that is different from my personality in history. I'm quite sure that it is some transference of one's "real self" into the poem that makes it come alive: this is the mystery of the small house! The poet's skill has to do with ability to turn spirit into words and word-music. I used self-hypnotic trance techniques writing *Mysteries* and felt I was in contact with a literal, tangible substance of spirit—there is no good vocabulary for these things—which became bound up with what I wrote. Now that I've said this it's material for the historian and for history—and people need to know such things have been said—but history is the least of what it is. A poem is written, and at best read, in a different kind of time from historical time, even if it sounds like its time and even if a good part of what the reader gets from it is bound up with what's going on in time . . . Writing poems gets done in a strangely isolated nontemporal space as all poets know, but I'm not really trying to claim anything "special" for the poet. I think anything we do could be like this; but poetry is especially meditative. The historian could not discuss this terribly well. The historian is, it seems to me, absolutely incapable of dealing with the role of sound in poetry and doesn't try probably, though sounds change from era to era. The historian can't deal with what it feels like to write or read a poem, and that's what poetry is all about. On the other hand it's interesting to read poetry from a historical vantage—poetry of the more distant past—to contact the sound of another time. And it's fun to read contemporary poetry for gossip value. Everyone bought the Ted Hughes book on Plath to find out what had happened! I have no idea if they found out since I haven't read the book. I've thought for awhile it would be great to write a book of poems that contained some sort of information that the public could only get by reading that book. Most poets leave so much out though. They think they've told everything by putting down about ten words.

MAUREEN OWEN

EF: Some of the *Talisman* interviews, like the ones with William Bronk are printed literally verbatim. There's not a change from what he said. Others are modified, or corrupted if you will, by second thoughts—people thinking, Well, maybe I should have said this or that; let's pretend I did. There's no real agenda in this interview or in any of them. Things should go, and perhaps be changed, however you will—meaning is there anything you want to talk about here.

MO: Well, I didn't think about that. I just thought we should do it.

EF: OK, in that case . . . . you come from Minnesota?

MO: Yes.

EF: Why?

MO: Why? Because my mother's family, my uncle and my grandmother and my aunt lived on a family farm there. And my father was in the Air Force, so he was away, and my mom came home to the farm. Actually she'd never really left. So I grew up there on the farm for about the first six years of my life, and then we moved to California, just my mom and my brother and me. So my uncle and my aunt and grandmother were still on the farm. And my middle brother and I often went back in the summers. Even though I left when I was six, I have a deeper connection to it because I've spent a lot of time there later.

EF: An isolated part of Minnesota?

MO: I guess you'd say so. It's kind of where the map bumps out and becomes South Dakota. Just across the lake is South Dakota. It's all farming country. I don't know what the population of the nearest little town, Dumont, is. One of the towns nearby was, like twelve. But Wheaton, which is about ten miles away has a population of about 2,000. And dropping now. So it was pretty small. But at that time there were so many family farms that it felt like at every corner of every section there was a farm. But then the big co-op farms came in and bought up all the land. Now there's almost no family farms up there.

EF: Your mother had grown up on that farm, hadn't she?

MO: Yes.

EF: Had her grandfather or grandmother?

MO: Well, actually she started out on a farm on the neighboring section of land. That was my grandfather's farm, her father's farm. He raised big draft horses, Percherons and Belgians and basically the tractor came in, and he said, No, it will never replace the horse. Whoops. And so, alas, it did. And they had been doing fairly well. They were fairly wealthy at that point, but then they lost everything. So then they had to move to this old homestead across the field, a pretty ramshackle place compared to the gorgeous farm they were on. And my mother was the youngest of the kids; there were four kids. And so she was pretty little when that happened. Everybody else had had a high life; my aunt never recovered from it as she was the oldest. I think she (my aunt) was permanently traumatized by it actually.

EF: What did you mother remember of it?

MO: My mom really didn't experience it that much being so young, and she grew up in a working environment. She did a lot of field work. My uncle Bud who was the second oldest son, took over the farm after his father died.

EF: And was he the one who was working the farm at the time you were living there?

MO: Yes. My grandfather actually died in his forties. I was just born. Everyone on that side of the family had a heart attack. I'm knocking wood. And my mom, who's just incredible, always exercising and hiking . . . . Last week she went up in a balloon ride in Truckee, California where she lives, and she's seventy-seven. So she's really healthy. But my uncle just died last November. He was in his seventies. But my aunt died in her fifties, and my grandfather died in his forties, and my grandmother died in her early sixties. And it's all pretty much a heart thing.

EF: Well, there's more than genetics . . . .

MO: I know. My grandfather worked hard, and had all the trauma of losing everything . . . .And my grandmother worked insanely hard.

EF: This must have been just after the depression began.

MO: Actually this was right before, because during the depression (my mother remembers this really well), they were living on the dilapidated farm and there was a huge drought, and it must have been the weirdest time because the wind is always blowing in Minnesota, and . . . . I love it there. But then the wind blew forever, and there was dust in the air, so you couldn't really even see. They used to wrap themselves in wet sheets at night to sleep. They had to let all the livestock loose because they had no water to give them, so they just let them run wild. They were running wild and finding water where they could. And the wolves came down from the north, and my mom would lie in bed breathing through a wet sheet listening to them howl at night. A pretty weird time.

EF: What's it look like now?

MO: It's pretty remote. I inherited the farm from my uncle when he died. He had sold all the land and pretty much retired. And he was just raising some pigs and chickens. But he left the homeplace of ten acres to me. Or to the family really through me.

EF: Then you still stay there?

MO: It's so far away. I wish I could just go there for a week-end or something. And now it's just sitting there abandoned. The house is falling apart. I was there in November. I was hoping to go this summer, but I have a full-time job and I was doing all these things. It takes a full day to get there. You fly into the twin cities, and then you have to rent a car, and it's a good four hour drive finally on gravel roads. My uncle used to joke because the road out past the farm down to the lake was always gravel when there were lots of people living there. After the small farmers were driven off the large co-op farms, because they're trucking everything, paved the road. And ours was the only farmhouse left on the road, so you get this incredible paved road from Dumont out to the lake. So my uncle used to say, "They paved the road just for me," and that was nice. But it's still pretty remote. And I love it.

EF: Why did your mother take you to California?

MO: She remarried. She'd divorced my father. I think they just didn't see each other; the war was on, and they just didn't know each other that well. And she married this fellow that came from a pretty big family, who also was living in that area of Minnesota. His people were horse people, too, but thoroughbred horses, running horses, and they were a race track family. They had race horses. And so they all went out to California to the race tracks there. She married him, and we all went to California. And I pretty much grew up on the race tracks of California. We'd winter at Santa Anita and do the fair circuit up and down the coast in the summer. I went to so many different schools, because we'd have to leave early in the spring to follow the tracks. It was a gypsy life. I'd go to a strange school and not know anybody and leave after three weeks and go to another strange school. So it was kind of crazy. I'd have this little window of stability because at least we'd winter in one area.

EF: You're the kind of person I envied. I lived almost all my life in one little farm town, and I'd go to the county fair and see these kids who'd act wild and crazy. And they'd live in trailers.

MO: Oh, yeah, well for a kid, you know, it was fine. And I loved horses, and my mom was wonderful. And my stepfather trained race horses, and my mom did some training and worked with the horses. I really loved horses, so it was great for me as a child. The fairs last like a week or two, and then you're off for the next one. It was a nomadic and rather manic life tho.

EF: But pretty wonderful. You're truly the kind of person I used to envy. As if you were in Oz. And somehow I'd think you were still out there, running the race track. But you're here—in Kansas, so to speak. What happened?

MO: Well, we lived in southern California for a while, and then we moved to northern California. And that year we moved to northern California, I went up to Seattle University. The Jesuits.

EF: A Jesuit school?

MO: Yes, Seattle University was a Jesuit institution. I was a very devout Catholic, Irish Catholic. I was in parochial schools when we weren't moving around. But as I got into my teenage years, I started to have all these questions, and didn't have, wasn't getting any answers. And that was why I went to the Jesuits and how I went to Seattle. And they were so wonderful and answered my questions. But it was a traumatic time for me, and I quit the church. Because all the answers were just as I suspected.

EF: You're saying the Jesuits were too truthful?

MO: The Jesuits are great. But I came back, and I didn't want to go back to school in Seattle because I no longer wanted to be a Catholic. Then my mom and my stepfather were having problems, so I was working nights helping the family out financially and going to San Francisco State in the daytime. Then I became involved in Civil Rights causes and demonstrations and in a time of great conflict moved into my own apartment in San Francisco and met the father of my two eldest sons. He and I were both interested in Zen, so we decided we wanted to go to Japan. We were saving our money to go to Japan, and saving forever, and we had enough for one person round trip passage. In those days to get a visa, you had to show that you had return passage. So we both took the same money and went down at separate times and showed we had return passage. We went on this Japanese ship, the Sakuramaru, and sailed under the Golden Gate Bridge and off to Japan. It took like two weeks to get there, really incredible. We were down with the Japanese people in third class, so we were already in Japan in a way.

EF: And you lived in Japan?

MO: We lived in Japan for about two-and-a-half years, and my two oldest sons were born there. We came into Yokohama, which is a vast, crammed city and we didn't stay there very long. We left and hitchhiked. We hitchhiked all over the place and we ended up in Tokushima, a port city, on Shikoku, a southern island. We stayed on Shikoku for quite a while and traveled around and ended up teaching English at local schools. Once you got out of the bigger cities, you'd just be hitchhiking, which nobody understood. They'd just stop and kind of ask us what the heck we were doing, and then they'd give us a ride. You'd come to these little towns, and English was taught as a second language, but the Japanese professors who were teaching the language had never heard a native speaker before because they were all local people from these little villages. They were very excited to be hearing two Americans, so they'd invite us in to talk to their class, and then they would cook us Japanese dinners and put us up for the night. They were so nice. So we wound up staying there for a while and teaching English. It was a day-to-day affair, living. But then we had a two-month visa, and we kept having to renew the visa, which the Japanese authorities were not happy about. You're not suppose to do that; they figure you're not putting money into the economy; you're just being there. So finally they said, All right, you guys gotta go. And we had not enough money to get back home.

EF: And this is two-and-a-half years on a two months visa.

MO: Yes, and this was after about two years and two months. So we thought we've really got to make some money, because the money we're making in the little towns teaching English was just enough to buy groceries and for a place to stay. So we went back to Tokyo, which was, like, trauma. It was almost like leaving Japan. And so we both got jobs teaching English in a Korean business school. Teaching business English to Japanese people. And there were teachers from all over the world at that school and they were all in the same position we were in, needing money for passage out of the country. Half of them didn't even speak English. It was amazing. There was this Australian guy, he was Australian, but he was from Germany. His English was so bad, I said to him, "How can you be teaching English?" And he said, "The best way to learn a language is to teach it." And the Korean fellow who ran the school was a real character. But after six months we had enough money to come back.

EF: Had you studied Zen while you were there?

MO: Yes, we traveled all around, and we went to a lot of Zen temples and talked to a lot of Roshis. Now I wonder, why did they ever bother to talk to two crazy Americans with two little kids. But they were so nice. They'd invite us in and talk to us. It's like the Pope talking to you. Really serious Roshis. We would stay sometimes a few days. Unfortunately, Suzuki, himself, had died just as we arrived in Japan.

EF: I thought he'd been living in New York.

MO: I think he was back and forth, and he may have died in New York. I don't know. But he did go back to Japan occasionally. Of course, we would have thought of encountering him there.

EF: By this time, you were writing.

MO: Yes, I started writing when I was pretty young, not quite yet a teenager First I started oil painting. And one of my mother's brothers, my uncle Pat, he was a house painter, but he loved art, and he bought me all these art supplies and oil paints. But then when I went to Seattle University, I stopped painting and started writing, and since then, I've been a writer, but I was writing when I was younger, too. I guess I was doing both because in a period of time when I was , like, eleven, I remember forcing my younger brother to listen to me read my poems, long epic poems, tho I hadn't ever seen any actual poetry in books. There were hardly any books on the farm. There were a few children's books, but they were unusual ones, and I memorized them basically. There was a wonderful book, I wish I still had it. I'd look for it there, but I'm sure the mice have eaten it long ago. But it was about a Navaho family, a grandfather, a boy, and a girl. And all I remember from this story is that they were endlessly searching for piñon nuts for dinner. But they had great adventures. There were wonderful illustrations. But we had so few books and no poetry books. There was, one day when I was rummaging around in the attic, I found a songbook of Irish ballads. That was the first poetry I'd ever seen. I was about ten or nine or something. And I thought, Wow, this is awesome, this is really amazing. So that was my first venture into poetics, and so I wrote these long ballads about butterflies or whatever. And they were endless, and they all rhymed. And they would just go on and on, the way an Irish ballad does. And then later when I discovered Thomas Wolfe, I was writing . . . I don't think you'd call it prose. Just this kind of writing and writing and writing. Nothing ever really ended. But then I wrote a few short stories and they had a beginning and an end.

EF: But you weren't doing the completely distinctive "Maureen Owen."

MO: No, not at all. I wrote a lot of haiku when I was in Japan. That was one of the wonderful things about being in these little towns. Every time people would get together for dinner, everybody would recite haiku. And they would recite their own haiku, and they were completely unselfconscious about it. It was just what you did. So I was writing kind of journal things and haiku in Japan. But I still wasn't. . . . But earlier when I'd gotten very involved in the civil rights movement, I had started writing poems with a political feeling, but they had kind of wild, rambling lines, but still kind of a narrative. I think the reason I ended up writing is interesting because I'd grown up on the farm, that wonderful thing: you're out in the middle of nowhere, totally desolate. You can just get one channel on the TV. So people would just come over to my uncle's; he was very gregarious with wonderful, funny Irish stories. He'd tell the same story four nights in a row. He was hilarious. Then the other farmers would tell stories too. It was definitely oral history in the making. The daily goings on of each other and the lives of the locals became hilarious tales. So I loved those stories, and I loved the humor in the tragic situations that you find in the Irish. They need to find humor in tragedy. If it wasn't for their tragedy, there wouldn't be such a use of humor there.

EF: I was married for twenty-seven years into an Irish Catholic family, so I know what you mean. My father- in-law, at his best, was the funniest man I ever met, but the world gave him lots of reasons to be unhappy. And maybe he was, but he didn't think it necessary to inflict the rest of us with his feelings. Instead he used humor to tell us what he'd learned. Humorous stories. That seemed to be the soul of his Irish humor, deeply serious but very funny.

MO: It's wildly funny. My uncle was a great, great storyteller. I always wanted to tape him, but it seemed intrusive. And then I thought, the stairway of the house came down right behind him where everything happened in the kitchen, and I thought . . . . But I couldn't reconcile the dishonesty of taping without him knowing. But I wanted to record the stories somehow. So, anyway, what I think happened to my writing was that I wrote a lot of stories and I didn't think they were very good at all because I was bringing in a lot of description, and I was trying to write a sophisticated story. So I think what I started doing was incorporating into my poems short stories, short-short stories, and that really worked for me because I could sort of hit the nail on the head, and then I could roll on. And it was a poem, but it was like a little story. It was like little rivers that ran through, but they were shorts. So there are a lot of stories in my poetry, and humor is really important to me. And it's not funny. A lot of it's serious. And that's hard, I have to say, because if you write and you're successful at being funny, it's like taking the Irish story out of its context. People don't get it somehow, that it's funny but it isn't funny. It's hard to use humor unless you're just trying to be funny because a lot of people don't get it, and you're kind of branded. It's, like, humor just isn't good enough; it's just funny. It's not serious; it's not hardcore.

EF: Meaning that people will misread you or mishear you? That they'll not know what you're saying.

MO: People will come up to me, and they'll say, that was really funny, only it stops there, they don't follow it through to the tragic. And that kills me. And I sort of blame myself, because it is funny, too. Only its got another side and I think they've missed it, they only have half of the story, only half of the way I felt about it.

EF: I think people always thought my father-in-law was just telling jokes. But I used to watch his eyes, and they'd sparkle, but they'd also tell you it wasn't just a joke.

MO: Exactly. It's not a joke, and you have to get that somehow. I'm actually like him (my uncle]) in a way, because I had the Irish stories, and the farmers, you know . . . some of them Swedish. There were a lot of Swedish farmers, too. But most of the farmers we were close to were Irish. They were wonderful story-tellers. I think the desolation of where they were, the flat prairie. . . . That was their whole oral history, telling the stories about themselves and other people and never bad-spirited or mean-spirited, all just completely hilarious no matter how horrible the other person might have been. And on the racetrack at the end of the day during the fair circuit all the trainers and hot walkers (people who walk the horses to cool them down after they've been exercised or run a race) and grooms would often get together in the shedrow or in front of the barns. And it was summer, and we would all just sit out on the bales of hay and tell stories. My God, those racetrack stories, I wish I'd written some of them down, but you couldn't have; it was just the thing of the moment, you know. There was this one man, a good friend of my dad's. His name was Tucker Slender.

EF: Tucker Slender?

MO: Yah. . . . no, Charlie Slender. His son's name was Tucker. Charlie Slender. And his wife was, like, a full- blooded Cherokee. Her name was Irene. She was wonderful looking. She had this face, and it was, just like, so incredibly beautiful. And she was just a great person. They were really a cool family. Tucker was a great trick rider in the rodeo, and he was amazing on horseback. He did tricks on horse-back, galloping across the big arena. Anyway, Charlie Slender could tell the stories. You'd be sitting on this pyramid of hay with a bunch of other kids and suddenly laugh so hard you'd bounce off the hay all the way down to the ground. It's like at a slumber party when you laugh so hysterically you can't even pick up a pillow. It would be that kind of thing. Some people are so amazing. And they're just sort of gone today.

EF: It was a kind of art.

MO: Yes. But it is also like an oral history. I don't know if it's a lost art because there's all this technology, and there aren't those pockets of people anymore. And in a lot of places like rural Minnesota, there aren't even as many people as there used to be. And they just don't know each other in the same way. The families that were so close are the families that sort of grew up together. It's not the same now.

EF: So how did you get to New York, leaving all that—Minnesota, the racetracks, storytellers, Japan—behind?

MO: Well, so then we came back from Japan, came back to San Francisco, and I was with Lauren Owen, and I had my two sons, Ulysses and Patrick, and Lauren's father, who was a professor at Tulsa University, had a place that he had bought—this is a great story—for back taxes during the depression, and it was about 136 acres along the White River in Missouri, just wild, but it was a bluff and bottom land, and then there was the White River. And at that time he was still teaching at T.U., but he would go there in the summers and Lauren had been there as a boy, growing up. So we decided we would go to New York just because we hadn't been to New York. And this is kind of an interesting connection. So on our way we first went to the place in Missouri to visit, and there was literally nobody there in the winter except Lauren's grandmother who was living there year-round all by herself. Lauren's dad would come on week-ends. She was, like, ninety years old then. She was an amazing lady. So we stayed one whole winter there and just kind of helped her. That was extremely interesting. The land was along the White River; the cabin—it was just a cabin really—was on top of a hill. Across the river was the School of the Ozarks, and the town right there is Branson, Missouri, which is now the Country/Western music capital of the world. When we were there, thirty, twenty-five years ago, Branson, Missouri, was like Wheaton, Minnesota, like a thousand people if even. The only thing there that was of note in any way was that Nyhart who wrote Black Elk Speaks had lived there. There was a plain little green house on the edge of town and I think there was a small plaque.

EF: I don't know that name.

MO: Well, he was a great writer. He wrote stories and was famous for that book, So there was a little house there, Nyhart's house. You know, a little sign that said "Nyhart Lived Here," or something, and it wasn't kept up. It wasn't a museum or anything. It was falling apart. It wasn't attractive, but it was like, Oh, wow! Nyhart lived here! Otherwise there was nothing in Branson, Missouri, but it was beautiful, you know, and we were definitely sort of hippies at that point, and we were living off the land, eating wild asparagus and dandelion greens. Letting the children run wild, and it was a perfect spot for that. But then Lauren was from Tulsa. He'd grown up in Tulsa, and he was sort of a child prodigy and he'd pretty much skipped high school and gone to college when he was fifteen. And I think probably because he was an oddity like that and a writer, he fell in with Ron Padgett, Ted Berrigan, Dick Gallup. He knew all those guys there. Then he got a Fulbright, Lauren did, to go to school out in Berkeley, the University of California at Berkeley. But this is a tragic story, because you can't skip high school because of the socialization it provides to a teenager. So he went out to Berkeley with his Fulbright and realized he wasn't a complete human being; he was just, like, this scholar that had no life. So he dropped out of school, and that was when I met him. But he knew Ron and Dick and everybody, and they had gone to New York. So from Missouri we thought about going to New York. Well, we were that year in Missouri, and then we weren't sure. We could go back to San Francisco where we knew Charlie Plymell, and Ginsberg was there. And Neal Cassidy.

EF: And you knew him?

MO: I met Neal Cassidy for the first time in Lauren's apartment, all those guys kind of hanging out together. All those Beats. So the question was: should we go back to San Francisco or should we go to New York? And we went to New York because we hadn't been there. And Ron Padgett was so generous, and we stayed in his and Patty's apartment part of that summer.

EF: This was about '65?

MO: No, it was later. That was the summer of '68. The year of the horrific convention in Chicago. And from that time on we lived in New York. We got an apartment on the Lower East Side. The people in the literary community in New York around St. Mark's. . . . That was kind of the place. I was just so impressed, because when we were in San Francisco the Beats were . . . . Well, they were
on different drugs, but they were all kind of paranoid. When we came back from Japan, it was all the Summer of Love, but earlier everybody was kind of paranoid, nervous, and you could get arrested easily for smoking grass. When we came back from Japan people were smoking grass on the streets in San Francisco. We thought Wow what has happened in two-and-a-half years! This is great! So it had been more of a suspicious community before; it was just a different atmosphere. And so, then, in New York, it was so great. St. Marks. After I had been there a little while, I met a few people, and I'd go to some readings. And then I met a few women writers like Rebecca Wright and Rebecca Brown. And I asked Anne Waldman if I could use the mimeograph machine to do a little magazine. There were people that weren't getting published in The World that I thought were really good. There were a lot of people around, and The World wasn't big enough to publish all the writers. So anyway, I asked Anne if I could do a little magazine, and I knew nothing about it. It was just, like, this would be cool, because I'd gone and helped collate a little. But she was so nice, and she said, Sure, you can use the mimeo machine, and I said, Wow. And so then Tom Veitch was there. Do you remember Tom Veitch?

EF: No.

MO: He was a really sweet guy. I don't know where he is now, but he agreed to help me run the first issue of *Telephone* off, because I didn't know how to work the Gestetner, the mimeo machine. And Larry Fagin was actually quite helpful because he told me the kind of stencils to get, and said this is what you have to do. So I put this little magazine together, typing stencils, and I had two little kids. I got a stylus, and I drew illustrations for the magazine by holding the stencil up against the window and drawing on it. So I got it all together, typing stencils. Have you ever typed stencils?

EF: Sure.

MO: Oh, boy, they're hell. Oh, such a pain. So anyway, I got it all together and took it over to the church, and Tom Veitch helped me print it, really he printed the first issue for me and showed me how to do it. And we ran it off, and I can't even describe to you: I'd done all this work, and I knew how it should look, but I really didn't think it would. It seemed as if some kind of miracle had transpired, changing lead into gold. It just came off the press, this beautiful white piece of paper with print on it. I was amazed. I was so excited.

EF: And that was the beginning of your career as a publisher.

MO: I started doing the magazine and then the books, and I loved doing it. You could do things so fast, and you had such control, and it was so good to get it collated, and, of course, things would get collated upside down and whatever, but it was still cool. It just seemed such a wonderful, fast way to get work into people's hands, the hands of readers. St. Marks' was just wonderfully open in that way, and I think they still are. It's a generous place for just allowing people to come in and use things. I can't think of any other space that's like that. Open, you know. Other places would probably let you use things, but they'd stand over your shoulder. But Anne just gave me the keys because I would put the kids to bed and go over to the church and mimeo a lot of the issues at night. I would do it way into the night. I was the only person in the church, and it's a spooky place. I was just, like, "Was that Stuyvesant's ghost?"

EF: But why did everybody leave, except for Ron Padgett and a few others? Ted and Alice to Chicago and England. Others to San Francisco. You to Connecticut. Anne to Boulder. And then some people came back, but they didn't stay.

MO: Well, Anne was there a lot of years. I think things just happen in your life, like for me I was happily working there for a long time. I loved that job, but I ended up moving up here, which was another story, because I was doing a book of Susan Howe's and I was living up on 110th Street. I was still with Lauren, and we were poor, and the kids were in public schools.

EF: So this was '74.

MO: Yes, probably, '73 or '74. I was living up on 110th Street. The schools were difficult, and the streets were dangerous. And I was working at St. Mark's. So I did this book of Susan's, and she had moved up here because her husband, the artist David von Schlegell, had gotten a prestigious position in the sculpture department at Yale, so they'd moved up here, like, only three or four years before. And I hadn't known her; I'd just seen her work. So she was coming in to meet with me, and I was living up on 110th Street. You have to know Sukey pretty well to appreciate this. She arrived at our door, just in a state, saying things, like, Oh, my God, it took forever to get here; the train broke down; I can't believe I live up there; I miss the city so much; this is just hell; I can't believe I'm living so far away. Finally then we had tea and started talking about the book, and so a couple hours later, we're kind of breaking it up, and we're talking again, and I said, I hate to say this, but I really have to think about moving out of the city. Lauren and I weren't getting along so well, and I was worried about the kids in such a rough school. I said, they shouldn't be in public schools, but I don't have any money, and the schools aren't so good up here. And they couldn't go out on the streets because kids were being held up at knife point. So I was saying all that, and then Sukey said, Well, my God, come to Guilford; it's beautiful! It's wonderful! The train goes right into Grand Central; it takes you not even two hours, the easiest trip in the world. Just delightfully funny. It was a complete 180 degree . . . of everything she said earlier. So then some months later, like maybe even a year later, actually, I'd broken up with Lauren, and I was going with Ted Mankovich, and we came up on Memorial Day just to visit Sukey and David. And so we came up and stayed that week-end, and we did kind of like it. So then some months later I came up, and I rented a little house in the winter out on the shore, but in the winter you can do that for, like, really cheap. And so a year or so later, we bought this place, and Ted had moved up. This was, like '76. But I was still commuting to New York.

EF: Working at St. Mark's.

MO: Yes, for a long time, like for four years. And I would go in, and the Schneemans, Katie and David, were so sweet. They'd let me sleep over for the night. But I'd go in and out every day, and stay over one of the nights. And then Kyran was born in '77. At some point I thought I was missing his childhood. And I felt a little schitzoid, like being in the city and then I'd get on the train, and I'd get out here. I was, like, leading two lives or something. The problem wouldn't have been so bad, but I had my children and we needed more time together. So then I got an NEA fellowship, and I thought I could quit work for a year. So I did, and after about three months, I realized how out of touch with myself I'd gotten. I'd just been sleeping four hours a night or something, commuting, a whirlwind in the city, coming home. I was exhausted. I was so exhausted I didn't even know I was exhausted. I didn't even know what it was like not to be exhausted. I was sleep-deprived. I realized after about three months, I'm feeling really off, I'm feeling really different, and what it was, was I was awake. Not that I hadn't been awake of sorts, because I'd steal little naps on the train. And I would be in New York, and it would be late. I was, like, you know, doing everything. I was doing Telephone Books and the magazine. I was overdoing everything actually. So I began to think, I don't want to do that. I want to be awake.

EF: So that was about 1980, when Inland came along?

MO: So then it just happened that Inland Book Company was starting, yes, '80 or '81.

EF: Had you known David Wilk before?

MO: Just a little bit because I'd been on the CCLM board of directors, and so he had been at the National Endowment, and I met him there. He was the director of the Literature Department at the NEA.

EF: But Truck?

MO: He'd had Truck Press, but I didn't know him then at all. But I knew Truck Press, but I'd never met him. He was also Truck Distribution and then Bookslinger took it over. So I'd met him at a few meetings of CCLM, just meetings like that, so I hadn't really known him. But he knew me a bit, too, so he and his partner, Steve Hargraves, had opened this book distribution company. I thought, Wow, I could get a job working with small presses, which I liked, and distributing, which I thought was such an important thing to do for small presses, because that was where it all fell apart. You'd do these books, and they'd sit under your bed for the rest of your life or in your garage or something. The hard part is distributing. So I thought, What a great opportunity, so I took that job, and it was great. You really felt like a pilgrim or a savior of small press and independent publishers. And Inland, when it worked, was wonderful. It did put a lot of small presses on the map. Although tragically, then it collapsed. So then I worked up here and taught workshops in the city.

EF: But you decided not to stay with the Inland people when they went to LPC.

MO: No, for a number of reasons. I didn't want to go to Chicago, because Kyran was still in high school. And the whole dispersement, the whole falling apart of Inland was pretty sad for most of us. The whole thing was so tragic. It had been so incredible, and part of it was the people who came to work there. They really loved books; everyone really loved books. They were totally involved with small presses. It was like some kind of vortex. Everybody got along. A great group of people. And then the whole thing just kind of fell apart, and it took about two years for it to do that. We all felt bad; we felt bad for the presses that were really getting left in the lurch. So the heart kind of went out of it. But one of the women who worked in the catalogue department, Jean-Marie Dolan, went to Chicago, was I guess the only other employee who went besides David.

EF: But Ann Grossman stayed.

MO: Ann Grossman stayed because they had a Milford office, and I worked in the Milford office for a while, but then I got another job.

EF: If places like Inland can't survive, and apparently they can't, what's going to happen to small presses in this country? I mean if you were starting out again, would everything seem very bleak, or just bleak? It's not the same thing when you've got something on the internet.

MO: No, it's not a book. I don't know. It's a complicated time in a way because of the superstores. Perhaps I shouldn't say this, but I was rather heartened to read in *PW* this week that Crown Books went bankrupt. I was like: Wow! That's a switch! I mean things are interesting. You have these big superstores. They move next door to some wonderful little independent store. And it's all over for the independent. Superstores have done some irreparable damage. And they're filled with people selling books who don't know anything about the books. And that's a very strange situation for a bookstore.

RON PADGETT

RP: This is an interview with Ron Padgett, conducted March 30, 1991.

EF: A nice spring day with snow in the air . . .

RP: . . . outside his lovely apartment on East 13th Street in New York. The End.

EF: That was nice. I enjoyed it, but it's very short, and some people will be disappointed. Maybe I should ask these questions on my notecards. I've got them in chronological order.

RP: That's a good way.

EF: The first one will probably be meaningless.

RP: The first question is almost always meaningless.

EF: Well, this will be very meaningless: what was it like growing up in Tulsa, Oklahoma?

RP: Meaningless. I don't know. I can't remember. That's a big question. But I'll talk for a minute, and then we'll get used to the idea that you're asking me questions and I'm answering them. I suppose it was different for everybody. For me it was a normal mixture of good and bad. But basically more good than bad, I'd say. It was kind of a nice town. Smelled good.

EF: But it was small?

RP: I can't remember what the population was in, say, 1950—I was born in '42—it was probably something around 180,000. Tulsa had lots of movie theaters and even an occasional touring ballet company. Things like that. In high school, we started to get foreign movies at one theater. But I think Tulsa was sort of an average-type place. Democratic in its politics but basically conservative. A lot of birds and trees, quite green, unlike the Dust Bowl image. My mother, my father, and I lived in a blue-collar neighborhood. Then, when I was six, we moved into a brand-new, middle-class house, red brick, with big elm trees outside, a lawn, and a big back yard, all on a tree-lined street. Kids could play from yard to yard on the block. My best friend was Dick Gallup, the poet, who lived across the street. His family had moved there from Massachusetts when he was in about fourth grade. And we became pals.

EF: But meanwhile, if rumor is correct, your father was a bootlegger.

RP: Yes, I seem to be quite proud of this.

EF: How did he do that? The sort of thing with shoot-outs, midnight runs?

RP: Oklahoma was, until 1959, a "dry" state. It was against the law to sell alcohol, except very weak beer. Most, if not all, of the other states around the country had repealed prohibition. During the Second World War, my dad was working at a gas station, pumping gas, and then he started selling hooch by the bottle on the side to his gas customers, and he realized it was a much better way to make a living. So he went into business selling whiskey, which he would buy up in Missouri, about a three-hour drive from Tulsa. He sold wholesale. That is, he sold it to other bootleggers (who sold it by the bottle) or he sold it to other, more well-heeled customers, like the mayor, chief of police, and lots of respectable citizens.

EF: Seriously?

RP: Sure, because they knew that the liquor laws—backed by religious fundamentalists—were absurd. He made a good living that way, but he did have a reputation as a criminal.

EF: He did?

RP: Yes, and the papers made much of it. But he had a lot of friends in the police department. They had all grown up on the same side of town—the rougher side—and most of them became manual workers, blue-collar guys, welders, race-car drivers, cops, or crooks. Everybody knew everybody, and they knew he was not a bad guy. And one of his best friends, one he used to go bird-hunting with, was a cop. There was no problem. But there was one division of the police department—the "raiding squad"—that insisted on raiding our house occasionally. But we were always tipped off about the raids, so they never got any evidence. My mother was the bookkeeper and took the phone orders. And she was a housewife and a mother. That went on until the state went wet. At that point it became a federal crime—like being a moonshiner, which he wasn't—so he decided to get out of the liquor business. He didn't like the idea of having a legal liquor store, standing behind a counter, a little bit too calm for him. So, yes, he was a bootlegger, for around fifteen years.

And he was also, I should add, a Robin Hood kind of character, a stand-up guy, who was honest and loyal to his friends. But he was also not to be messed with. He carried a gun in his car, and he slept with a revolver under his pillow.

EF: The real West.

RP: Well, he did a cash business and sometimes had large amounts of cash about him. It was necessary to have a gun for self-protection. He never shot anybody, but he let it be known to would-be highjackers that he carried a gun. So there was a little bit of Wild West, a little bit of old cowboy, there.

EF: How did you get from there to poetry and the *White Dove Review*?

RP: There does seem to be quite a distance, doesn't there? Especially as my parents were not at all literary. The only way I've been able to explain it to myself is to think about the image of my father as an outsider, a dashing figure who was willing to defy the social and legal conventions to do what he thought was right, and to that I link the image of the romantic poet, a Rimbaud-type figure—an outlaw character, a renegade, an individualist who is willing to go against the grain. That's one way I've explained it to myself. I don't know if it's true or not. Also, I was a sensitive kid, perhaps made sensitive by my father's profession and the social stigma attached to it. The third thing that comes to mind is something that seems to run through at least one branch of our family, through my father's mother and her father, who was a self-educated justice of the peace and a socialist in Oklahoma back in the 1920s and '30s. Apparently he was an omnivorous reader. He read Homer, for instance. There was a series of books back then called the Little Blue Books, published by E. Haldeman-

Julius, who may have been a socialist himself. You know the series? There were literally hundreds of these little tracts and books—excerpts from George Bernard Shaw, how to raise bees, selections from Baudelaire—just an incredible variety of books. I think my great-grandfather must have read a lot of those. So there's some kind of weird strain that got through the family, maybe, to me. I don't know.

EF: Did you know him?

RP: When I was a kid. He lived to be something like 84. As I boy, I remember going up to the nearby town of Claremore, which is where Will Rogers is from, and visiting him. He lived in one of those old frame houses that had an icebox, literally an icebox, not a refrigerator. He was nice to me, and he gave me a book on the life of Eugene V. Debs. So anyway that's my hypothetical explanation of how a Tulsa bootlegger's son becomes a poet.

EF: When did you start reading poetry?

RP: It must have been in junior high school, which is when I started reading "seriously." Most of my reading before that was of comic books. I read a Lone Ranger book and a couple of dog books by Albert Payson Terhune, but basically I didn't read "children's literature." I wasn't into reading books, but I liked comic books, and I read enormous mountains of them, and my father kept me endlessly supplied with any and all of them. I mean he would come home with twenty or thirty comic books at a time. He himself did read a little, now that I think of it. He read westerns. He liked Zane Grey, people like that. But I started reading poetry in junior high, when puberty made me even more sensitive, and at that point it was pretty clear that I was smart, too. I made good grades in school, and my parents were very proud of that. In junior high, I had the same English teacher for seventh, eighth, and ninth grades, Miss Lillie Roberts, who was a wonderful teacher, and who encouraged me to read more and write more. She made me like English. She had us keep a three-year reading chart of all the books we read, and the first year, I read the minimum two books (*The Mickey Mantle Story* and something else equally inane). But the second year I sort of blossomed, and I read the *Iliad* and a book about Einstein and others, even *Romeo and Juliet*. It was in through there, about the eighth grade, that poetry started to mean something, but still less than science or fiction. I think my real interest in poetry must have crashed through my brain about the age of thirteen or fourteen. I started writing poetry at thirteen or fourteen.

EF: Who were your models?

RP: Oh, very bad ones. Rhymed verse by the kind of authors who appear in volumes such as *The Best Loved Poems of the American People*: "The Cremation of Dan McGee," the old chestnuts, which I haven't dared to read since. I'm afraid they might be good! But my introduction to modern poetry came a little later, when I was fifteen and working in a bookstore, the Lewis Meyer Bookshop, run by a very nice and highly literate man, who was also a writer. It was there I found out about e. e. cummings and T. S. Eliot. Then I learned about *Evergreen Review* and suddenly started reading all these modernist poets such as Leroi Jones and Frank O'Hara, and I subscribed to the magazines advertised in *Evergreen Review* like Leroi Jones's *Yugen* and Wallace Berman's *Semina*. And when I looked at magazines like *Yugen*, I saw they were just little things stapled together, and so I went down to a local printer and asked, How do you do this? And he said, Oh, it's nothing—it's real easy. So I decided to start my own magazine. I invited Dick Gallup, who was still across the street and was writing poetry, to be co-editor, and Joe Brainard, who was the best artist in school, to be the art editor.

EF: It must have been about that time that you met Ted Berrigan.

RP: Yes, I met Ted in the spring of 1959. I was working in the bookstore, and Ted walked in with three friends of his.

EF: He was stationed in Tulsa.

RP: Yes, he was still in the army, but I think he was in something like the reserves. He had enrolled at the University of Tulsa under the GI bill, and he lived near the college campus, as did I. I was a junior in high school. It was partly through Ted I met other poets and artists at the University of Tulsa.

EF: Who, for example?

RP: There was a poet named David Bearden, who was a friend of Ted's at the time. And there was a painter named Johnny Arthur. And there's a sculptor named Gordon Boyd, who eventually worked at the Gotham Bookmart. There was a whole crew of young artists and wild people, sensitive, creative people. Ted seemed quite a bit older than me. He'd been in the army, for god's sake—he'd been to Korea. He'd grown up in Providence. He'd been to Japan. And he knew a lot of things I didn't know, so he was in many ways a mentor to me and to Dick and to other young people.

EF: And then Columbia, how did you get there?

RP: I applied to Columbia for two reasons: one, I knew that Kerouac and Ginsberg had gone there, and that sounded pretty good; and, two, it was in New York, which also sounded pretty good. The next thing I knew I was on my way to New York on a train, and then, boom, here I was.

EF: 1960.

RP: The fall of 1960.

EF: And Dick Gallup came, too?

RP: No, actually Joe Brainard and I were the same year in high school, and Joe had received a scholarship to the Dayton Art Institute. Joe and I left Tulsa together on a train for Dayton, Ohio, where he rented a room, and then we took a Greyhound bus to New York, right through the Lincoln Tunnel. Joe stayed here for a couple of weeks, and then went back to art school in Dayton, and I started classes at Columbia. Dick was a year older than us. He had left Tulsa the year before and gone to Tulane.

EF: So how did everybody converge on New York?

RP: Not too far into the first semester, the Dayton Art Institute had an outdoor art show, at which all students and faculty were invited to exhibit their work. Joe exhibited some nude self-portraits, there on the sidewalks of Dayton. The school told him he had to withdraw them. He said, OK, went back to his room, packed his bags, and just disappeared. He came to New York immediately. Dick came here in the summer of '61 and spent a couple of months, where he met up with Ted, who had come here around Christmas of '60 or in early '61. Ted was sharing a storefront apartment with Joe on East 6th Street, and then he stayed on. Dick kept bouncing back and forth and sometime in his junior year dropped out of Tulane and moved to New York. So we all eventually gravitated toward New York.

EF: Did you know Kenneth Koch was at Columbia when you decided to go there? Or was that something you discovered when you arrived?

RP: I did know that Kenneth Koch was at Columbia, and I had read his poetry, but I wasn't particularly taken with it. I didn't dislike it. I think it baffled me. I didn't understand contemporary comic poetry.

EF: You?

RP: I was very serious. My models were Pound, Eliot, Ginsberg, and the Black Mountain poets, in which there wasn't a lot of humor. I was a real serious kid. But I was assigned to Professor Koch for freshman Humanities, and I thought, Oh, that's good—he's the poet Kenneth Koch—that should be interesting. But I wasn't really as excited about it as I would have been later. It turned out to be a great year, and it was a wonderful way to read the classics with a teacher who is that bright and that enthusiastic. He managed to make me really like Saint Augustine and other writers you don't ordinarily like when you're that age. It was great reading the Bible under Professor Koch.

EF: He was also teaching at the New School, wasn't he?

RP: Yes, but I never took any of those courses. No, I didn't have to because I could take courses with him at Columbia. One of his courses was called Twentieth-Century Comic Literature. It was the first course at Columbia to teach the work of Gertrude Stein and to read *Ulysses* as a comic novel. It was great because I was reading *Ulysses* for Professor Trilling's modern fiction course at the same time I was reading it for Kenneth's Twentieth-Century Comic Literature course and getting these different points of view, both of which were valuable. In Kenneth's course we also read Ronald Firbank, whom I'd never heard of, and Alfred Jarry and Aldous Huxley and Evelyn Waugh. And I also did extra assignments—like reading Raymond Roussel.

EF: And now you've translated Roussel and other French authors from that period. Was it under Koch that you started reading French poetry?

RP: No, I started reading French poetry in high school. The first French poetry I really got interested in was Rimbaud's. Difficult poetry, of course, but you know that fascination . . .

EF: You mean your French at the time was poor?

RP: It was rudimentary, but I was determined to make it better because I wanted to read Rimbaud. I wanted to understand him: what the hell is going on with this guy?

EF: But by the time you graduated from Columbia, your French must have been reasonably good—good enough in any case to get you a Fulbright.

RP: Well it wasn't actually, but I did get a Fulbright to go to Paris because of Kenneth's help. He and F. W. Dupee wrote glowing recommendations, and then for the language requirement part, Kenneth sent me down to a colleague of his in the French department, who gave me a good recommendation, and I got the Fulbright. I went to France just to be a young poet in Paris. I didn't really go to study French literature, but it turned out I did an enormous amount of work studying French literature, all on my own. I spent many hours in the library researching and reading and translating.

EF: What were the conditions of the Fulbright? It couldn't have been a teaching . . .

RP: No, I was a student, Fulbright student.

EF: At what university?

RP: I made a feeble effort to enroll at the Sorbonne, but then I completely lost interest in it, and school didn't seem necessary. I don't mean to brag, but I did learn a lot in the Bibliothèque Sainte-Geneviève, which has a special collection of French modern manuscripts and books. It was extraordinary what I was able to examine and read there.

EF: So you had a year just to read modern French poetry.

RP: Yes. It turned out that I was less interested in Dada and Surrealism than I thought, and that what interested me most was the work of Apollinaire, Max Jacob, Pierre Reverdy, and Blaise Cendrars. But I liked certain Dada and Surrealist works, and I got to read a lot of great books, first editions of beautiful books by Man Ray and Eluard and Max Ernst. It was quite an education. Not to mention the great joy of being in Paris and suddenly getting interested in history for the first time in my life.

EF: But the people you mention were all dead by this time, and their work was in the past. Were there others . . .

RP: No, Man Ray was still alive.

EF: Of course, but Reverdy and Cendrars and Apollinaire . . .

RP: Yes, Apollinaire was long gone. Cendrars was barely gone.

EF: '62, I think.

RP: '62, yes. I went there in '65, and Reverdy had died in '60—on my birthday. But there were a lot of people still around who knew him.

EF: And you met them?

RP: I met some people, yes, and I actually got a letter from Apollinaire's wife. And also I imagined or fantasized the old Paris that seemed to be still there, in the architecture and the buildings and the signs and the feel of the place. The same old métro cars that were originally installed in the North-South line—that Reverdy named his magazine after—they were still working. And you could still go in these old cafés and restaurants that had an incredible fin-de-siècle feeling. Philippe Soupault was alive, but I didn't meet him at that time. And André Breton was alive, too, but the idea of meeting him scared me. But I did see characters like Raymond Duncan, who was Isadora Duncan's brother, in the street. So I felt connected to the past.

EF: So in a sense the world you were living in was French modernism of, say, around 1915.

RP: It was 1909 to 1917 that I found really attractive.

EF: And that's still the center for you?

RP: To me, it has been the most consistently interesting, yes.

EF: Would you say it's the same, or something in that vicinity, for John Ashbery?

RP: I don't know.

EF: That period does seem something of a common denominator for New York School poetry.

RP: To some degree. With John, there's also the interest in Roussel, who was writing around that time and later, but who is such an unclassifiable oddball that you can't really situate him with any group. And there are other French poets that would interest John, too. But you'd have to ask him.

EF: How is it in that poem by Frank O'Hara—"My heart is in my / pocket, it is Poems by Pierre Reverdy."

RP: Yes, Frank liked his work, too, and Kenneth a lot.

EF: So what is the connection between the Paris poets and those in New York? It's fifty years later, and it's a new culture, a different language.

RP: In the first place, those three poets all read French. You have to, because if you depend on the translation you can be in trouble, especially with Reverdy, who's so hard to translate. But I don't know—I'll just give you the kind of standard answer that would spring into anybody's mind, that the poetry's so exciting and so beautiful, so open and still fresh. There's a certain amount of high energy in it.

EF: Why weren't you more interested in contemporary French poetry?

RP: I don't know. I guess the lives of Reverdy, Cendrars, Apollinaire, and Max Jacob paralleled mine in some ways. That's to say, maybe I felt a sympathy for them because I was a little displaced. I was an Okie living in New York and then Paris, as Apollinaire was originally of Polish-Italian extraction. He wasn't even a French citizen, until later. Cendrars was Swiss. He wasn't a French citizen either. Jacob was a Jewish convert to Catholicism. And Reverdy felt real displacement in coming to Paris from the South. Also there was a certain amount of poverty, or at least a bohemian life. I mean, here I was in New York: I had very little money, and I was a poet, and I didn't care if I had any career or money or anything like that. I just wanted to get by, to eat, and to pay the rent. We lived close to the bone: we didn't go without anything, but we had no luxuries. We weren't as poor as some of the French poets were, but I sympathized with their condition. And also I liked the fact that those guys were all involved with painters, and I liked painting a lot. And also I guess those fellows felt to some degree they were doing something new and interesting. And unfortunately I seemed to feel I was, too!

EF: Unfortunately?

RP: Oh, yes. It's the kind of assumption you make when you're young that enables you to do things you can't otherwise do, whether or not the assumption is based on a reasonable premise. I felt that Ted and Dick and Joe and I and other people at the time were doing something new and interesting in poetry. It's a claim that I'm loath to make now.

EF: But it enabled you . . .

RP: It gave us the guts to try something.

EF: How did you feel it was distinct from what Ashbery and Koch and O'Hara had been doing a few years before? Weren't you concerned about that?

RP: How did I feel at the time? I'm not sure that I even thought about it. In many respects, it wasn't different.

EF: It was not?

RP: No, because we were all influenced by them so strongly that sometimes our work was too imitative. But at the time I wasn't worried about any of that. I was just writing on waves of language. I could tell sometimes pretty quickly if I thought the poems were any good. Somehow I knew I was being influenced by those three writers and by James Schuyler a little bit later, but I didn't think the influence was harmful. You know, there would be a turn of phrase or a certain rhythmical shift or something that sounded like Frank O'Hara in my work. I wasn't really too concerned with that. I was happy because I knew that I was getting something from it. Something was rubbing off. And some of those poems that are highly imitative I never published, or I published them in little magazines and put them away forever because they just were not good, but after that I started to feel a difference or to notice a difference between their work and mine. My work was a little more "down home." It seemed to come more out of the working class. My Arkansas Ozark ancestors are wandering around in my work. The work of the others was more sophisticated, urbane, and witty. But my work was quick and light, with a lot of the cowboy-hillbilly that was natural to my feeling, that I didn't find in theirs. It isn't an accomplishment, it's just something you get, by being who you are.

EF: Could a similar description be applied to Ted's work—the sense of working-class background?

RP: Yes. Ted had a blue-collar background also, and he was a guy living on the edge, an outlaw type. And there was a lot of spunkiness and orneriness and street urchin bad-boy stuff in there that you don't get so much in the older poets that we admired so much. You get it in Frank some. Frank liked to be naughty, but in a little different way.

EF: They were all at some point at Harvard, and that can make a difference.

RP: All except Jimmy.

EF: But there's no connection like that within your group.

RP: No, I was the one who went to an Ivy League school, and so there was a bit of rub-off there. John and Kenneth had gotten degrees at Columbia also. So maybe I was more comfortable around them than I would have been if I had attended a less illustrious school. What was it?—Kerouac had been sent the galleys for one of David Shapiro's books, and had made a comment, something like, This book is full of that good old Columbia wit and charm. And at the time I remember thinking that there was something to that idea, that there is a kind of tone to schools. I'm not sure that wit and charm is the perfect description of Columbia or the people who have attended it, but there was something, a certain kind of sophistication.

EF: So in any case, you began reading Reverdy and Cendrars about this time on your own, not because someone suggested it or you knew others who were reading them. Are you saying there was no influence—no New York School influence?

RP: Well, no, Kenneth Koch had pointed me toward Reverdy, Apollinaire, and Max Jacob, but not Cendrars. He had mentioned them in his courses and talked about them, and in fact I'd taken an independent study course with him, in which I would go to his office once a week for an hour or two. He would look at the translations I was working on, and we would discuss them, and he would tell me how to improve them. In general he pointed me in the general direction of those three poets. Apollinaire's work was so exciting, big, expansive, fresh—poems like "Zone," for instance. It's just a wonderful poem. Or the strange highjinks of Max Jacob in *The Dice Cup*, which I think is a great book, an extraordinary book, still extraordinary. And in that black and white moodiness, that angularity and mysteriousness of Reverdy and the sonority of the work in French. Once you're pointed in that direction, that's about all it takes, I think. I didn't have to be convinced or encouraged very much.

EF: What did you bring across from those poets to your own work?

RP: I don't know.

EF: You wouldn't say that your earlier work was more like Cendrars and recently it has been more like Reverdy?

RP: No, I think it all reverberates back and forth through time. I pick up Reverdy from time to time, get interested in him again for a month or so, and even translate some more poems or dig a little deeper. I've just finished this Cendrars book, translating all his poetry, and so the last four or five years I've been involved with his work, thinking about him, reading about him, studying him, retranslating his poetry, researching, whatnot. Somehow I don't think it's changed my poetry or the writing I've done over the last couple of years. So I go back and forth to those guys, depending on how I'm feeling at the time. Anyway, I've gotten confused about who influenced me or when or what or how. It's all this big swirling jumble, which is the way

I like it.

EF: In *Great Balls of Fire* you mention Reverdy several times.

RP: That's true.

EF: Yet it doesn't seem a Reverdy book.

RP: No, it isn't at all. It's strange, isn't it? I love the idea of him, but I felt I couldn't write poetry like his. It's too hard. I mean in the first place usually it doesn't sound very good in English. It gets real flat. It loses its sonority, and also you have to make it more explicit than it is in the French because of certain words in French that would sound silly in English. He uses a word like *esprit* that can mean about twenty-five different things—*mind* or *wit* or *intelligence* or *feeling*, or, you know, *soul*, *spirit*—you're going to have to pick one in English. You don't have to do it in French. Or the French word *on*—*one* does this. You can't translate Reverdy's *on* as *one*: it sounds like you're posturing, and it doesn't in French. So anyway I didn't see any way you can write like him in English directly. Also there's the matter of his ear and his subtle use of rhyme—a lot of his free verse poems are actually rhymed. If you lay the lines out differently, they're pretty standard-looking arrangements, and you can't rhyme that way in English without sounding ding-dong. So I never did try to write like him, but somehow the figure of Pierre Reverdy grabbed the back of my brain and wouldn't let go. I was very interested in this guy. I couldn't figure out who he was, what it felt like to be around him.

EF: Totally without a sense of humor. Unlike your work.

RP: Yes, the opposite of me in many respects. He was grim, possessed by religious anxiety. He had an explosive temper, wanted to fight, punched guys in the nose occasionally, and was very set in his ways, firm about his opinions, dogmatic even, and never seemed to crack a smile. Somehow that interested me because I was quite the opposite. It's a little bit like his description of the power of the literary image: if you can bring two disparate things together and make them work together, the further apart they are initially, the more powerful their combination is going to be.

EF: Yes, you mention that definition at the end of *Among the Blacks*, but I'm not quite sure what you meant there—I mean in that context. As you use it, it seems so different from what I would understand by the word *image*. In that book, you bring together two prose works, two narratives, and Reverdy was talking specifically about the image. I have a feeling he was describing something similar to montage in movies.

RP: All I meant to do in that afterword was to point out that the Raymond Roussel story I translated, "Among the Blacks," and my own memoir, to which I gave the same title, were very different, and that I wanted to put them together in the same volume to see what would happen, and that reminded me of Reverdy's definition of the image as being more powerful once you'd somehow united two disparate things. *If* you can unite them. In fact, if they don't unite, if there's no rapport between them, then there's no power whatsoever. And I was saying in this afterword that I didn't know if these two pieces that I was bringing together would fit or not, but I was going to give it a try. I still don't know, but I like them together in the same book.

EF: And your work was in no way a response to his?

RP: No, not at all. I simply happened to have these two pieces around. Once I had written my piece I had to give it a name, and then the title of Roussel's story occurred to me. I thought, Well, this is a good title. It would fit my piece, too, so I used it, and then I realized that it would be funny to have them in the same book. And then I wondered, Well, *would* it be funny? So I put the two pieces together and looked at them and thought, I think this is interesting, and Stephen Ratcliffe at Avenue B Books wanted to publish it but asked me to write a little note explaining why these two are in the same book. That's what I tried to do in the afterword.

EF: Well, it would be impossible to duplicate your tone in French, and I think it would be impossible to write naturally in English in the tone Roussel used.

RP: Very, very hard. Harry Mathews has almost done it in his fiction, in a book like *The Conversions*, but, no, Americans don't write fiction like Roussel's.

EF: Cendrars's admirers in this part of the world include Dos Passos and Miller and Padgett. Put those three together . . .

RP: . . . and you have an illness.

EF: What does this writer have that attracts such an incredibly diverse group?

RP: In the translator's preface I've written for the University of California Press edition of Cendrars's complete poetry that is going to come out soon, I point out that to me Cendrars always sounded like an American writer—unlike, say, Reverdy. There seemed to be all kinds of connections between Blaise Cendrars and America. He wrote poems about America; he traveled here extensively; he lived in New York for a while. He translated a book by a guy who had been in jail with O. Henry, an Oklahoma outlaw named Al Jennings. Cendrars even went to Hollywood and met Jennings and got his revolver as a present. And I was from Oklahoma. And Cendrars's work itself, certain of the works anyway, were flat the way a lot of American speech is flat. And he also seemed to have some of the rambunctiousness that I associate with the frontier mentality. He wasn't entirely that way, of course, but that was my impression at the time. So I sensed something American about him that I didn't see in Apollinaire or Max Jacob or Reverdy. When I translated his poetry, it sounded OK in English. He has a book, for instance, called *Kodak*, which is made up entirely of found poems, it turns out. If you don't know that, it doesn't hurt because the poems actually read quite well anyway. I really like those poems, and the fact that he had done something so bold—very bold in the early 1920s—seemed extraordinary to me. And the more I looked at his work, the more I saw that in each work Cendrars was doing something quite different from what he'd done before. I like his willingness to try some pretty wild things, which weren't wild in the same way the Dadaists and Surrealists were wild. I think he was so avant-garde that he was off the graph.

EF: Maybe this is the place to settle once and for all the question whether there is, or ever was, a New York School. A few people still seem to feel it's a great and burning issue, and it's true that some of the poets you and David Shapiro included in your anthology have more than geography and friendships in common. And then there's the St. Mark's group, and some people have said that there are similarities in style and so forth among poets associated with the Poetry Project there.

RP: First of all, I doubt that it's a great and burning issue. There are some connections between poets we included, but notice that David and I titled that book *An Anthology of New York Poets*. It's not called *The New York School*. It's not called *The New York Poets*.

EF: But that's what people said when they read it.

RP: That's their problem. In fact we anticipated that, and in the preface we said that the connections were tenuous in many cases. We did not make a claim for a school. I don't think it's all that interesting to generalize about poets by putting them in "schools." It's better just to read the work and see what it says and how it says it, and then sometimes you can have the delightful experience of reading a poet who supposedly belongs to a school you are not supposed to like and you find the work is quite interesting. You hear people say, Oh, I hate poet X's work, and I think, Right, I don't like X's work either. Then I realize I haven't read it for twenty-five years. I'm different now; I should read that work again to find out if my old opinion still carries any weight. I'm not sure it does. So I'm skeptical of those categories that are chiseled in stone—opinions, schools. Opinions and "schools" are boring.

EF: This is from a interview with David Shapiro a few years ago: "I'm not sure that anyone in my generation has made a structural achievement in the way that I'm sure John Ashbery has." And then he goes on to acknowledge you as "a fine kind of poet," Joe Ceravolo as "a very fine Pierre Reverdy-ish cubist," Bernadette Mayer and Alice Notley as "extraordinary and very talented." But then he continues, "Too often the poets of the second generation seem like corollaries to corollaries, as it were, to the adults," and then he says, "I'm not convinced yet that my generation has produced a work that will last." He's saying several other things on his way to that conclusion, but I think that pretty well summarizes his basic argument, and I was wondering if it seemed adequate to you. To me there seem to be remarkable differences between the so-called first and second generations, and it would seem that what you've done, for example, is not an extension or corollary to someone else's work, whatever the debts may be. Padgett is finally not Koch or O'Hara any more than he is Cendrars or Reverdy.

RP: I'm of two minds. I'm going to be diplomatic and agree with both you and David. I agree with David in the sense that if you had a father that you admired, you're never going to feel that you can be as great as him as long as you keep that same father-son relationship. I once told Kenneth Koch that I couldn't imagine ever writing anything as great as Frank O'Hara's poetry. That's the kind of thing you say when you're feeling that you're the junior—and that's one legitimate way to feel.

Perhaps David was feeling that way, at least in the quotation you mentioned. On the other hand, we not only follow people, we move along beside some, and we precede others. I've finally gotten old enough to realize that it's pointless to measure myself against my own personal pantheon—the legendary Frank O'Hara, Kenneth Koch, etc. I just turn around and think that certain people of this so-called second generation of the New York School, such as Joe Ceravolo, have created some wonderful poetry. I think a book like *The Sonnets* by Ted Berrigan is an extraordinary book. Is it better than *Lunch Poems*? I think that kind of comparison is unproductive and invidious. Tennis commentators are always asking, Do you think Ivan Lendl could have beaten Bill Tilden? Is Homer greater than Dante? What kind of question is that? If I had to write while thinking I'm a "second-generation" person and that nothing I write is going to be as good as X, Y, or Z, it would be a terrible way to feel. It seems useless and neurotic. It would make us stop writing. Neither David nor I have stopped writing: that's the real test of how we feel about this whole question.

EF: *The Big Something* has a different tone from *Great Balls of Fire*, and that difference seems to me to be centered in the poem "Who and Each," that wonderful, very comic poem about using the *O.E.D.* But the reader reaches the bottom of the first page, turns it, and there at the top, reads, "Thus I spend my days waiting for my friends to die." And I wouldn't expect that in anything you've written before.

RP: No, I couldn't have written it before, but there are little hints of that theme in *Great Balls of Fire*, a certain preoccupation with death that I wasn't even aware of until later. There's a poem that says, "Coming out of the bathroom" . . . blah, blah, blah . . . "I've never been able to make any really reasonable connection between love and death." There are also similar references in the poem "Tone Arm." It begins, "The clouds go rolling over / the rooftops of the 17th / 18th or 19th century buildings—/ They are really rolling // You people of the future / How I hate you / You are alive and I'm not / I don't care whether you read my poetry or not." So there are hints of it in there. Is that what you mean?

EF: Well, "waiting for my friends to die" cancels out everything that has happened in "Who and Each." The humor's gone, and the tone is deeply serious. It is something like what you find in O'Hara's "A Step Away from Them," where he has been talking about pleasant things, a general kind of revery, and suddenly he gives you the words, "First / Bunny died, then John Latouche, / then Jackson Pollock." But then the poem seems to reverse, and yours doesn't. It brings everything up short and then ends—as if what it's finally said can't be overcome.

RP: It's kind of a slap in the soul. My poem is rather odd. The first part of it is just a transcription of what happened to me thinking about certain Latin words and looking up their English equivalents in the *O.E.D.*, looking up each and finding an extraordinary list of variant spellings and pronunciations that belong to the history of that word. And I wrote all that down, and when I got a certain way down deep into the poem and looked at it, it seemed rather insane to me—that a person would write what I had just written. I hadn't done it consciously, but I suddenly became aware of the fact that I was a grown-up human being, reasonably intelligent, sitting at a desk writing this bizarre stuff, and it seemed not only crazy but absurd, and so the diction changes: "Thus I spend my days . . . "—an elevated diction that the poem didn't have earlier. And I'm actually making fun of myself as if I were a nutty Victorian scholar: "Thus I spend my days whiling away the hours with my lexicon." And suddenly it hit me that the poem had been influenced partly by the death of Frances Waldman, Anne Waldman's mother, who was a great stickler for accuracy, and who would often come back at you with a quotation from the *O.E.D.*, saying, This word does not mean that—you *did* misuse this word. She was very nice and funny in that way. She used to edit the *Poetry Project Newsletter*, and poets would send her these vaguely worded reviews that would drive her crazy. I liked her a lot, and she had died not too much before I wrote this poem. There was also Ted's death. Yes, I must have written this poem after Ted's death. The death of my friends kind of erupted at that moment—the absurdity of sitting and worrying about words in Latin when actually what was on your soul's mind was the fact that you were getting older, and not only the fact that you were closer to your own death, but even worse, that your friends were dying. That was how that poem happened: I wrote what was there, and then suddenly there wasn't anything else to say.

EF: But the tone in those final lines seems to emerge many times in the book, and it makes the title of the book, in one sense, seem very serious.

RP: It *can* be, except *Something* doesn't need to imply *death*. The title didn't come by with my thinking about death. Actually I think the title has a comic overtone. *The Big Something* is kind of a parody of *The Big Sleep*.

EF: Which, of course, is death.

RP: Yes, but the idea of calling something *The Big Something* seems funny to me. How can you use an adjective to describe something when you don't know what it is? I like that idea. Maybe I should have called it *The Medium-sized Something*.

EF: You end the book with a piece in which you say that men once left home saying they were going to get cigarettes and then just never came back. The last words are, "They left, and they looked, but they never did find that pack of cigarettes." It seemed a particularly dry way to end the book. It seemed a very Reverdyish solution.

RP: How so?

EF: Well, I suppose I'm doing more with the piece than you intended, but still, it suggests to me the way things are now: I'm sure that men leave home just as often as they ever did, but they don't have to make excuses anymore. There's nobody left to make excuses to. The way that piece ends reminds me of what has happened to us, what has happened to all of us, and it leaves things suddenly empty.

RP: I put that poem at the end simply because it has somebody leaving. It's just that I like the idea of the character in this piece not only going out the door—he's already gone. All you have is the sense of the back door slamming. I like that kind of exit for the book: the guy's gone before you know it. The book is over before you know it. I like that. "Smoke" is just a little prose piece. I didn't mean anything metaphoric. I almost never do. I don't like metaphors all that much.

EF: Nor did Reverdy, of course.

RP: I mean I like them. I like them as an idea, and I am very happy they exist. It just occurred to me as I was looking at you that there's another way of having the force of metaphor be throughout an entire poem without its being metaphoric. I'm not sure I know what I mean, but . . .

EF: I remember Ashbery once said something about how Reverdy gives things their true names. Isn't that it? And that's, therefore, what that piece at the end of *The Big Something* does, at least for me. He returns things to their true names—or he returns the true names to things. It's been a long time since I saw that, but it stuck with me as something poems can do, and that it has to be a great poem in order to do it. And that's the opposite of metaphorical, I think.

RP: I don't know the comment.

EF: I think it was something he wrote just after Reverdy died.

RP: Perhaps in the *Mercure de France* homage to Reverdy. Yes. I think that is true in some of Reverdy's poems. There are others that are metaphoric, clearly metaphoric, but that's not really what he's best at. The thing he's best at was more along the lines of what I think John might have been saying. Ted once told me, Ron, you're really good at simile and metaphor—You really have a knack for it, maybe too much of one. Meaning I had an ability to make similes and metaphors so naturally and quickly and easily that it became a mannerism that kept the work from developing. Right after that, I wrote a line that said, "The ball lay there like a ball," in response to what he had said, to make the dumbest possible simile I could imagine. Besides, I like the idea of something being like itself.

ARMAND SCHWERNER

EF: You mentioned yesterday the piece that you read by Ted Berrigan . . .

AS: Oh, that was in Moxley and Evans pamphlet series. You've seen what they're doing?

EF: *The Impercipient?* Yes

AS: I try to keep up with what's happening with people in younger generations, so. . . . I guess you've read this one

EF: Yes, I have, but I don't remember that he quoted Ted Berrigan

AS: Here it is. It's from Steve Evans' essay on "The Dynamics of Literary Change," where he reports a conversation between Berrigan and Clark Coolidge about *The Sonnets* ,the book that brought Ted relatively early to renown. Berrigan finds himself wondering whether he will "ever be able to do another work like that." He concludes that he will not. ". . . There is no having back the work that came out of *nowhere* and landed itself and its maker *somewhere*. "If only one could be nowhere again, that would be really fantastic," Berrigan says. . . .

EF: nowhere, again?

AS: "If only one could be nowhere again." if one could regain a radical innocence, avoid a growing awareness of a certain kind of historical sense. The theoretical and seductive purity of beginnings.

EF: A return—meaning that you no longer speak from an accustomed place. Maybe no longer being aware of speaking from any particular place—just speaking.

AS: Yes, and your term is reminiscent of Zen phrases like just-sitting etc., because if you are just-speaking, you're not outside, making a distinction between the self/producer and the self/analyzer. These matters relate also to the poet's sense of his or her audience. Take Jerry Rothenberg. Early on, I never understood his starting to make manifestoes. Deep Image. Ethnopoetics. Primitive is complex. I was always uncomfortable with such formulations. Jerry was right. He'd read the culture early, knew it wanted food. And he saw no reason not to give it what he himself was in the course of preparing for himself. And I notice in Jerry's recently published master-anthology *Poems for the Millennium II* that he and Pierre Joris have a section entitled "The Art of the Manifesto." But it wasn't my thing. For so many years, I'd been deeply convinced that everything should go into the poem, that there should be no need for external divagations. And then, years after that profoundly held belief, I added "Divagations," a long section of citations and commentary as an appendix to *Tablets I–XXVII*. And I've recently spent a fair amount of time writing about what I've written! So much for consistency. Do it; don't talk about it, I used to feel and often still feel that in this part of our century, a kind of brass age, we announce rather than personally blunder into and through. So that the poem often turns into a versified argument. Odd, to think how close much of our production is to eighteenth century modes. a century toward whose creative work we often experience aversion.

The foregrounding of methodology often trumps the slow painful availability to unsuspected and intuited connections. Why bother with the necessary labyrinthine work in the psycho trenches if the connections can be accessed through random digit tables, themselves then representing arbitrarily assigned values? Or through some kind of poetic "sampling," deriving major poetic elements from the circumambient whirligig of demotic language. What I'm saying is that it's incredibly hard to live meaningfully within the rooting and branching of connections; we pay lip service to Emily Dickinson's slow watchful waiting. . . . Almost as if the hyporcritic litcult says: See, thou slug, worship, and do other! I'm driven sometimes into frenzies of rebellion against poetry—what is that—and into feelings of disbelief that so many poets and critics can take part in the proliferating verbosities *about* poetry. . . . How is it possible to remain obdurately outside unitary tropism of poetic reaching? What else matters?

EF: Well, how do you respond to critics who are very careful to put you into the category "postmodern" with the theory and assumptions that implies?

AS: In the colleges and universities an important aspect of the modern rage for categorizations, I might almost say for nosology, (which refers to classification of diseases) rests on trumping, on unwitting creation of "new" and exploitable lines of thought. More name chairs. More tornadoes in the departments and in the Pied Piper value of professorial prophets. More young acolytes for the universities intent on survival and the overcoming of competitors' advance men and women. No one's immune; I listen to my own righteous sound and call to mind my pleasure when Brian MacHale was good enough to show me an early draft of his essay on my *Tablets*. What was that pleasure? It was that my work deserved the soubriquet "postmodern," as opposed to the work of some other interesting poets who are involved in a modernist enterprise, what Brian calls "archaeologies of knowledge." Seamus Heaney's bog-men, or the digging-spoons of Eliot, or Geoffrey Hill's anthropological resurrections (and I love his *Mercian Hymns): these works assume that digging, associating dug materials, play out some highly important, real, revelatory skirmishes of soul and dream and cultures.

But in fact, as McHale points out, *The Tablets* are involved in wave after wave of denial about any significance in all the looking, checking, interpreting which their own Scholar/Translator apparently embodies. Not only is there no there there, but the very bases for the ideas and constructions of jokes or woes or civilizational particularizations, these founder endlessly. No Kung-Fu-Tse behind the Poundian arras, no Anglo-Catholic deep thumpings to sadden the reader into a melting sense of loss to be overcome by the music of eternal verities behind the sucking sounds of the Waste Land. All is ego and all founders, although *The Tablets*' humor and litanies and erotic intensities go on in their susurrations on page after page of text.

"There are no issues," Cid Corman says in "The idea of a Mandarin Orange." That's true isn't it? That issues resolve into *gnothe seauton* , "know yourself."? And then comes the buzzing trouble, endless, about the solidity of that self. I'm not happy that there are no issues. My pleasure at Brian's identification of my "position" brings in its wake, immediately, its commensurate pain. What else is new? Wallace Stevens says somewhere in the *Necessary Angel* that the problems of the normal (whatever that is) require from us everything that we have to give, implying it seems to me that so much of Otherness which is so hard sought in our arts is nothing but a metaphor for the endless transmogrifications of ego.

Well, that's a long divagation. You asked about me being put in the post-modern slot. So I just want people to read what I do and for their intellects and hearts to be touched by it. This comes very close to what I was thinking about when I was waiting for you this afternoon. All founders, and also all is by necessity, deep necessity, and for the avoidance of spiritual fascism. While I was waiting for you I was thinking about the nature of "interview." (This is strange. I hadn't thought we would be talking about the doing of what it was we were supposed to be doing.) "Inter-view": that is, I always have felt uncomfortable taking a position, partly because out of emotional spurts I found myself suborned into positions that immediately became turf that I'd have to defend, ignoring the fact that there is no turf, or that it changed right away from a golf course to foul dump. Anyway it seems to me that everything is mercurial, can be gas, liquid, solid. Depends. That's why I love Henri Michaux particularly. His work is both the result of looking at the culture and an endless greasy sliding between percepts and experiences—a sort of Mallarméan technical clowning brought into the world of comedic preferences with ambiguity piled onto ambiguity.

So, what am I doing with this interview? I've done a good number of interviews before. Is this going to be interesting for me? Am I going to learn anything from this? And what about you? Who's going to read this? Is it going to be useful to anybody? In what way? What's the intention of this? For the poet? For the reader? My intention is someone who's constantly doing a drama. So you start the tape. Is there such a thing as the real?* Or the really real? Or the truly real? And so "interview": I looked it up and, very interesting: "inter" doesn't mean only "between." But also: in the midst of; within; mutual; reciprocal.

EF: To what do those additional meanings point?

*After the tape recorder had been turned on but before the interview had begun, Schwerner and the interviewer had talked about a nineteenth-century American mystic and poet, Manoah Bodman, who believed that he talked with Satan and that Satan was literally part of his daily world. His neighbors also believed these experiences were "real." The interviewer said, "He was part of a culture that saw evil as an active embodied presence in people's lives—a presence that did not necessarily have a cause, at least one that an individual understood, but that had to be constantly resisted. So it asks the question all over again, 'What's real? Is it true that the real is more or less a convention?' Or is calling reality a convention, itself merely a convention?"

AS: If Martin Buber's right, and I hope he is, nothing's more important than the *I and thou* relationship. All aspects of which mean beginning again and again. What's my sense of an interview? Partly it has to do with you and me. It also has to do primarily with different aspects of my self-presentation, and having to choose between four or seventeen possibilities of what I will be able to say. What decides things? How does one begin, from where? Is any beginning fresh? What decides things is partly how you or my readers or myself perceive me. Well, that's pretty heavy, because usually in conversation we don't think too much about that. We do a fairly graceful dance, ignoring the complexities of intentionality and choice. And here I sort of decided: Well, I'm going to think about the form of what we're doing. I'm not sure what Rilke meant when he said "I'm a perpetual beginner," but I've always liked the sound of that, however suspect self-intuition is, and it is very suspect.

Two words come back to me: "interview" and "amphibian." And they basically are cognates, right? "Inter": that which is between x and y. "Amphi-bios": the Greek means "living a double life," usually living in either water or on land. Incredible radical antithesis in one life. In that sense, the power that is in each of us. Or another image I often come to, which also plays a role here, which is "chiaroscuro." None of these terms involves a set position of one kind.

Somebody whose work I like very much, who was a kind of mentor and who is not a simple dualist, George Oppen, nonetheless had certain set positions, and certainly he was constantly working processually, but there he was. There was still a sense of place from which you could talk. I think George always did have the sense that you had to inquire, as Mike Heller says in his book on the Objectivists. He says Oppen wasn't interested in the effect of society on self. He was interested, courageously, in the nature of that society, not just his narcissistic dream. He was constantly concerned with what the society was like—the pressure of the real. So I often have the sense with George that one are talking from some place. I don't think there *is* a place from which things come. That is precisely one of the grounds or non-grounds, emptiness—for investigation. So "inter," "amphi," "chiaroscuro," consider the bizarreness of exercises of self-presentation and supposed information. But hell, it's never a matter of being able to avoid position is it?

EF: Yes. And you're in the middle of a paradox. You can't not take a position; on the other hand any position is an issue, and "there are no issues."

AS: Only through that paradox is life possible. And if I do have a poetic "issue," I suppose it relates to the importance of incarnating that paradox in the poem. I remember in my early days as a Zen student there would be other beginners, literally beginners, some even up to say five years in the process of their beginnings, who had made this joyous discovery, that nothing has its own essence. They translated that into a dance of Nothing is Real, and celebrated the discovery . Of course the accomplished students appreciated soon enough that their discovery had to be paradoxically supplemented by the understanding that everything perceived by the sense is in fact real. And that only in this tenuous balance lay sanity. Great poetry does that dance.

EF: if identity, or the self, is somehow intermediate, what is it that is identified by others, if not by you, as the point from which they speak of uniquely enter the world?

AS: It's a philosophical assumption. And experiential.

EF: But what postulates that point of view?

AS: It's a problem for me

EF: Perhaps questions involving origin may be somewhat deeper than we're supposed to think right now. That might be one reason poets are so curious about their procedures—that it's not enough to do the work and leave the rest to readers.

AS: I've felt the necessity the last ten years or more to talk about or write about what I do. The first essay in that new Australian magazine which is dedicated to Charles Olson. . .

EF: *Boxkite*

AS: Right. In *Boxkite* I wrote a longish essay to discuss textures and the motivations for the late *Tablets*, XXVI and XXVII, which have a lot of different kinds of graphics. I usually tend to do such explanatory essays a *contre coeur,* as if they had to be done, as if they had to be set forth, whereas my deepest belief is that everything should be implicit or overt in the poem and not require supplemental glosses. Ironically I entitled the *Boxkite* essay GLOSSES, a kind of identification of myself with the aggressor, which in this case is the self-conscious, uneasy, invasive World Prober, Homo Fodens, Man the Digger. Hardly a pure stance, right?

EF: How do you understand that, Homo Fodens?

AS: Psychoanalysts are pretty well agreed, finally, that what matters is not what "really" happened, but what are the constructive or self-defeating behavioral traits and aptitudes with which one navigates in life. So if you're healed it means you've been able to rewrite your filmstrips, or reorder them or transmute them into something rich and not too passing strange. The poet is Homo Fodens, cautioned ceaselessly by the accepted constraints of his own body and the body of the world. That is, no poet in our tradition, that is the West anyhow I suppose, can credibly absent himself totally from operating room procedures on syntax and semantic variables; but neither is he or she free from submitting humbly to the human condition from which—in a slightly altered image stolen from my good friend Mike Heller—he can't leap out scot-free in the service of some post-romantic operational revisionism on language. And a proffered application of any encompassing socio-economic teaching can't act as substitute. That is, Digging is limited not only by the awestruck sentimentality of the frightened science-fiction protagonist; it can't help being subjected to the phenomenological surround of the Digger. The more care-worn the actor, the greater the inspiriting wisdom. The fascination with what's difficult or, as Brian McHale has it, *The Obligations Toward the Difficult whole. . . . I* started by talking about poetic textures and motivations, didn't I?

EF: To avoid being misread, I guess. Is that what you're addressing? A person may not want to infringe on the world, but he doesn't want it to misrepresent him.

AS: Ah you're posing a cutting problem relating to the lines of force between the person and the society or the idea of the society. I think I'm talking about the ways my personality impels me towards the kind of ambiguity which I think for instance *The Tablets* embodies, as do some of my other longish poems like "the work," "sounds of the river Naranjana," "the triumph of the will," "the Bacchae Sonnets," "Prologue in Six Parts." (Those will be available again in my *New and Selected Poems*, coming out next year.) I think the reasons for the particular kind of texture or existence or deep-structure questions of penetrability and historical treason in *The Tablets* have to do with precisely my desire, "inter," "amphi," to not put myself into the poem, to hide, as it were, behind the arras, or to understand and accept the fact that creating all these figures, these archaic figures whose very gender is unknown, whose very provenance is unfindable . . . There's a kind of micro-history here, maybe a little like Fernand Braudel's superb *The Structures of everyday Life from the 15th to the 18th Centuries,* but without the attestations, and bounded by barely available proto-historical records. Beginnings again, in a pseudo-world of crypto-historical beginnings.

EF: What can the reader know about the protagonists who inhabit *The Tablets* ? Or, say what should he or she know?

AS: The reader doesn't know whether they're telling a truth or their truth or aspects of social verity or as it were inventing parts of a world; you don't know whether they're the object of scribal emendations; you don't even know whether the whole sequence has any kind of verifiability. But the work doesn't exist in a realm of fantasy; there's too much deep structure of familiar archaeology and palaeography and ritual for that easy course, and thus the work is continuously subject to anchoring constraints. The satire in the work, a simple brass ring for the merry-go-round reader, exists as the condition of loss and the conceivableness of emptiness. In spite of the unverifiabilities the human figures are *there*. So the reader's constantly "inter," and as the Tibetan teacher Gampopa says, "irrigating one's confusions." And that's, I think, the most consistent climate from which the need to write poetry comes. In any case mine.

Looking over the contemporary ground, my problem with some of the Language Poetry activity—and as in all generalizations this one is problematic, given significant exceptions and the difficulty of assigning place or even the worthiness of such assigments, as in the case of Lynn Hejinian, say, whose work I like a lot—my problem then is that I see much of the work as programmatic. It's a funny disjunction. On the one hand, they can be very programmatic; on the other, their frequent and useful intention is to dynamite any preliminarily held point-of-view because they want to get down to the cleansing destruction of syntax and the socially and economically conditioned aspects of human emotionality. Like Pierre Joris, Jerry Rothenberg, Mike Heller, Anselm Hollo, for instance, I subscribe to the Buffalo Poetics email list, and I find—I assume like them—useful book and periodical references that I download and sometimes order and which keep me in touch with ongoing poetry matters I'd otherwise be ignorant of. In that sense I find that group of poets and critics giving and sociopoetically valuable, but I must add that some younger poets and I myself at times have experienced a certain lack of openness and generosity, a deeply centrifugal tropism in members of the group acting in great sober publicity concert. I know art "movements," so-called by self or history, try to create turf and identity, and I also remember the sometimes deadly power applied against some individual artists by such figures as Andre' Breton, the pope of the tight clutch of the European Surrealists, so I'm not starry-eyed about poetry schools; they're not eleemosynary groups.

But I'm not invoking heavily oppressive paradigms to apply here. In general, I'd say that some of the L=A=N=G=U=A=G=E philosophical and aesthetic suppositions are insufficiently self-aware. I was particularly upset at their attempt to claim George Oppen, at least the Oppen of *The Materials,* as a fountainhead. At Royaumont was it? George, the hardscrabble phenomenologist painfully slow in his speculative gleanings and so ill at ease when faced with the self-presentational complexities which went along for him with giving readings, which I remember clearly he so disliked doing. . . . The task of the poet these days is all the harder because of our almost insensate desire, or need, not to be had—whether by political shibboleths, acquisitively subtle advertising deployments or the desiccating divorce between holistic and environmentalist intuition and the depradations of what the wonderful poet *Chuck* Stein calls the *"sad machines,"* the *sadness* of the Samsaric world, illusion born of grasping. I can't think of a better shorthand expression, a kind of syncretist Buddhist mathematics, of both the pain and the hope implicit in our condition than Chuck's comment in the notes at the end of his collection *The Hat Rack Tree.* I'll get it; here's the passage:

> . . . [intuitionist] mathematician L.E.J. Brouwer thought that our world has been compromised by our power to construe being in terms of regular numerical series. These series, when correlated with the world in a certain manner, yield what we think of as temporally extended objects and, when correlated in another manner, yield causal chains *of* events. The construction of such series gives us the capacity to dominate nature technologically but distracts us from our immediate connectedness to both the being of the world and our internal spiritual sources. The world we produce for ourselves with this capacity is "The Sad World.

EF: Getting back to our allusion to L=A=N=G=U=A=G=E poetry, there's also an absolutism or tendency in that direction, coupled with a deep, deep lack of concern for what's being taken away or denied—ways of thinking and writing that are actually quite profitable to others. It's as if problems could be solved in a theoretical rather than a human way. I know that's not what you were arguing, but. . . .

AS: It's cognate though.

EF: Much of their argument is absolutely correct, but there's also a moral arrogance such as in any missionary ethos.

AS: But their concern with the elemental aspects of syntax and expressivity—I share some of them, so I don't like to sever myself from their tendencies to experimentation. Also, we have to note that contiguity and accident play a large part at least in the initial stages of the formation of any artist's identity and relationships, crucial connections, with other artists. We poets are such a small group of people in this culture that we can't afford really what we often engage in—feelings of outrage, feelings of entitlement, feelings of constructing the ramparts and then defending them in turn, which in Buddhist terms we may understand as ego invents turf, ego invests in castle, ego invents moat, and defends it to the death, and the irony is there is no turf, no moat, no castle. What you're eventually left with, if you're lucky and assiduous in your life-practice, as in the last of the ten Zen Ox-Herding poems, is Man in the market place as Old Dog. So we're a small group of amazingly persistent fabricators and makers and finders in a culture which doesn't seem to need us in any way but which, nevertheless, continues amazingly enough to harbor us for whatever embedded reason. The more inventive and intense the techno-electronic contributions to the culture at large, the more deeply felt the need for the poet taking the phenomenological measure of the whole.

EF: When you say there is no turf, or that the ego creates it, I assume you're talking out of your Buddhist training.

AS: Well, I think everything I've done since at least 1971 is involved with, relates to, the fact that I had a Tibetan Buddhist teacher, Chogyam Trungpa, from 1971 to 1976 and then a Zen teacher, Roshi Glassman, from 1980 to 1985. I guess I'm no good for institutional membership for more than five years at a clip, but I can't conceive of the way I am or the way I think or the way I write outside the phenomena of these experiences, and a lot of my poetry is tinctured at the very least with my being a student of Trungpa's and my being a student of Glassman Roshi and being a friend of the monk and philosopher Lou Mitsunen Nordstrom. "Everything changes," is the golden lesson of Buddhist practice and Buddhist teaching. So there's a constant paradox in holding to that and looking at the fact that there are things that are things. There are books, there are sweat pants, there are intellectual positions, there is a body.

EF: Intermediate or both. Chiaroscuro.

AS: Both positions. And this really bothered me, because I didn't know how to resolve this problem. The illuminating Buddhist teaching on this knot is that there are the absolute and the relative and that they are paradoxically coexistent. So that's a way to deal with the incommensurate paradox of these two states of being, as it were, these two states. I think it was mostly in the Zen situation that there were students who were so taken by the idea that everything was empty, that is to say that nothing has self-essence, that everything is unalterably related to everything else. "Dependent origination." It was a kind of Zen sickness, that unilateral emphasis on the emptiness of all phenomena, ignoring the fact that it hurts when your foots kicks into a rock by accident. Yo, that's a rock.

EF: Does *The Tablets* operate within that Buddhist notion?

AS: Well, *The Tablets* was begun partly in the matrix for which emptiness and fullness were somewhat the guiding metaphors. Kenosis and Plerosis. I found them first in Theodore Gaster's *Thespis: Myth and Ritual in the Ancient Near East.* Those are great overarching ritualistic terms of being.

EF: Sumerian

AS: In general in Ancient Near Eastern texts. Part of the ambiguities and the lacunae and the slippages, metaphorically and syntactically, relates to the paradox of emptiness and fullness. But I do think you veer towards a philosophy partly based on your character, your predilections. I've never been able to sunder Kierkegaard writing from my sense of who he is, or Nietzsche from my sense of who he was and what he needed.

EF: Implying that spiritual notions are essentially historical?

AS: Whatever you think now or whatever you adopt as your philosophical or religious, quote/unquote, ground probably has to do with who you've been since the age of two. I don't think we change that terribly much. We make adjustments, we find walking spaces within the weathers of terror and confusion. An intensified and abbreviated process of that sort happens in psychoanalytic therapy, where with luck we exchange the viable story for ineffective narration. We appreciate the possibilities for minor transformations. But I think we're given one overarching sense of reality, and we work with that.

EF: Which in your case includes not having been born here or even having English as your first language?

AS: I came here when I was nine, and I have a very bad memory, extremely spotty memories of anything that preceded that.

EF: You were born in Belgium?

AS: It was Belgium

EF: And at first you spoke. . .

AS: I spoke only French until I was nine, and then I was thrown into English, and I learned it in six months.

EF: What was the reason for coming here?

AS: My father was in the human hair goods business in Antwerp with three of his brothers, Hirsch, Jacques and Moise. The other brother, Henri, was already in New York with that branch of the business We were greeted in 1936 when we came in on the S.S. *President Harding* ,which I think served as a troop ship later and was sunk during the war. I think we were picked up by my uncle and a chauffeur and a big car. My father went to work with his brother in the New York office on East 22nd Street near Broadway by the Flatiron building. The firm made wigs, the employees were almost all women, weaving wigs by hand on wooden heads. I used to go there occasionally, the long benches with the women intently working hairs into fine hair nets. There was also a huge vat, magical to me then, where Nick the chemist would process the hair. With one exception, it was all human hair, from nuns for instance who would cut their long hair when taking orders. Chinese hair would differ in texture from Italian hair and so forth and Nick was the expert in working with the raw materials. The only animal hair used was yak hair, long enough and ductile enough for use.

EF: So there were women walking around New York wearing . . .

AS: Wearing Yak heads. Orthodox Jewish women among others, with yak hair on their heads

EF: Was that the primary market?

AS: I think it was a significant market, but there were different kinds of diseases where you lose you hair. Then of course there were women who wanted four or five kinds of wigs.

EF: So your family lived well even during the depression?

AS: My father worked extremely hard after we'd arrived in New York, traveling all around the country and Canada representing the business and making a living with great persistence. He attained a reputation as an expert in his specialty. He was gone a lot. Things got better, and then years later, the business went bankrupt, destroyed by something called I think kenikulon, a plastic substitute for hair, much much cheaper and not totally horrible unless you were really wedded to real human hair. In the early days, a good wig could cost several hundred dollars, a lot at the time; and a plastic wig you could get for fifteen. Now I read that human hair wigs are back. Many people have money and they want the real thing.

EF: What was the reason for your family coming here? Because of the business opportunity?

AS: I have understood that we came because of the business opportunity. But my family did not engage in family councils or exchange information about much of anything. I think my mother wanted to leave Antwerp, in which she was increasingly uncomfortable, I'm not sure exactly why. The Jewish population was a small ingrown group, most of them working as diamond dealers. My father was neither a diamond dealer nor a diamond cutter and shaper—*schleiper*, they called it in Flemish—Much of the block around is it 48th Street in Manhattan is a center containing hundreds of diamond dealers.

EF: They're from Antwerp? The whole community came from . . .

AS: Many of them, I think, have those connections. My mother's brother now in his nineties is still engaged in the business in Antwerp. But to the degree that I had met a number of them, I had no real feeling of connection with their concerns, what interested them. As far as I can understand it, in my coming here at the age of nine, which probably saved my life, was a historical accident. Before I left in 1936 there was already in Belgium a fascist movement called the Rexists, headed by Leon Degrelle. But I don't know how big an influence that was at the time. I certainly had no sense of this devastating horror that was already five years old in Germany. I had two cousins, Norbert and Harry, not so much older than I, who were either killed at home or deported to concentration camps with the take-over of Belgium by the Nazis a few years after my mother and my two siblings got underway to meet my father who'd preceded us in New York City. I have a very large sheaf of letters in French and Dutch and German written by relatives in what was then called unoccupied France, where people had gotten there, to my father asking for food or packages or asking for his intervention and to go to Washington and try to get them visas, which was very very difficult. His mysterious visits to D.C. to try to help were never really explained to me at the time. Some of my relatives managed to get out and there would be circuitous routes through Spain, Cuba, Portugal before reaching the haven of the U.S.

EF: What was it like for you to enter into a culture, suddenly, so different from what you must have known?

AS: Well, I was thrown into an American language public school, total immersion you could say, and I learned very quickly. No question it helped that both my parents were fluent in English, as well as in French and Flemish and German and Dutch.

EF: And what happened to what you'd known in Belgium, the French language, the culture?

AS: French I wanted to drop as soon as I started becoming an American boy. I wanted to forget it. I used to play in the street, on Ocean Parkway between Ditmas and 18th Avenues in Flatbush, in front of the house whose top floor we had rented, and my mother would call from the window and I would yell back, "That's in French, I don't talk that." I didn't want to be different. That changed. When I got to high school, I took French, but I'd lost my instinctive knowledge of French grammar, so like a foreigner to the language I'd have to study what conditions governed the use the subjunctive for instance. A lot stayed with me though. I spent my junior year as an undergraduate at the Universite de Gene ve, studying philosophy and French literature. At Columbia, I majored in French literature.

EF: That's when you started doing translations?

AS: From the French, and from there eventually to doing lots of work transforming archaic and tribal materials into poetry, and worked from 11th century Tibetan

Buddhist texts some work from classical Greek, Italian . . .

EF: In translating Dante, your Italian is . . .

AS: Adequate to that kind of work

EF: But that work, or interest, came much later.

AS: Came much later, but I took Italian at Columbia as an undergraduate. Tibetan I didn't learn in school.

EF: You speak it?

AS: No.

EF: But you can translate it?

AS: I can translate it. Speaking is not required. I studied Tibetan at John Giorno's loft for about two years, every week. There were about seven of us, our teacher was Arthur Mandelbaum, who had a degree in Tibetan and I think Sanskrit in India. Arthur's a Tibetan Buddhist practitioner and a very good teacher.

EF: Any relation to Allen Mandelbaum?

AS: I never heard that he was. You mean the translator?

EF: Yes

AS: Arthur, who should have a chair at a prestigious university in Tibetan, is teaching high school in New York. Remarkable teacher. So it was partly language learning, partly teachings. Of course, these were religious texts, and Giorno is also a practitioner. And there was me and a few other students. And there was Betty Ann Lopate, the sister of Phil Lopate; she was a brilliant student.

EF: Do you personally think it's necessary to know the other language when you do translations? I remember once a couple years ago hearing you criticize Robert Pinsky for not knowing Italian yet not hesitating to translate Dante.

AS: Well, again as in so many matters having to do with poetry and poetics, L don't want to issue fiats. That is to say, I don't think you absolutely *have* to know the language in all cases. I'd like to leave a little space for that possibility and there are examples which could support that contention. I'll go as far as that. I don't think if you have a special talent or intuition and humility and a sense of song and a great attention to sonic value in language and a great sympathy for the culture within which the poem had its birth—I think if you have all that, you can do an incredible job with trans/lation, or a certain kind of translation. An example of that is Christopher Logue. Do you know his work?

EF: Sure.

AS: I understand Logue doesn't know Greek. But from what I've been reading in this new anthology *World Poetry* that Norton just put out, his Homer is superb.

EF: I don't know the anthology.

AS: It's not in the bookstores yet. And it's an incredibly daring . . .

EF: Norton's answer to Rothenberg?

AS: Nothing like that. This book includes poems from the the time of Sumer to the present, every continent, dozens of languages and cultures, many in very good translations by poets, George Economou's wonderful new *Piers Plowman* for instance, Paul Blackburn's great work from the Provençal, Logue's Homer, Samuel Beckett's Alfonso Reyes, Rothenberg from the Sumerian, Anselm Hollo's Alexander Blok as well as his translations from the Finnish Paava Haavikko, Snyder's Han Shan, Andrew Schelling's early lyrics from India, my Dante, work from my *Tablets,* some from the French and the Tibetan and the ancient Greek . . . Getting back to the question of what does the translator have to know: Washburn has included a powerful, movemented segment of *The Iliad* by Logue, full of pith and sinew. Take just the one line,

> Leaving the tall enemy with eels at his white fat

microcosmically suggestive of the rich vowel variety in Logue's *Iliad.* In general that *Iliad's* music's extraordinary. The discretion evident in the choices, the rapidity of verbal change, just remarkable. And in fact a friend of mine, Brian McHale, who is writing a book for Duke U. Press—this includes a long consideration of my work as well as that of Howe . . .

EF: Susan?

AS: Susan Howe And Bruce Andrews. . . . It's a wide net.

EF: I'll say.

AS: And Geoffrey Hill, whose complex evocations in *The Mercian Hymns* are a real turn-on. Anyway Brian sent me an email a few days ago that he sensed a kind of sympathetic commonality between Logue's *Iliad* and my Dante. Which I think is true. I think we try to do some similar things, like positioning the words idiosyncratically on the page to give a sense of the dance of language. In the case of my Dante, dialogue on one side and non-dialogue on the other. An excerpt in this issue will present that and implicitly I hope the rationale for it.

So I want to stress that anything can be done. It's not just because Pinsky doesn't know Italian that his translation doesn't work very well. I think basically it's because almost every translation of the *Inferno* that I know, however different in quality and reach, they seem to me to be recycling former English or American versions of the work and don't constitute a direct confrontational sort of adventure, risks in facing the Italian and in allowing the echoes of one's own past scurryings in American and English poetry to enter in, as Dante allowed entrance into his *Commedia* to so many internal errant voices in himself, from Latin or Italian sources.

So it's one of the wonders of poetry and the high-wire act of translation that almost anything can be done. Generalizations can be made but they're very dangerous. So the attempt to catch the process of translation, as Blake might say, in flight, is what I try to do in the "translator's process notes," of which I give a sample in this issue of *Talisman,* so that the reader can get some sense of the transformative fight informing the translator's possibilities.

Working with the Dante, I always have on my computer four immediately available windows. Very often when I'm considering options, all I have to do is click onto the window to add to the Process Notes for that Canto, and be my own secretary, since various considerations are in my mind right then and there; it does take a certain balancing discipline, to make the notations while I'm in the very preoccupations of choices. I immediately type out in a sort of rough, and then go back to the text, with another click to the page of text, and then I just keep going back and forth that way. You might see it too as a kind of practice submitting to an idiosyncratic kind of double text. The third window is the window of my Italian/English, English/Italian dictionary, which I use not so much for vocabulary as for occasional checks for grammatical forms and inflections. And the fourth window is the extensive version of the computerized *American Heritage Dictionary,* which has lots of etymologies and I use that all the time too, because that leads me into different possibilities and cognates. A sort of semi-aleatoric blundering sometimes results in happy *trouvailles.* I'm particularly interested, as I think Logue is too, and Basil Bunting, in populating the poem with words alive with Anglo-Saxon echoes because in this case particularly I think they're close to the American/English reader's sense of epic. And I think using archaisms—as Pound allowed himself to, through the diplomacy of his mind ear—that's perfectly fine if one thinks of them as contextually validated and working with colloquial American either companionably or by useful friction.

EF: But in this way you also avoid the French side of the English language.

AS: In this case, probably, but some Latinate and French-derived nouns and verbs, if discretely embedded in a context of informing surprise, those are ok too. I think of Stevens of course, so enamored of the French side. You can do anything

EF: Yes there's much ore to be said for it than some poets would have us think.

AS: I've been less enamored of it because I felt such ambivalences about French when I was younger.

EF: What initiated *The Tablets?*

AS: There's the proximate cause and there's the ultimate cause. The proximate cause—am I using the word right?—that is to say, the thing that spawned the beginning stages of that work was occurred when I was a graduate student working in the Columbia Library. At the end of one of the long stacks I stuck out my arm to rest it on one of the shelves for a moment, looked at what I was covering and there was a large format edition of Samuel Noah Kramer's translation and transliteration from the Sumerian. I interpreted my experience as an omen. I have never forgotten the power of that initial charge. Charge in both senses, both electricity *and* the responsibility for a task I hadn't yet formulated.

The family of more diffuse causes had to do with my discomfort with a lot of what was going down as poetry in the late fifties and early sixties. I'd begun to learn from Blackburn and others what was possible in poetic construction, song and what is now called multiculturalism, and I reacted vividly to my sense of the exciting ferment of that time, leavened by—particularly—the initial experiments and concerns of David Antin, Jackson MacLow, Jerry Rothenberg. I wanted among other things to find a form sympathetic to the oral, informed by the variety of linguistic possibilities and receptive in its construction and in its notations to the riches of chance occurrence. In addition I could find a way to harbor my sympathies for the animistic and embody that sympathy in form without having to say somehow in a poem: as if. I didn't want an 'as if.' I wanted to make a world both archaic and entropic.

EF: And about beginning the work on the *Inferno?*

AS: Here too there are both proximate and ultimate causes. My first translation, which I'd gotten more than forty years ago, was the very first ever done in English. I don't know where I got the book; I know I hadn't bought it but I have no idea how I came by it. That was the Dante I read first, in some ways my favorite for a long time, in spite of its expectable early nineteenth century turns, a slighting of the colloquial, inversions of a habitual not a stylistically necessary order. But the translator chose blank verse rather than go toward a doomed effort to ape a *terza rima,* and effected a rather accomplished blank verse. By the Reverend . . .

AS: Cary.

EF: The Reverend. 1802, think. In fact I'd loaned it to somebody some twenty-five years ago, who promptly lost it, and I was really despondent at that and I said, "You've got to find me another copy of this translation and with the same early nineteenth century dark rust brown hard cover." It took him two years and he found a copy somewhere, not exactly the same edition; mine was printed in 1901, but near enough. Anyway that was my first Dante. Before I'd bought the Ciardi, the Mandelbaum, the Lawrence Binyon, the Lawrence Grant White with the Doré drawings, the Dorothy Sayers. . . .And in many ways Cary was still my favorite.

The immediate cause for my turning to doing Dante was an invitation a few years ago to read at the St. John-the-Divine Episcopal Cathedral, which takes place every year, April. Katharine Washburn, who edited the *World Poetry* anthology, wrote and asked if I'd like to go and read somebody's translation of a Canto from Hell. The whole *Inferno* was to be read, and each canto was to be read in whatever translation the reader chose. So I said fine. The readings start around 9 PM and go until after 3 AM, somewhat romantic and certainly in some ways interesting. And stone church clammy with early April.

Then, I thought to myself, Wait, I'm a translator. Let me see what's happening here. So I tried my own version of the Canto I was assigned, XV I think, which didn't work as I wanted it to. During the week after the reading, I got to work , feeling intensely, almost epiphanically, chosen to do this work. I had no publisher. I had nothing except my intention. And now I've finished almost half of the *Inferno.* That's the immediate beginning. Katharine used to say to me: this is the most marvelously mercurial enterprise I've ever seen. I appreciated very much her enthusiasm and her sharp critical capacity. I would send her versions as I worked and she never stinted in her attention and her useful commentaries. So that's one my tasks for these years. I'm going to finish the forty-four Cantos. A university press is interested, and I assume that will go OK. After that's finished, I'm going to do a book of translations from the poetry of Pierre Ronsard.) People in the literary and translation community have responded very favorably to my versions of the *Inferno*. One of the essays in this issue addresses the Dante translation.

EF: It's absolutely appropriate—the work of an exile.

AS: Yes. Dante was in exile most of his life. I'm in a kind of exile. Dante was on the outside, but I think you are too. It would be hard to find a poet who doesn't feel somewhat displaced, exiled, barred from the action fields of the larger culture. It's just somewhat in our nature, plagued by this outsideness. But who doesn't feel that? Plumbers, poets, police on horseback, fundamentalists. . . .

EF: Though one should never see it as romantic.

AS: Yes, that's another door to a whole bunch of problems.

ANNE WALDMAN

EF: And so this is the very place it began, Macdougal Street in Manhattan.

AW: This is Aaron Burr country. We're sitting in my ancestral home, 47 Macdougal Street.

EF: Just south of Houston, west of Broadway. And not terribly far from St. Mark's Church In-the-Bowery. How did you and your family end up in a location so perfect for a poet?

AW: Well, it's an interesting story. My mother lived here with other bohemian ladies during the war. Their men, husbands, lovers, were caught up in military service. My father was at Fort Bragg in North Carolina. Frances lived here. This was basically a rooming house owned by an Italian couple, living elsewhere.

EF: This whole area was Italian at that time, wasn't it?

AW: Especially this little block and the immediate environs. We have St. Anthony's Church around the corner on the next block, and St. Anthony's parochial school right across the street. There's a convent attached to the church. Italian restaurants, cafés, pasta and bread shops. Many of the elders are still around, people I used to see as a child, and there's a community "club" on the south corner.

EF: So how did your mother find this place?

AW: Through a woman friend, I believe, the bohemian grapevine.

EF: This was after she came back from Greece?

AW: Yes. My mother had lived in Greece a decade before in an earlier marriage with Glaukos Sikelianos, the son of the Greek poet Anghelos Sikelianos. She'd dropped out of Vassar at age nineteen and sailed off to Greece.

EF: And your father?

AW: He was a swing piano player. It wasn't until after the war that he went to college on the G.I. Bill—went to NYU, Columbia, eventually getting his doctorate in education, literature, and started teaching at Pace University.

EF: And then started working on rapid reading?

AW: He was getting his Ph.D. in education. With Evelyn Woods, he wrote that popular book *Rapid Reading Made Simple*. I was an early guinea pig actually for him, taking some of these tests where I had to read pages and pages, be timed, and then be tested.

EF: And this was when you were quite young?

AW: Eight or ten—probably closer to ten. So I would read a story, usually some prose text—essay, story—then be tested on my comprehension. My speed was good, but my comprehension was about 60 percent. Ha!

EF: Was this place still a rooming house when your father got back from the war and your parents started living here?

AW: By the time he got back, they had the top floor. I'm not sure when that transition occurred. Other friends lived below. My mother Frances worked at Bell

Labs, which is quite near here, where Wesbeth Housing Complex is now, and also at a tie factory, painting ties—the sort of work you had during the Depression and later during the war years. And we lived on the top floor until I was about thirteen and then moved downstairs.

EF: Took over the whole house?

AW: Took over the whole house, but began renting the top floor to friends. Two Smith College ladies. The Italian family—they had a grown son and daughter but no children after that, and the neighborhood was changing—were anxious to move to the suburbs, and they sold the house for $14,000. It took my father about fifteen years to pay that off. Amazing to think of now.

EF: So you went to local school in the area?

AW: P.S. 8, the public school around the corner, which folded years ago. It's now full of condos. I went to Grace Church School for two years, right across the street from where Frank O'Hara lived on Broadway, and then to Friends Seminary after that.

EF: And then Bennington.

AW: Yes.

EF: And when in all this did poetry become the center of things?

AW: I was very interested in poetry in grade school, always participating in the Arbor Day contest where you had to write a poem about the joys of trees! I enjoyed public speaking, writing things of my own in seventh and eighth grade to be read aloud. An early interest, always attracted to the literature classes and reading poetry. I had a wonderful teacher in high school who read a lot of Wallace Stevens aloud to us, which was quite unusual. Jon Beck Shank. Also a Latin teacher who was quite hip to contemporary poetry. And a close schoolmate was Jonathan Cott, who's a critic and writer himself now. We almost had a literary club together, exchanging and discussing books. He gave me *Sonnets to Orpheus*, *Illuminations*, *The Dream of the Red Chamber*. And there were other comrades in a love of theater. We'd get together and read plays aloud. My mother, of course, had an eclectic library, and Gertrude Stein's work was on the shelf. Frances was very excited about the New York School poetry—this was later as things were being published. The Don Allen anthology was, of course, important to many poets of my generation but to my mother as well.

EF: Your mother was aware of it when it was originally published?

AW: She was well aware of it. We were friendly with Eli and Ted Wilentz, who ran the Eighth Street Bookshop and who later published me and many others under his Corinth Books imprint. We subscribed to the *Evergreen Review*. Certainly growing up in this milieu, there were a lot of possibilities for exposure to poetry. We started going to poetry readings. My mother took me to hear Robert Lowell—it must have been when I was in high school—when he was reading at NYU. And later we went to hear Marianne Moore, others.

EF: Your mother was an extraordinary woman.

AW: She was really an autodidact. She had dropped out of college to go to Greece with her first husband. You know Sikelianos was a fairly well known Greek poet, so she was in an artistic milieu there and quite closely involved with Sikelianos's wife, her mother-in-law. Eva Palmer was a Maine heiress who had taken up with the prodigious Sikelianos. She donned the ancient Greek garb which they wove themselves. My mother learned how to weave in the traditional style. And Eva had long red hair down to her ankles, and they wore the sandals based on an old Greek design that Raymond Duncan, Isadora Duncan's brother, fashioned. He was married to Anghelo's sister. So it was a nostalgic and eccentric return to the Hellenic golden age.

EF: And is that how your mother became interested in translating?

AW: My mother started translating Sikelianos in Greece—and subsequently, too, got more serious about that. Before she died, I brought out the little book of her translations of Sikelianos, *The Border Guards.* She also knew some French, and she had done a book of translations of Cesar Moro, who was a surrealist based in South America, and wrote both in Spanish and French.

EF: So poetry was in some sense always around you when you grew up.

AW: I think I was born with a karmic link to poetry and particularly a sense of an oral tradition theatrics.

EF: Were there poets your family was friendly with—poets who would have been around when you were growing up?

AW: Jonathan Cott knew Ted Berrigan and Ron Padgett at Columbia University, so I was getting their *"C"* magazine at Bennington, and my mother saw that. And my mother, while I was at Bennington, started going to the New School. She went to a class with Bill Berkson and through that met Kenneth Koch and others. And I remember when I was still at Bennington coming into town and going to a party at Bill Berkson's, and Frank O'Hara and Larry Rivers came. I'd already been to Berkeley.

EF: To the poetry conference?

AW: Yes, I was still in college when I went to the Berkeley Poetry Conference in 1965. And missed some of the great readings because I was first experimenting with LSD. I remember valiantly thinking of trying to get over the bridge the night of Allen Ginsberg's reading. There had already been some connection between us. I had tried to get him to visit Bennington, so we'd had a phone call before he went to India.

EF: What other early connections did you have to the poetry community?

AW: Paul Blackburn and Robert Kelly when I was in college. Lewis Warsh, who I met at Berkeley. . . . He was actually a friend of a friend of Jonathan Cott, who was at Berkeley studying, and Jon was very au courant with a lot of these up-and-coming magazines and writers and so on. So I met Lewis there at a Robert Duncan reading during the conference, and there was an instant connection and excitement about both being from New York, and we decided to start a magazine, basically on the spot—*Angel Hair* magazine and books. The title came from a poem of Jon's: "angel hair sleeps with a boy in my head." But it was also the pasta and the wonderful junk you put on Christmas trees. It comes out of an aerosol can now.*

EF: And so you returned to New York with Lewis?

AW: Well, I was planning to go back to college, so I was just out there in the summer. I kept thinking, Should I drop out now, and my father was basically supportive. Do what you need to do, he said. I was already going in some direction of my own. I was writing poetry seriously. Reading poetry voraciously. I'd dropped acid. I'd hitchhiked to Mexico, and founded a literary magazine. I didn't know one made a career of writing poetry or that it was the only thing you might be doing, but now that I look at my life with some distance and panoramic sense I see the different strains, the different paths that have been continuous my whole life, with poetry at the center.

EF: For you, it seems, poetry has always been particularly involved with communities.

AW: Berkeley was extraordinary that way—you know, it was a community event, and you could see the wonderful web-work of a world of poets. I took a vow then and there to exist inside poetry and a community of poets. These were all poets in what we at Naropa have termed the "outrider" tradition, outside the academic mainstream. These were the most exciting writers. At Bennington I was working with Howard Nemerov. We were reading Robert Lowell and having visits from John Berryman. I remember asking about Stein and Pound, and there was a paranoia there about Pound's anti-Semitism.

EF: And yet Bennington—I grew up in that part of the world—seemed very radical compared to other colleges. After all, these were the days of Sandra Dee and Annette Funicello, and it was enough to turn one's hair white, I mean the local people, just thinking what the women there were doing.

AW: Bennington seemed academic compared to what my mother was onto—at least her taste, her openness, whatever. She was reading John Ashbery and listening to John Cage and Cecil Taylor, remember. These distinctions were blurred. You didn't think about academic poets and outrider poets. These things were coming your way, and you were seeking them out, just reacting very personally, and in an intimate way to the work.

EF: The first year you came out of Bennington was also the time the Poetry Project got under way, wasn't it?

AW: Yes, so I was right on board from the start. In an out-of-residency term back in New York, I got involved with Theater Genesis at St. Mark's, and Theater Genesis was doing the first plays of Sam Shepard and others, so I must have been about eighteen or nineteen. I was in a production at Theater Genesis, and I remember Sam Shepard and Charles Mingus, Jr., jeering at me from the back, teasing me during some rehearsal. The poets had just moved from the Metro Café, and Paul Blackburn

---

*Note added by AW in June, 2000: "Lewis and I are working now on a huge Angel Hair anthology with Jon's line as its title to be published by Granary Books in the next year.

POETRY AND POETICS IN A NEW MILLENIUM

had brought the open poetry readings into the St. Mark's vestibule, into the parish hall. This was all prior to the funding from the Office of Economic Opportunity, which came through in 1966.

EF: You were one of the organizers for the project, weren't you?

AW: I was hired as one of Joel Oppenheimer's assistants. And then within two years Joel's energies were shifting. He was writing for the *Village Voice*; he was in a new marriage, young children and so on, spending a lot of time at the bar where the *Village Voice* crowd used to go, the Lion's Head. He was very warm, a generous witty man with a lot of support from the younger crowd, but he wasn't really happy as an administrator. So I had all the energy and was ready to go: "I know how to work the machines," I triumphantly proclaimed in the poem, "Fast Speaking Woman." And so quickly it became obvious that I was the one with more energy in terms of being there full-time and running the place.

EF: And worked there until you became involved in Naropa and the Jack Kerouac School?

AW: The Naropa project began in the summer of '74. The institute seemed as if it were really going to develop. I didn't really move to Boulder until the winter of '76. Naropa was basically a summer program at that point. So I could manage both for a while. But there was a time where I was travelling back and forth too much. I was officially the director of the Poetry Project until '78, I think. But by that time things had shifted. More of my energy was going into the "academy of the future" on the rocky spine of the continent. I was very excited by the landscape "out west." Living in the mountains. Back at home an advisory committee was forming at St. Mark's, and there were community meetings, and it was definitely time to pass on the wand.

EF: But you kept your apartment on St. Mark's Place and basically lived in New York up through '84 or so.

AW: Yes. I kept that apartment until, I think, '84. I tried to hold onto that apartment on St. Mark's Place that originally Lewis had found as long as I could. My son Ambrose was born in Boulder in 1980. I met Ambrose's father, Reed Bye, in '75 in Colorado, and we eventually got together. We came back to New York to be close to family, although Naropa was still very much part of my life, and it was obviously going to go on in some form or another. But we came back with our child and settled back into St. Mark's for a spell.

EF: And began teaching with me at Stevens. 1981-82, I think.

AW: Ted died the year after my mother's death in 1982. '82 was the summer of the Kerouac Festival in Boulder, so I went back for that shortly after her death and then went to San Francisco where I taught for a semester at New College, and then came back to New York.

EF: How involved with Buddhism were you when you went to Naropa in '74?

AW: I had met Chögyam Trungpa, the founder of the institute, earlier. I'd met him in 1970. I was already interested in Asian thought, philosophy, having had an excellent religion teacher at Friends Seminary who was a Quaker, but very scholarly. We were studying Buddhism, Taoism, reading in the *Upanishads*. Dr. Hunter taught a great comparative religions class. I had already read some texts, and the poetry was interesting to me. I didn't have a clear distinction, philosophically, you know—the nontheism of Buddhism as compared to the theism of Hinduism or Taoism. I hadn't read enough to experience the distinctions philosophically or psychologically, but that started to get clearer as my interests expanded. I credit that early teacher: he was really a kind of boddhisattva.

EF: And that interest in Buddhism put you very much in the center of things that were beginning to merge in the 1960s.

AW: There were some auspicious connections going on. You know, hints and murmurs in the *Evergreen Review*. Zen was very much in the air. Alan Watts was popular. Some version of the *Tibetan Book of the Dead* around. The songs of Milarepa. Texts were becoming available. John Cage's interest in Buddhism as a kind of background for his work.

EF: And yet that's all very different than. . . .

AW: Than Tibetan style? Well, it's still Buddhism. Buddhism assumes different shapes. Vajrayana Buddhism seems more audacious perhaps, but it's no more outrageous than Zen.

EF: When did you turn toward Tibetan Buddhism?

AW: We have to backtrack a little. In college I had a close friend who had come from Harvard, Tom Griffin, and he was close to several other fellows—including the translator and scholar Robert Thurman—who became students of a very important Mongolian teacher, a Tibetan Buddhist from Mongolia named Geshe Wangyal. Geshe Wangyal had come to the U.S. on a Tolstoi Foundation grant and settled in Freehold Acres, New Jersey, not far from Philadelphia. This was in 1962. He had some young monks there working on translation, and some of these Harvard fellows were very attracted to the study and practice of Eastern philosophy. So my friend, who was by then a student at Bennington, introduced me to some of this world during the summer of '63. I went to Philadelphia and worked in an arts project in a Quaker Friends Community Center, teaching poetry and theater with children from the ghetto. This was a tense time (still is) in urban America, summers of so-called riots (which should more appropriately be called "insurrections"). Tom Griffin had already become something of a student of this Tibetan Buddhist teacher who lived nearby, close to Philadelphia. So at the age of eighteen, I went with him—I was probably one of the few women around—to visit the "pink house" as we called it. This was my first experience of a Tibetan lama. Suburban New Jersey. But inside you had a vivid Tibetan shrine with colorful terrifying deities glaring down from their tangkas, pungent incense, candles burning, deep, guttural chanting.

EF: So what was Wangyal like?

AW: Wangyal was impressive. He was the quintessential teacher who mirrors back your own mind. When you'd ask a question he would give you the environment to have you see your own energy and neurosis or whatever it was. The whole Hindu guru trip was popular, fashionable, and we saw it in the injection of the Hindu style—clothing, beads, incense—into the hippie culture. There was a blurring of distinctions, but Wangyal was not a Hindu teacher—he had a very, very different style, and I personally found it more appealing It's always very hard for me to relate to the more devotional—it's called bahkti—path where you're basically in a subservient mode, sitting at the foot of the teacher and chanting for hours and hours. It's a very genuine path, however. There is a lot of devotion demanded also in the Tibetan Buddhist tradition, but it's very different in tone and flavor, and yet it has—you know, like a Catholic Church does—these wonderful trappings and ritual and vividness and strong sexual imagery. And I started to understand that the iconography—the mandala paintings, say, or images of the deities—these were to be understood as representations of your own mind, the psychological states of your own mind, those different distinctive kinds of energies. So if you saw a red figure, this was representing a very passionate and seductive consciousness, whereas a white version was calmer.

EF: And from there, the more serious interest developed?

AW: These early epiphanies were at the same time exotic and curious, but the idea was to supplement them with some sort of grounding in text and practice, understanding the psychological underpinnings, the "view," so to speak. So I started looking into that. And also I had the sense of the Vajrayana tradition as a long, unbroken, ongoing tradition of practice and study and enlightened mind. So that by the time I met Trungpa in 1970. . . .

EF: How did that happen?

AW: I was with poet Michael Brownstein and had been visiting friends in Vermont: Joe Brainard and Kenward Elmslie. An English student of Trungpa's had shown up in New York City and was talking about his Tibetan teacher who was coming over to the States, and how some students were starting a community in Vermont. I was also very politically active and was planning to go to Cuba, through the auspices of Nancy Rubin, Jerry Rubin's wife at the time, who was organizing a cultural trip the summer of 1970. I thought to go through Vermont first, stop at the Buddhist Center and then visit playwright friend Sam Shepard in Nova Scotia, and then get to St. Johnsbury in Nova Scotia and then get a boat to Cuba. So we stopped at the little Buddhist farmhouse in Vermont, and Chögyam Trungpa was coming in from Disneyland that night, and since we had the only functioning car on the premises, we met him at the airport. A drunken Tibetan got off the airplane, and he was very amusing—a very funny character. And he had some of these trappings I'd experienced years before around Geshe Wangyal, and so I already understood something about the hierarchy and what a guru or lama was supposed to be in this tradition. Basically unpredictable. Trungpa was even more iconoclastic. He was talking about the holograms of Casper the Friendly Ghost at Disneyland, perhaps seeing them as Sambhogakaya emanations. In any case, we ended up staying because he was teaching a seminar on the yogin poet Milarepa. And stayed there a couple of weeks, and that delayed this other trip although we did visit Sam (the boat that was coming to get us from Cuba never came in). And I remember you could talk to the teacher in short darshan sessions. I was already writing poetry, and my first book was coming out from Bobbs-Merrill.

EF: Politics, poetry, Buddhism—all at once.

AW: And I was thinking at this time it's time to get out of New York City for a spell—people were moving "back to the land," back to the country. I remember Trungpa saying, Go back to New York. Stay in New York City; it's a holy city and needs you—something to that effect. So I worked eight more years at the Poetry Project, and then, dovetailing a bit with that at the end, twenty years at the Naropa Institute.

EF: I'd always assumed it was Allen Ginsberg who first brought Trungpa together with poets.

AW: Actually I met Trungpa before Allen did. I remember telling him about Trungpa. He'd asked, What is it like up there in Vermont? Are they sitting with their eyes closed? Is it like the Zen scene where you sit facing a blank wall? Allen had been to India and certainly knew the difference between the Tibetan and Hindu and Zen states were. But he was looking for a solid teacher (smarter than he was!).

EF: And you in the meantime felt more in common with the Tibetan tradition?

AW: I was more attracted to that wild vividness, the colorfulness of the Tibetan tradition, the depiction of energy in the texts, and the sense of working with what is called Crazy Wisdom and the sense of being impeccably on the spot. Vajrayana Tantric Buddhism is fierce and cutting. Maybe you can wake up. You can benefit others. Your fathomless energy becomes skillful means or *upaya*. And it seemed to offer more to a woman in some ways—something about these Tantric dakinis, these red-skinned deities stomping on the corpses of ego with skull cups in their hands, with bone necklaces around their necks. Something I felt close to, close to whatever that energy seems to imply. More than shaving my head and putting on a black robe and sitting facing a blank wall.

EF: Which you feel is more masculine?

AW: It's not that it's more masculine, necessarily. But less sensual. The trappings are more stark, quiescent, and I felt at least at the time all this is going to change. Buddhism's just arrived in America, and it's going to take completely different forms and shapes, and will require improvisation as it develops. Not the pith of it; that's genderless. It seemed to me there were more gateways for my particular female energy—which is not a male or female thing—my feminine energy. *You* could have more feminine energy than I do at some point. So it is not a matter of being a man or a woman necessarily to understand this energy.

EF: What about poetry and attitudes towards language within the Buddhist universe?

AW: Well, there's a notion of sacred body, sacred speech, and sacred mind, so from some point of view everything is sacred. There's mantra—mantra's basically sound. It's words that confer a certain kind of intensity and energy, and it evokes energy centers in your own body, wakes you up, and in a way poetry does that as well for me. You know that early experience I describe often hearing Wallace Stevens. It's like Allen's Blake "vision." It was "Idea of Order at West Point." The teacher was reading, and it was something about this repetition of the words "sea," "she," and "sang." It was immensely engulfing. I mean maybe it was the particular way this person was reading it or that particular day and so on. But I didn't know what it was about. It wasn't necessarily appealing to logopoeia. It was much more on the level of melopoeia and phanopoeia, the images and the sounds evoking a response whether you describe it as a feeling of oneness or wholeness or aspiration to a realm of knowledge. So I had various experiences of "satori," around poetry.

EF: Is the word "sea" then separate from the object, the idea of the object?

AW: Well, it is and it isn't. I mean it probably wasn't in that experience. But the "sea" became absolute.

EF: As a result of Buddhist. . . .

AW: Well, you get into Madhyamika philosophy now. It's very interesting because you're looking at things basically as they are, but you're always aware of absolute and relative reality. So you're existing in a state of "Negative Capability." Seeing things from these two vantage points. It's like being alive but seeing your own death, your own corpse at the same time, *all the time.*

EF: Is absolute reality essentially a verbal reality, something existing essentially in words?

AW: No, not to me, *essentially.* But I feel it is such at times through a verbal exploration or sound. The sound *unlocks* the experience of "absolute." The image unlocks it. You can finally *see.*

EF: Then if the absolute is beyond or outside words, the materials with which poet works must lie in relative experience. And that raises questions about the value of poetry within the Buddhist tradition. What is the place of poetry in Buddhism?

AW: Within traditional Buddhism?

EF: Yes.

AW: Ultimately very high, but traditionally and historically there's some question of fear, because of the ego and the body. Poetry is powerful! (And poetry, from some point of view, is a wisdom tradition as well. Buddhism doesn't have a particular corner on wisdom or enlightenment, you know!) And certainly the monastic tradition was trying to keep a lid on. There was all that erotic Hindu Sanskrit poetry to contend with. Yet there's an amazing oral folk tradition of off-color eroticism Gelek Rinpoche just clued me into. And "yum-yab" songs of women yogins and expressive "dohas" of all kinds.

EF: Nagarjuna raises questions there, and I think what he says is implicit throughout Buddhism. The Dharma has to be apprehended directly; you can't get there simply by analyzing words. But you can't escape the paradox: you have to use words to say don't use words—like Thomas Aquinas reasoning brilliantly to prove in the end all that matters is belief.

AW: There are many different schools and disputes within these different schools so when you get to what's called Mahamudra, words become wild, outrageous poetry, filled with contradiction, and you *can't* analyze it. You're saying one thing and taking it back all the time. Ulatbamsi, or upside-down language:

> A barren woman gives birth!
> A chair dances!
> Because cotton is expensive,
> The naked weep!
>
> Amazing! An elephant sits on a throne
> Held up by two bees!

These lines are from a song of the woman adept Laksminkara, translated by Miranda Shaw.

EF: So as a poet, Buddhism has particular value for you as access to a certain energy—crazy wisdom.

AW: There's an organic connection for me surely, and one didn't come before the other. It's not as if I discovered Buddhism and my poetry changed.

EF: Your first book is very stark in some ways, Williamsesque, at least compared to the most intense, fiery pieces you were doing soon after.

AW: Well, the longer pieces, and the chant poems are modal energy constructs, it's true. But it was Kenneth Koch and Allen Ginsberg and others telling me to go on, push your voice. I remember Kenneth talking about my great vibrato, and letting my vibrato work for me, and Allen saying, Keep going—don't stop yourself short; you have a beautiful voice and range. And Ted Berrigan telling me to be Mayakovsky. And Edwin Denby saying I had the power of a Greek tragedian.

EF: Then where does Buddhism have its effect?

AW: Trusting the passion, becoming the fierce deity, trying to manifest energy on the spot (in performance). The Tibetan form—the *doha* form—which is a Tibetan form of realization. But it's also very traditional. Traditional in that they speak of meeting the teacher, and the trials you go through and the levels of realization you have, and they read like formal structures, and, of course, some of these poets are better at this than others. You know there's a rigidity there, and even within the spontaneousness there are still catch phrases and ways that you can label your experience. And that isn't so interesting to me as the more Zen approach: it's just empty mind and then what comes up. But that was too staid for me.

EF: But I come back to wondering if there is a traceable difference in your work between the early poems and those after you were more seriously committed to Buddhism. Is it the spontaneity?

AW: Spontaneity is perhaps part of it, with the oral pieces, especially in performance, but it's more complicated than that. Study, practice, retreat, travel, other writing, language, family, love, death, separation, dream, hallucinogens, vision, fantasy, history, gender, politics all play in the work some kind of insight, one hopes. The long *Iovis*, which continues, is a weave of many strands and increments of language. It is also speech, is also argument, is also palinode, contradiction. Early poems from college years were dense, abstract, imaginative, on a kind of dark ominous emotional edge. Words as "things" in them have a kind of film noir quality. I've recently unearthed a manuscript my mother kept of my poems from 1964-66. Here are some lines from "Cusps," circa '65:

> The desks were metallic calendars
> long before his birth, received him in a way
> no mother could,   taught him
> the meaning of receptacles
> the days passed casually in chips,
> then slowly into dust.
> I mean there was a certain point
> a passing,   one character into the next
> and substances would change
> as those children right there do
> right before our eyes!
>   not stumped
> as trees and points are left rising
> toward us
>   they call it the "shark"
>   they call it "magic hand"
>   they call it "black breast"
> always some comparison as the mouth is ripped.

Why is the "mouth" "ripped," what was I getting at? Some horrific vision of what being a poet means?

I was reading Spicer, Ashbery, although I don't think there's significant influence there, and exploring my dreams and reveries. They are quite absent of personal detail—experience is filtered through some romantic lens. There poems are filled with parings, keyholes, the Cosmic Parcel Company, metronomes, suicides, palates, glimpses, impositions, references to Africa, travel, relationships (quite muted) and are on the whole quite evocative and atmospheric. I have a series of three "Hostilities." I am impressed with my own language—the specificity there—images, the sense of "story," character, with some sophistication. From the "Voyage of the Legend":

> Her fingers let slip the consonant "oh"
> and we all tried to say "fish-church"
> before the final take

Well, you'd have to hear more. But from the Buddhist standpoint I was already inside sense perceptions in the language and had a sense of words as "things," as tangibles. And thoughts as "things," too, you could catch and let go of. And that mind was discursive and all over the place. And that the poem was a glorious matrix of fragments. And a sense of multiplicities: that you could say one thing and then contradict yourself, and this didn't make you a terrible person. That was your right and power as maker of the world. So words were clearly not things I had to be attached to. The sounds were freeing, the effect was freeing. And I could create whole little universes, I could travel. But I guess at some point I clicked into my own dumbness, and let go some pretensions I probably had. So Williams was important as impulse to get "close to the nose." And then the New York School influence of play, and immediate surroundings and the sense, too, of writing for and to others kicked in. All the occasional poems. And I was curious to track my life as young woman in the center of a lively scene. Humor was more important then. So there's a light, more airy touch in the work—speedy, off-hand. Poems in the books *Baby Breakdown* and *Giant Night* are the best of that time, and maybe closer to who I was. But I cringe often at the blind youth there, and how—and I remember this from that period—I intentionally wanted to "forget" my education for a spell. I'd been studying Yeats and Blake and Milton! There was an almost anti-intellectual tone in the downtown New York scene.

But I was already playing with tape recorders and chant and repetition. There's that list of *baby*s in "Baby Breakdown," and the poem "Tape" was actually composed with a tape recorder which was picking up snatches of information and newscaster-speech off the radio, plus telephone calls and the like. Not to mention the sounds coming in from the windows on St. Mark's Place. I was writing a lot at night; there are many mundane references to what I'm reading, who's coming by. There's a journal-like quality to that whole period and the poems in those books read together as one long book.

EF: And into this comes your Buddhist training?

AW: But, yes, Buddhism. Sure there's a confluence with my own mind and experience—remember Buddhism doesn't require "belief"—and in that way it's more a philosophy than a religion. And there are particular later poems which have a Buddhist "view" or cast to them. Explicitly exploring Buddhist thinking. "I Digress . . ." from *Makeup on Empty Space* is a trip through the Abhidharma, one of the Buddhist "tripitaka" or three bodies of teaching. The Abhidharma deals with the five "skandhas" which represent the constant structure of human psychology as well as its pattern of evolution in the world. It is a very precise way of looking at mind. *Makeup on Empty Space* is basically what "prajna" or feminine principle does—it adorns empty space and then deconstructs the form it creates, "Helping the Dreamer" is a poem that expresses a panorama of tenderness and generosity to the phenomenal world. And the section from *Iovis*, "Self Other Both Neither," is an excursion through Madhyamika philosophy in which you realize that things do not come from themselves, nor from things outside themselves, nor from both, nor from neither. In Madhyamika you go to great pains to analyze this question, such as where does a baby come from. Is it a replica? Are any two things alike? I love these modes of thinking, although my kind of intellect is more sweeping and emotional than scientific. *First Baby Poems* is a book that transcends the categories and definitions of Buddhism. It is maybe the most grounded and yet ecstatic of my books. *Troubairitz* is a love poem for Andrew Schelling, written over forty-nine days, the traditional time in the "bardo" in Buddhist thinking, a period of "gap" between death and birth.

But I think the influence one gets from tantric Buddhism emanates from the concurrent desire to get on stage and manifest various states of energy and have the pieces—the poems—what I like to call "modal structures"—become ritual enactments of these very powerful states of mind. And carry an efficacy as well. As poets we can be more powerful. We have a duty here, like the monks mumbling mantras in hidden caves that keep the world spinning. That counter the violence and misery of "samsara." Why not try one's magic power? Work spells, charms, curse the devils in the Pentagon, become red-skinned vajra yogini with her tongue of fire and skull cup of blood, stomping on the corpse of ego. When I say, "I'm coming up out of the tomb, men of war, just when you thought you had me down, in place, hidden," I am the chthonic goddess with her claws and barbs. Or shouting to the censorious ones, Jesse Helms and others, "I'll make your semen dry up / Your genitalia will wither in the wind," I mean it; I'm serious. But it's humorous, too. "Paean: May I Speak Thus?" is a litany against AIDS and speaks of spreading "the merit in ten directions," which is something you do in all Buddhist practice; you dedicate the merit of your words, your actions.

EF: So then at the center there's magic.

AW: I guess magic is the key for me. Tantric Buddhism is filled with white magic. And of course the words you invoke, those sounds, whether it's "CRRAACCK in the world" or "ennnnndometriuuum shedding," are efficacious. They create the event. They actualize the state of mind where these events occur. All those phones and phonemes carry energy and power to push against the darkness. I am obsessed with the color of words and their magical capabilities. In Buddhist practice you invite the energies to descend. You visualize the deities; you become the deities. You might walk around the city like a blue (Sanskrit) "Hum" or "Hung." The deities or syllables enter into you, or rather they confirm your energy. It's not some outside "ghosts" or theistic goddesses or anything like that that you become possessed by. The whole business is a struggle with ego, with the *kleshas*, or obstacles to awakened mind, awakened consciousness. Rather you're possessed by your own sanity which takes vivid forms. When you prostrate in Buddhism, you're bowing to your own enlightened mind and the sanity possible in the world. Poetry practice is much the same. You're synchronizing your body, speech, and mind to refine your expression, your manifestation in the world. And I've worked in my writing to be in touch with the patternings in my own nervous system, the grammar inherent in my own thinking. It's a changing manifestation, and a changing world. I am simultaneously that young schoolgirl and the wizened hag. Dharma is never out-of-date. Poetry is never out-of-date. You want to ride the fierce winds of cause and effect, to become the pulse, the throb inside your psychophysical being, your mind/heart (which are married in tantric practice) efficacy, and spill your insight with skill onto the page, and into the space around you. Charged, electric. You're there to wake people up and to disappear. And you dedicate the merit: May all beings enjoy profound, brilliant glory.

[The following portion of the interview was done at the Jack Kerouac School in Boulder, Colorado, 29 July 1994. A short distance away at Folsom Field, the University of Colorado's football stadium, 52,000 members of an all-male organization calling itself the Promise Keepers were holding their annual meeting. Founded by (the now former) UC football coach Bill McCartney four years earlier, the Promise Keepers are evangelical Christian men who want, among other things, to bring the world into line with their "family oriented" ideals. According to the Boulder *Camera*, "McCartney called his wife, Lyndi, on stage and, embracing and dipping her backward, delivered a long kiss to the delight of the [audience]. The coach prayed over his wife on stage last year." Meanwhile, airplanes circled the stadium with banners displaying messages like "Only weak men fear strong women."]

EF: *Chain* is probably the most interesting new magazine around, but I wonder if it's always a good idea to separate things according to gender. Insist on those categories, and sooner or later the right wing will be back.

AW: Well, this is a group of very strong women who feel that there are stories that need to be told and possibly wouldn't get told unless there was a specific forum forgrounding women and their experience. Women editors, publishers, serious writers. Up and coming literary women!

The next round table in *Chain* is documentation. They want people to respond to the notion of documentation—film documentation, verbal documentation, and what one's notion of "documenting" is in the first place. And the projects I've looked at and the people I've noted who were doing documentation, and with whom I've worked collaboratively, are often male. There's no distinction for me, and so the information I'm providing in this roundtable discussion is not bound by gender. And reading over a lot of women's statements and histories and experiences in the first issue of *Chain*, they weren't only about other women or work with other women, so I don't see that as a problem. But if it were just a magazine of women writing about *being* women, it would be like other soapbox feminist magazines and, by definition, limited. They're trying to do something else.

EF: *Iovis* and Dodie Bellamy's *The Letters of Mina Harker* appropriate male voices and male energy, and that seems a lot more interesting than women writing basically for women, men writing basically for men. I think of Susan Howe's statement that poetry transfigures beyond gender.

AW: I totally agree with that. Poetry doesn't have a gender, but I think you naturally write *out* of your gender at times. It's one of the physical energy sources. I am more wired like a "woman." I sound like a woman when I read aloud and perform. As I say in my piece in *Chain*, I'm all for unbound imagination. The statement in my new book entitled *Feminafesto* is about writing beyond gender—what you were saying just now: writing that's transformative, or transsexual poetry, whatever terminology you want to use.

EF: What about *Iovis*?

AW: I don't consider *Iovis* just a strident feminist argument or challenge to male energy. I do appropriate a lot of other voices, closely examining the males around me and my world. When you go through experiences like motherhood and being a daughter where you do have a close relationship with your father and then brothers and lovers where your reflection is constantly coming back at you, channeled through whatever their maleness might be, your poetry responds out of them. And I don't mean content. It's more subtle. There's a lot of reference to World War II—that language seems quite gender specific. Or the current arsenal of weaponry. Those names carry historic "male" aggression as I see it.

EF: How do you respond to claims that gender is somehow essential—that an individual is essentially male or female?

AW: New biological research indicates that there's a specific gene for femaleness that sits on the X chromosome and that can reverse the sex of the fetus. This contradicts the theory that the default mode of the fetus is female.

One of my closest friends in recent years is a transsexual who went from a female body to male, which is less usual, and his description of actually being born a woman and feeling it was not the body he was supposed to have is intense and terrifying. Tried to change the shape of his body—binding his breasts and then actually seeking out the specific operations. Somehow being in touch with this person's story and history and being sensitive to these issues and also trying to understand—is it physiological, is it a karmic thing—has been an interesting meditation. This person's situation "stopped my mind." It seems to be a combination. In Buddhism, you supposedly come in with only 25 percent of your inherited tendencies—this is aside from gender—and your mind is completely free. You mind is unconditioned.

EF: Fertile ground, alas, for Promise Keepers.

AW: But it's not a physiological thing. It's a relief. And then you can enjoy the relative differences. And you don't have to be conditioned by neurosis. The Promise Keepers are hung up on patriarchy and a male godhead. They are just poor couch potatoes who want to bond. The leaders, unfortunately, are savvy right-wing fundamentalists who use religion for political power. They prey on the fear of "difference," of "diversity." They're getting on schoolboards, running for office. They have a fascist agenda.

EF: They certainly seem to be people who want to make the world go their way, who insist that there are certain ways for men to behave.

AW: Listen to their rallies! There are thousands of people among them who are homophobic and chanting the name of "Jesus" like Nazis shouting "Seig heil"! Some of the directions this culture is taking! It's just more political work to do: as writers we have to stay alert, engaged. There's no "break" from samsara! I also want to be supportive of all the different poetry scenes and publications and magazines. I know *Chain* has been a place where Katie Yates and Rebecca Bush and Lee Ann Brown—many younger writers can talk about what they're doing. And Lee Ann's Tender Buttons is a terrific press for women's writing. It's been a delightful series.

EF: So then there are certain things that remain fundamentally male or female—things beyond some kind of control: women deciding how men should act, men deciding how women should dress.

AW: Well, there are experiences in the body and sexual experiences. In Buddhism, there's the idea that there are millions of ways to make love and zillions of different kinds of attraction to people, which is why I love your recent piece for Ted Berrigan, because it's a transformative love poem. It's conventional friendship, but it's more than that. It's almost erotic, and that for me is an unusual connection, thinking of you and Ted in that way. So I sense that in you and in myself. I love people. It's not a gender distinction. I think bisexuality is the actual mental condition. That's the true condition.

LEWIS WARSH

EF: I remember years ago you saying that you went to the Berkeley Poetry Conference in 1965. You were there with Anne Waldman, weren't you?

LW: Well, we met there. We didn't go there together.

EF: I think it was then that you and she decided to do *Angel Hair* Magazine, wasn't it?

LW: Not that summer. We returned to New York together, I still had a semester of undergraduate work at City College, and Anne was entering her senior year at Bennington. I'd visit her on weekends and on one of our trips back to New York from Vermont we decided to do a magazine. The idea of calling it *Angel Hair* occurred on the same trip—our thoughts were running along parallel tracks at that time. "Angel Hair" was part of a phrase in a poem by our friend Jonathan Cott—"Angel Hair sleeps with a boy in his head"—and since it was through Jonathan that we'd met, it seemed like the appropriate title which somehow included Jonathan as well, a kind of invisible third editor. Anne was editing *Silo*, the Bennington literary magazine, and she had access to a printer up in Williamstown, The Chapel Press. In Spring '66 I found the apartment at 33 St. Mark's Place and when Anne graduated we began living together. And by then the first issue of the magazine had appeared.

EF: To go back to '65 for a moment, what drew you to the conference? It wasn't something most people your age would have known about, I think.

LW: I'd decided to go to California even before I knew there was a poetry conference in Berkeley. I wanted to visit Liam O'Gallagher and Robert Rheem, two friends I'd met when I was in San Francisco the summer of '63, and for the first part of the summer I took courses at San Francisco State, I was still an undergraduate, but mostly I just wanted to get out of New York. In a recent autobiographical piece Anne writes that I'd come to San Francisco to "sit at the feet" of Jack Spicer and Robin Blaser, but nothing can be farther from the truth. I never met Blaser until the early 1980s, and then only briefly. I'd met Spicer in '63 and he seemed like a very formidable character, not someone I'd purposefully seek out for direction as a poet or otherwise.

EF: A poet in fact whose work seems very much unlike yours.

LW: That might be true on some level, but reading his book *Heads of the Town up to the Aether* had a big effect on me. I read it when I was eighteen, when I was in San Francisco, it had just come out, and I think it made me realize that a book of poetry didn't have to be a collection of poems, that a book could be unified in some different way. I've always been interested in conceptual projects and *Heads of the Town* seemed like that kind of book, something without precedent. I remember denying to myself that it was interesting and then being drawn back to it over and over again. And the veiled eroticism—"I could have slept with all the people in these poems"—certainly intrigued me. The poet of that group who interested me most was Blaser, especially two poems that appeared in *Locus Solus* Magazine, "Cups" and "The Park." And Robert Duncan was a big influence. But that came later.

EF: San Francisco 1963. A completely different world. Kennedy's still alive, and so is Robert Frost. Most people think he's the great American poet. It's not a time most people who will read this interview can remember. They weren't born yet.

LW: I had a friend, Steve Lovi, a painter and photographer. I'd met him the summer of 1960 when I was living in Boulder, Colorado with my parents. He was renting an old American Legion hall on the corner of Fillmore and O'Farrell and he had turned it into four lofts. He invited me out for the summer because one of the painters who lived there was going to Alaska and I could have a whole loft for myself. I could spend the whole summer there. He and Harris Schiff, who I'd also met in Boulder, and had known in high school, met me at the airport. I was eighteen and it was the first time I was really on my own. They drove me into the city, and my first night there took me to Gino & Carlo's, the bar in San Francisco, as you know, where Spicer and his circle used to meet. I'd read Spicer's poems in the Don Allen anthology but going to meet him wasn't something I especially wanted to do. It seemed too loaded, like going out on a blind date.

EF: Even though at this point, as with any young writer, there's the chance that something can be learned.

LW: I think I'd put all the poets in the Don Allen anthology on little pedestals in my head and the idea of meeting any of them was too intimidating. I was incredibly self-conscious, to begin with, but mostly it didn't seem that important. I could read and absorb them from a distance. And also I wanted to meet them on my own terms, if it was ever going to happen. Regardless, entering that bar was my first introduction to a poetry world. A very drab bar with a lot of very unhappy-looking young men sitting around a table waiting for Spicer who was off watching the Giants game somewhere else. Finally he arrived and Harris and Steve introduced us. I remember reaching out my hand to shake his hand and stepping backwards in astonishment because here was this guy who was thirty-eight, which seems like a relatively young age to me now, but who looked about sixty, at least. There was a kind of grotesque feeling about it all. I ended up going to the bar every night, at least for a few weeks, and eventually began having conversations with people like George Stanley and Harold Dull, but the only person who befriended me in any real sense was Larry Fagin, who seemed to be one of the few "straight" guys in the group. I remember sitting at this table and Spicer sort of turning to me and asking me very sardonically what did I do. At that point I'd been writing for several years, poetry and fiction as well, and I said, "I'm a writer." And people started instantly kicking me under the table; it was the wrong thing to say. How could I say such a thing, because the answer obviously was "I'm a poet." Being there and observing the scene was more like a cautionary experience than anything else since I was thinking that yes I wanted a world that involved poetry but not this one. It was very much a group that seemed to be holding down a fort against the rest of the poetry world, and maybe I wanted a bit more joy and excitement. The back of that bar seemed like a very small world.

EF: And not a very promising one.

LW: I don't know if promising is the right word. Spicer is a great poet, but I needed a lot of support to feel comfortable in social situations in those days. I still do, sometimes. And I wasn't going to get that at Gino & Carlo's. I went back to San Francisco in '65 and actually spent some time in the bar but mostly I visited with Liam and Bob who I had met two summers before and who lived in a loft in Chinatown. This was the summer of the Berkeley conference, we seem to be shifting between these two years. Liam and Bob are painters, they'd studied with Hans Hoffman in Provincetown, and Liam's an interesting writer as well, mostly cut-ups and collages. They just kind of adopted me in some strange way, and when I returned to San Francisco they found me an apartment on Nob Hill. So I went from living in the Fillmore to living around the corner from the Fairmont Hotel. I was just staying there on my own, living on my own and going to school at San Francisco State, dropping by the bar occasionally in the evenings, seeing Liam and Bob, waiting for the conference to begin. Then a friend of mine from New York, Michael Bernsohn, came to stay with me. He wasn't very interested in going to the Berkeley conference but he had a friend whom he had a kind of crush on, Jonathan Cott, who lived in Berkeley. They'd known each other at Columbia. So he was always talking about going out to Berkeley with me in the hope of meeting Jon. So one night, the night of Robert Duncan's reading, Michael came along with me, and almost immediately we ran into Jonathan Cott. Jon was living at the time with Angelica Heinegg, who later married Tom Clark. And some time that same night, at the reading, Jonathan introduced me to Anne.

EF: Hadn't they been to school together?

LW: They'd been in high school together, at Friends Seminary in Manhattan, and she was visiting with him. Two weeks after we met Anne moved into my apartment on Nob Hill. I'd taken LSD for the first time, a week before meeting Anne. Liam O'Gallagher had guided me through this trip—he had taken it before with Laura Huxley, who had acted as *his* guide. In those days it was appropriate to have a guide when you took LSD, especially when you took it for the first time, someone whom you trusted and who would take care of you if you started to freak out.

EF: You mean the wife of Aldous Huxley? How did that happen?

LW: I think they knew each other in Santa Barbara, which is where Liam and Bob are living now. People used to say that Liam resembled Aldous Huxley, in manner and speech, but I can't remember the interconnections between them all.

EF: A distinguished lineage, from the Huxleys and *The Doors of Perception,* to you and Anne.

LW: As soon as Anne and I met we instantly started taking LSD together. She had never taken it before. I had taken it that one time with Liam. Getting together distracted us from what was happening at the conference. We were at Olson's reading but missed Allen Ginsberg's because suddenly getting from San Francisco to Berkeley seemed too difficult. After the conference ended we hitch-hiked down to San Diego and took a bus from there to Mexico City where we stayed for two weeks. Then we took a bus back to Laredo, Texas, and hitch-hiked from there to New York. And now we're back to your first question—stuck in the 60s—about how we started *Angel Hair*.

EF: Founding the magazine. But what I'd understood you to say once before was that the magazine and so forth had somehow come out of meeting Anne at the Berkeley conference—not just the magazine, but in some sense the writing, publishing. . . .

LW: I think one of the reasons I was so resistant to meeting Spicer was that it wasn't my world. The last thing I wanted was to be one of the guys sitting around that table in the back of the bar. So meeting Anne was important, since it was the start of my public life as a poet. I certainly felt comfortable about what I was doing. Anne and I embarked on our life together without hesitation. We met, we started living together, we got married, and poetry was always the central focus. It was like I was in my own skin, finally. But remember that I'd been writing seriously for over five years before we met. Living for most of that time in the weird ambience of my family's apartment where no one said anything.

EF: Where was this?

LW: The Bronx, near Pelham Parkway, not far from The Bronx Zoo. A tiny apartment where I shared a room with my older sister. It seemed like both my sister and I wanted to burst forth out of this very, very quiet environment. There was an undercurrent of repressed hysteria which is what happens when no one expresses their feelings. My sister eventually eloped as a way of escaping it all. My parents stayed together interminably. But nothing was ever said. My father was the principal of a public school in East Harlem. My mother taught remedial reading in a public school in the South Bronx. There was no sense of ever taking pleasure in anything so I guess I had to make up for it or become the "spokesperson" for this world and the way to do this, or so I figured out, was by writing. Most of my earliest poems were simply straightforward statements of emotions and feelings.

EF: But there was more than the family—friends, school. . . .

LW: I met a few poets when I was in high school, Jonathan Greene and Charles Stein, but they were a bit more advanced than I was, though we're probably about the same age. Knowing them spurred me on in some important way, maybe in some competitive way, since I always thought their poems were better than mine when in fact they were just different. Also Sam Delany was a year ahead of me in this high school we both attended, the Bronx High School of Science, and he had already written seven novels. He told me to read Rimbaud. He visited me at my parents' apartment in the Bronx and looked disdainfully at my meager bookshelf. That look, the casualest of gestures, changed my life in some odd way. Also, early on, I'd heard a record of Kenneth Rexroth reading his elegy to Dylan Thomas, "Thou Shalt Not Kill," one of those old Fantasy records, where he says "You killed him. . . .You son of a bitch in your Brooks Brother's suit" and that struck some interesting chord, again the possibility of saying anything given the big silence of my household intrigued me. I wrote a lot of Kerouac imitations. I bought the *New American Poetry* anthology when I was fifteen and by the time I entered City College in 1961 I was beginning to figure things out.

Probably the most important thing about the summer of '63 in San Francisco wasn't so much going down to Gino & Carlo's, but seeing the books that were coming out, the White Rabbit Press books. Books like "The wood climb down out of. . . ." by Harold Dull and George Stanley's "Pony Express Riders." And I remember Steve Lovi taking me to the Auerhan Press, and meeting Andrew Hoyem and Dave Haselwood, and looking around and realizing that a community of poets could exist through the actual writing and publishing of the work, and that the social scene—the back of the bar—was secondary to this other activity. Hanging out at the bar didn't mean you were a great poet. The only thing that counted was the work and getting it into the world. This is all pretty obvious but at age eighteen I wasn't sure since hanging out on this particular scene was fraught with dramas that weren't interesting to me at the time. It wasn't *my* scene. When I returned to New York in the fall of 1963 I signed up for Kenneth Koch's poetry class at The New School and while I was in this class I wrote a long poem, "The Suicide Rates," which was influenced by all the reading I had done that summer, Spicer and Blaser. And Kenneth's aesthetics at the time seemed antithetical to what I was interested in but he liked the poem nonetheless. I still have the copy of the poem with his comments on it amazingly. It made me wonder about all the boundaries that had been drawn by the Don Allen anthology, and elsewhere—this is something I'd begun thinking about—all the different schools that were enmeshed with one another but somehow at odds. I had the simple thought that if Kenneth could like this particular poem then those boundaries didn't really matter. It was the enmeshment that mattered. The night he read the poem in class Gerard Malanga was there & he waylaid me as I left the room and asked me to send him a copy. And a few years later it was published as a small book by a press in Oregon, by a person who I never met named Bill Thomas. It was Gerard who made that connection, my first little book. A couple of years ago Douglas Messerli unearthed the poem and published it in his anthology, *On the Other Side of the Century: American Poetry 1960-1990,* which made me happy. I was eighteen when I wrote the poem but I can still remember writing it. I can still remember that person.

Probably the most important experience between the years 1960-65 was my relationship with Allegra David, who I'd met in 1960 when we were both fifteen. By

1964 we were living together, with her baby Juliet, in a low income housing project on the corner of 125th Street and Amsterdam. We lived there from early 1964 until late spring 1965 when Allegra and Juliet went to visit Allegra's brother in France. Maybe if they didn't go I would never have traveled to Berkeley that summer. A typical day during this period involved getting up at dawn, changing a diaper, writing a few pages of whatever novel I was working on, walking up Convent Avenue to my classes at CCNY. During the afternoons we'd hang out with the baby, going to Riverside Drive Park, and at night, after Juliet was asleep, we sat around getting stoned and listening to the Beatles and Bob Dylan. For a while I rented a room on W. 112th Street so I could get some writing done and do some schoolwork in the afternoon. So I was learning about poetry during this time, and about love as well. School wasn't exactly the most important thing on my mind, as you can imagine, but I kept going. For a long time eating and sleeping didn't seem very important.

So this was my education up to 1965 and the Berkeley conference.

EF: All of which places you in a special position vis-a-vis poets who are beginning to work today. I mean people for whom Rexroth, Spicer, Donald Allen all belong to a time long before they were born. Who in that world did you especially care about, that was doing things you wanted to do?

LW: Let me avoid that question for a minute and backtrack a little. While I was reading *The New American Poetry* anthology, during the years 1960-65, I was also reading all the new French novels—Robbe-Grillet, Duras, Butor, Sarraute, among many others—and that was also influencing my fiction writing. I was going to college full-time during those years but my head was really elsewhere. I probably wrote more during those five years, both fiction and poetry, than I have in any comparable period. A real apprenticeship. And going to all the new French and Italian movies literally the day they came out. So except for the Don Allen anthology, and Kerouac, I was mostly involved in a tradition that had to do with Europe, European literature, European thinking. It wasn't until I was living on St. Mark's Place and doing *Angel Hair* and my writing began to change that I began to think of myself as an American writer. It had a lot to do with meeting Ted Berrigan, who was over at our apartment on St. Mark's every night. Ted tapped into my nonintellectual side and pegged me as this guy from the Bronx who had a secret fund of knowledge about popular culture. Which of course he did too. We had both read a lot of quirky American novels by people like Chandler Brossard and Vance Bourjaily. I'd always kept that part of myself hidden, as if it wasn't serious enough. I came out, so to speak, around Ted, and my poetry began evolving in some new ways. I'd written hundreds of poems since "The Suicide Rates"—between '63 and '67—but few of them were as good. And I began publishing a lot, not only in *Angel Hair* but in *The World*, the mimeographed magazine that was coming out every month or so from the newly formed Poetry Project. Tom Clark was editing *The Paris Review* and publishing my poems regularly and I was writing reviews for *Poetry* (Chicago) which still had some credence in those days. I cringe whenever I read my poems in the early issues of *Angel Hair* and *The World*—there was no time lag between writing and publishing. I still didn't know when something wasn't good enough. Around 1967 I began to realize I could use an *I* in my poems in a way I hadn't done before. The pronouns I'd depended on previously were "he" and "she," I was always hiding something, like characters in a novel who are really the author in disguise. When I was twenty-two or three I wrote this short prose piece about living on St. Mark's Place and standing outside the building early Sunday morning and then coming back upstairs. Our apartment was one flight above the street. I realized I could mention the names of people in my poems, something everyone takes for granted now, but which was for me a big breakthrough. And I discovered that I could tell a little story out of my direct experience. No need to hide, or obfuscate, or pretend I was someone else. And this led to a lot of other possibilities. Gradually I discovered I could write a kind of personal poetry that was different than Ted's, or Frank O'Hara's. There's a vast difference between being an Irish guy from Providence or Baltimore and being a Jewish guy from the Bronx

EF: So you were less French than you thought.

LW: I could have everything, it was all part of the same mix. You could read Samuel Beckett, for instance, and listen to Carl Perkins at the same time. The point was to be open about everything. The more sources the better.

EF: Well, most of your later work does seem very American, of course, very personal and somehow more about being in America now than French *nouveau roman* or New Wave movies. But what about *Methods of Birth Control?* It's all impersonal, like an abstract musical composition, a theme and variation or something.

LW: I never really thought of a musical analog in connection with that book. I guess there are motifs and fugues but it's different from the serial poem or serial composition. But the language is deliberately very flat. I didn't write a word of that book, it's all about choices, and the structuring of information in some new way. I was intentionally trying to keep myself out of it as much as possible. I figured that since I'd taken personal poetry to an extreme I might as well go in the opposite direction.

EF: How did that happen?

LW: Well maybe that impulse began back in 1970 when I was living in Bolinas and put together this autobiographical book called *Part of My History* which was later published by Coach House Press in Canada. It was my first attempt to take disparate pieces of writing and make a whole, I mean make a book that wasn't simply a collection of poems. This was different and would probably connect with Spicer, back to my first glimpse of *Heads of the Town*. I want to write books where from page to page you don't know what's going to come next. A book of poems that all sound the "same"—that's kind of inevitable, that's what most books of poems are. All my collections of poems are like that. But then there's another kind of book that you can do which is more diverse, more spectacular. A book of poems, journals, autobiographical narratives—that's what *Part of My History* is. It all adds up to something, hopefully. The structuring of a book like that is really what interests me most, and which is why I write novels. When I started writing the poems in *Methods of Birth Control* I was living in Lenox, Massachusetts, with Bernadette Mayer. We'd moved there in '76. And when I met Bernadette she was involved in conceptual writing projects, and I was the one writing the personal poems, and after we lived together a year or two we traded places, and she began writing the most personal of works, and I began thinking more conceptually. The lines begin to blur after a while. My goal in writing *Methods* was to see if I could write a poem about anything. There's a great local library in Lenox and I would take out four or five books on the same subject and make notes, bits and pieces of information which I would then arrange as poems. It was my chance to be a scholar at last, something I have no patience doing in a totally conscientious way. So I was approaching these books with a kind of dumbness, and reserving my intelligence for putting them together, for making something out of the information, which is what most scholars can't do. But musically, going back to what you said, it sounds a little flat.

EF: But very formal and very abstract. What is scholarship, after all, if it isn't about getting the right form? I remember a copy editor at a university press saying it was her job to make sure that authors said things in certain ways since scholarship depends as much on how an argument is phrased as on the argument as such. Which is conceptualism and formalism with a vengeance. Still, something remains of the writer, I think, no matter what the pattern, if he or she is any good.

LW: I like the idea of putting together books where I don't have to do much writing. My favorite book is the collection of letters written to me between 1960 and 1965, *The Maharajah's Son.* I wanted to do a straightforward autobiographical narrative about that time and couldn't do it. And then I realized that I had saved all these letters. I was living in Stinson Beach at the time and the letters were in a box in the back of a closet in my parents' apartment in New York. So my mother sent me the letters and I began typing them up. It seemed like they told the story better than I ever could. I didn't have to invent anything or do much editing. So maybe that was really my first conceptual project—a way of organizing personal material into some new form. A kind of epistolary novel, like *Les Liasons Dangereuses* or *Clarissa.* I liked the idea that here I was all of twenty-seven and I'd already put together two books of autobiographical writing. The idea was you wrote your autobiography when you were on your last legs and here I was with a few lifetimes up ahead. The way to do it was to work with a form that was at least as interesting as what I was writing about. I had the thought when I was typing the letters that maybe no one would be interested in this stuff in a million years but in fact it's probably my most clearheaded and endearing book. There's a lot of purity in the voices of the people writing the letters, unselfconscious and unabashed. And there's a lot of mystery in the book since my letters aren't included. No doubt everyone just threw my letters away. So

I had the same idea when I set out to write *Methods of Birth Control*: catch the sounds of a lot of different people talking, but in a totally different way. It seemed like a variation on something I'd done before.

EF: What was your life like during those years in Lenox?

LW: We were living in a huge apartment on the main street of town. 100 Main. Four bedrooms and a living room the size of a small loft for $250 a month. Neither of us had jobs and we were broke most of the time. Lots of food stamps, and for a while we were on welfare. When we first left New York we moved to a 200-year old farmhouse in Worthington, a town in central Massachusetts, and we stayed there a year, our first daughter, Marie, was born there. Then we moved to Lenox in '76 and stayed there for three years. Our second daughter, Sophia, was born in that apartment. Most of our days were divided between hanging out with the kids and writing. We had no social life though occasionally people would visit us from New York. Our only neighbors were Clark and Susan Coolidge and Paul and Nancy Metcalf. We'd have dinners together. It was as near-perfect a life as I could imagine, in many ways, and I don't think I've ever fully recovered. Bernadette and I spent 24 hours a day together every day for four years and this forever changed my idea of what a relationship could be like—a shared experience, on every level. People—our friends—thought we were crazy, and we did eventually pay for all this closeness when we returned to New York. Most days the big event was walking around the town, stopping off at the library and the bookstore. We managed to score a few grants when we were living there, bought a mimeograph machine in Pittsfield and started *United Artists* Magazine. So we kept in touch with the rest of the world in this way. I wrote *Agnes & Sally* and *Methods of Birth Control* and a million poems and Bernadette wrote *Midwinter Day* and *The Golden Book of Words*. And we collaborated on a book called *Piece of Cake,* a journal where we each wrote alternate days. The book is 350 pages and we barely made it through one month. We could have stayed there forever if we could have figured out a way to make money, even though the idea of raising kids in a small town didn't appeal to me much since all the teenagers looked so bored and part of me was pining for New York. Someone at the Welfare Dept. had the brilliant notion that I should work in a shoestore in Pittsfield but I didn't even apply for the job and they cut us off. Our idea was to spend all our time writing and hanging out with the kids and with each other. Finally Russell Banks called us up and offered us part-time teaching jobs at New England College in Henniker, New Hampshire, so we went, we relocated for a year. Bernadette was pregnant again and we were tired of being poor and teaching a few hours a week didn't seem like the worst idea. Max was born in New Hampshire and ironically we both got NEA grants that year so it seemed like a good moment to return to New York—with some money in the bank—which is what we did.

EF: What about a book like *Information from the Surface of Venus,* which seems more like your usual work? It's really a miscellany, an odd collection without that conceptual order.

LW: Well, on the surface it reads as a collection of poems, bracketed by the time period, 1976-82, the traditional "book" of poems, a type that everyone publishes. Poems that are selected from all the poems written over a period of time. I think the conceptual nature of such a book is more subtle given that books like these are involved with preoccupations that link the poems in a non-narrative way, a kind of unconscious cosmology. It's really up to the reader to develop the connections between the poems in such a book while the conceptual ideas of *The Maharajah's Son* or *Methods of Birth Control* are something I can talk about. Books like *Information* contain poems that are single entities. Not part of any conceptual project except the ongoing project of writing poetry.

I always think of writing as a series of possibilities. You can write single poems or you can write conceptual book-length poems and you can write novels and stories and plays as well. You can write autobiography. I'm always amazed that so many people haven't written their autobiographies. It seems like an option, right? There are these levels of experience, of being in the world, of living inside an inner world, which encompass all the other experiences, and which seem to me to add up to who you are, what it feels like to be alive. I've been preoccupied with this for years. *Part of My History* and *The Maharajah's Son* are just the first two books of an ongoing autobiographical project. In the early 70s, when I returned to City College to get my MFA, I wrote a book called *Earth Angel* as my thesis, a straightforward account of everything that had happened to me up to age fifteen. And my thesis advisor, Francine du Plessix Gray, thought I was a bit insane. Her idea was that it was pointless to write your autobiography unless you were really famous. Why would anyone be interested? And in the early 80s I put together a book of journals from the 60s and 70s where there are four or five narrative threads—a journal entry from 1962 followed by one from 1975 followed by one from 1967. Again, another project where all I had to do was type things up. And the book I did with Bernadette, *Piece of Cake,* is yet another volume.

EF: To some people, myself for one, that seems a strange way to think about writing —as a series of possibilities.

LW: I don't understand why. It seems like the ultimate way to go about doing things. The alternative is self-imposed limitation. Doing what you do best over and over again. And as I said, I never understand why writing one's life story isn't something in the air for everybody.

EF: I'm not arguing that. I'm saying that some people would say that they don't have a choice. They do what they're told, or as they might put it, what they're given to write. And that's what Spicer said, or at least claimed. Another person would say that when one starts making choices about what he or she writes, it comes with all sorts of conflicted personal matter, moreso than otherwise. And so the generating force of the work is not going to be apparent to the reader, who is left, at best, with a beautiful surface.

LW: Well, maybe it's not for everyone, but what I like to do—a big part of the writing process—is to unearth stuff, hidden stuff, and write about what I find, the memories behind the memories, to create this extra dimension. Which is why I like the idea of going through old letters and journals. I'm not interested in confession, it's more like uncovering something, the fact that you can say it, that you can blurt it out, that you can get close to people in this way. I don't expect everyone's poems to do this but sometimes poetry seems like "small talk" in relation to what it could be if it included this thing. And the great thing is that there's always another layer to explore.

EF: What about writing as therapy?

LW: A terrible idea. Anything you do that makes you feel good about yourself is interesting. That's a given. On the other hand, the truth isn't that interesting. The struggle to get it out is what makes it liberating. We want to know the truth so we go through this struggle, but it doesn't have to be painful, like Oedipus. How much or how little you participate in that struggle is the way you define who you are. Just the same way that if I were to tell you my secrets, you might be inspired to tell me yours. And then what? Maybe we'd fall in love and live together forever or maybe one of us would walk out of the room in horror. Freud's premise is that you can heal yourself by talking but I also like the Kabbalistic idea of repairing something that's damaged or scarred, putting the broken vessels back together again.

EF: This seems relevant to what you were saying before, your family where no one talked.

LW: So maybe, as you said, I didn't have any choice either. For all my talk of possibilities, I think I'm choosing but I'm not. Maybe saying "I'm a writer" back in that bar with Spicer *was* the wrong thing.

EF: The distinction between you and the Spicer group is clear. But what do you see as the distinction between what you and, say, Ted or Bernadette were writing?

LW: Ted and Bernadette are poets I feel close to. What they taught me is how to be more myself. How I could be in a room writing and not be this person who was wandering aimlessly in my head. Ted also told me things about my poems that were really useful. I'd show him a poem and he'd say: "Those asterisks make me want to throw up." I'd put these little asterisks in between stanzas and I looked at them again and he was right. They were totally nauseating.

I don't think there's much similarity between Ted's poetry and mine. The music is all different and he was involved in being part of a tradition in a way that was less important for me. But in comparison to Ted, a lot of other poets seem to be lurking in the background of their lives. Skimming the surface, so to speak. There's great beauty on that surface. It's a very tangible place to be. But it's not real. Denying that something exists can only end up being mildly entertaining. A good example are the two poems by Kenneth Koch, both called "The Circus," where the later poem is a commentary of how he wrote the first, which is an exuberant imaginative poem filled with a lot of exclamation points, somehow erotic and melancholy as well, and the second poem is a kind of memoir, what his life was like when he wrote the first poem, and what's different about his life now. The first poem was all about an attempt to stay on the surface, while the second poem gives itself up to the struggle to stay above ground. The first poem became useful in an almost mnemonic way since it created a new occasion, a companion piece which was all about process and nostalgia and loss. In the second poem he was attending to his darkness, so to speak. I was very impressed by that second poem. It meant that the memory of something was as important as the thing itself, which of course isn't true—but an optimistic possibility. It's also important, I think, to go from A to B, or A to J, to make some moves, but most poets get stuck in one place or stop writing. The paintings of Philip Guston are inspiring in this sense too. From darkness to light to something completely other. The surface—staying on the surface—is too limiting, too two-dimensional. You can only be *so* beautiful.

I've never had a poetry teacher, an older poet who I considered a teacher. But for a couple of years I let Ted get under my skin. As I said, we had a lot of similar interests, and he was much more open-minded about people like Spicer than many of the other younger poets associated with The New York School. And we went for some open place in our conversation, where we could say anything, so maybe this is what's similar about our poetry as well. And we traveled a bit together. I remember once we were in a hotel room together in Liverpool, England. Totally smashed. We had rented a car in London and drove across England looking for Swansea, Dylan Thomas's birthplace, but we took a wrong turn and ended up in Liverpool. It didn't seem to matter. On the way we took LSD, this is summer '69, and stopped the car on the moors and for a moment, as we started rolling down the hills, it seemed that we would stay there forever. A joyous moment. Somehow we got back to the car and ended up in this bed & breakfast where there was a copy of *Time* magazine with a reproduction of a de Kooning painting. And we spent most of the night staring at this painting in the magazine saying some of the most profound things that have ever been said about anything. I would say something and Ted would say, "That's the greatest thing I ever heard," and then he would say something. . . .

Bernadette too. I think we were all willing to go over the top, but in different ways. But they have a lot more glitter on the surface than I do. I think I'm more like the person who's going to fall overboard and that a lot of my poems try to trap that moment when I'm about to fall, that's the experience I'm interested in. It's like the Creeley poem, "I think I grow tensions. . . ." I think that's who I am. Trying to move off the surface and go somewhere else. The idea of not knowing is always tense and anticipatory. I think I'm settled but I'm not. The desire to be somewhere else is always a little nerve-wracking so I end up back on the surface looking down.

EF: The poetics of vulnerability, or so I think you've called it.

LW: Well, I was in China a few years ago, and Tibet, and I realized how adamantly I was this person, that I couldn't escape myself, not for a moment. Here I was in this place where I was as far as I'd ever be from a world which was familiar to me, but I was still the same person. And that was shocking to me. I was stuck in an elevator in Beijing, between the sixteenth and seventeenth floors, it was 90 degrees, the lights went out, almost midnight, no one could speak English. And I felt like I was falling, like I was slipping off the edge.

But I did learn one thing in Tibet. I learned to look up a lot. It's the highest point on the planet and the sky is really close.

Designed by
Samuel Retsov

●

Text: 9 pt Plantin

●

acid-free paper

●

Printed by
McNaughton & Gunn, Inc.